Themes in International Urban History

The city and education in four nations

Themes in International Urban History

Series editors
Peter Clark
David A. Reeder
The Centre for Urban History, University of Leicester

This series examines from an international perspective key themes in the historic development of cities and societies. The series is principally, although not exclusively, concerned with the European city, with an emphasis on the early modern and modern periods, and it will consider urban systems, structures and processes. Individual volumes will bring together and present in an accessible form the best work of the wide variety of scholars from different disciplines and nations currently engaged in research on urban history. The series is published by Cambridge University Press and Editions de la Maison des Sciences de l'Homme in association with the Centre for Urban History, University of Leicester. The first volumes in the series comprise collections of commissioned pieces organised around certain key themes that lend themselves to comparative analysis. Each includes a substantive introduction by the volume editor/s, making explicit linkages between individual essays and setting out the overall significance and context of the work.

Themes in International Urban History will interest scholars and students in a variety of sub-disciplines within social and economic history, geography, sociology and urban planning. It rides on the wave of important and exciting new developments in the study of cities and their history, and reflects the growing internationalism of this area of study.

The city and education in four nations

Edited by Ronald K. Goodenow
Professor (Affiliate) of Education at Clark University

and William E. Marsden
Reader in Education, University of Liverpool

EDITIONS DE LA MAISON DES SCIENCES
DE L'HOMME

PUBLISHED BY THE PRESS SYNDICATE OF THE UNIVERSITY OF CAMBRIDGE
The Pitt Building, Trumpington Street, Cambridge, United Kingdom
and Editions de la Maison des Sciences de l'Homme
54 Boulevard Raspail, 75270 Paris Cedex 06

CAMBRIDGE UNIVERSITY PRESS
The Edinburgh Building, Cambridge CB2 2RU, UK
40 West 20th Street, New York NY 10011–4211, USA
477 Williamstown Road, Port Melbourne, VIC 3207, Australia
Ruiz de Alarcón 13, 28014 Madrid, Spain
Dock House, The Waterfront, Cape Town 8001, South Africa

http://www.cambridge.org

© Maison des Sciences de l'Homme and Cambridge University Press 1992

This book is in copyright. Subject to statutory exception
and to the provisions of relevant collective licensing agreements,
no reproduction of any part may take place without
the written permission of Cambridge University Press.

First published 1992
First paperback edition 2002

A catalogue record for this book is available from the British Library

Library of Congress Cataloguing in Publication data
The City and education in four nations / edited by Ronald K. Goodenow and
William E. Marsden
      p.   cm. – (Themes in international urban history)
ISBN 0 521 41084 3
1. Education, Urban – Great Britain – History. 2. Education, Urban – United
States – History. 3. Education, Urban – Canada – History. 4. Education, Urban –
Australia – History. I. Goodenow, Ronald K. II. Marsden, W. E. (William Edward)
III. Series.
LC5136.G7C38   1992
370.19'348–dc20   91–43863   CIP

ISBN 0 521 41084 3 hardback
ISBN 2 7351 0473 7 hardback (France only)
ISBN 0 521 89291 0 paperback

Contents

List of tables	*page* ix
Notes on contributors	x
Series editorial preface	xiii

Introduction: problematics and domains: thinking internationally about urban education
Ronald K. Goodenow ... 1

Part 1 Research in national contexts

1 History, education and the city: a review of trends in Britain ... 13
   David A. Reeder

2 Education and America's cities ... 44
   Ronald D. Cohen and William J. Reese

3 The 'state' of the history of urban education in Australia ... 73
   Kerry Wimshurst and Ian Davey

4 Out of the shadows: retrieving the history of urban education and urban childhood in Canada ... 87
   Neil Sutherland and Jean Barman

Part 2 Approaches to the social history of education: ecology, choice and culture

5 Social stratification and nineteenth-century English urban education ... 111
   William E. Marsden

6 Compulsion, work and family: a case study from nineteenth-century Birmingham ... 129
   Christine M. Heward

7 Understanding irregular school attendance: beyond the rural–urban dichotomy Ian Davey and Kerry Wimshurst	158
8 Redoing urban educational history Barbara Finkelstein	172

Part 3 Needs and opportunities: policy and theory considerations

9 Theory in educational history: a middle ground Carl F. Kaestle	195
10 Approaches to urban education in the USA and the UK David Coulby	205
11 The uses and abuses of comparison in urban educational history David L. Angus	221
Index	243

Tables

5.1	Schools and social categories in the late nineteenth century	*page* 113
6.1	The sample streets	132
6.2	Mean rateable values of the sample streets	132
6.3	Household composition	136
6.4	Economic composition of households	137
6.5	Occupations in Birmingham	138
6.6	Percentage of children at home, school and work before compulsion	140
6.7	Percentage of children at home, school and work before compulsion	144
6.8	Results of the Birmingham Education Society survey, 1868	146
6.9	Results of the Birmingham Education Society survey, 1869	147
6.10	The effects of compulsory school attendance	152
7.1	Quarterly attendance rates, Hindmarsh Public Schools, 1884, 1889	163

Notes on contributors

DAVID L. ANGUS is Professor of Education Policy and History at the University of Michigan at Ann Arbor. He has written widely on the methodology of the urban history of education and is the author of a range of articles on the methodology of the history of education, on comparative urban education, on the politics of education in the ante-bellum and progressive periods and on the nineteenth-century urban history of education. He is currently planning a comparative, longitudinal study of education in Hong Kong and Shanghai.

JEAN BARMAN teaches the history of education at the University of British Columbia, and worked with Neil Sutherland on the Canadian Childhood History project. She is author of *Growing up British in British Columbia: Boys in Private School*, *The West beyond the West: A History of British Columbia* and senior editor of the two-volumed *Indian Education in Canada*.

RONALD D. COHEN is Professor of History at Indiana Northwest, Gary, Indiana. He has published widely on the history of urban education in the United States, including most recently, *Children of the Mill: Schooling and Society in Gary, Indiana, 1906–1960*. He is currently writing a history of popular music in the United States, 1940–70.

DAVID COULBY is Head of the Faculty of Education at Bath College of Higher Education. He is a co-author of *Urban Schooling: Theory and Practice*, *The Education Reform Act: Competition and Control* and *Contradiction and Conflict: The 1988 Education Act in Action*.

IAN DAVEY is Dean of Graduate Studies in the University of Adelaide. Well known for his pioneering work on the history of urban education in North America, he now researches on issues of class, gender and nineteenth-century school systems in Australia. He is currently co-authoring a book on the origins of mass schooling entitled *Assembling a School*.

BARBARA FINKELSTEIN is Director of the International Center for the Study of Educational Policy and Human Values and Professor in the

Department of Educational Policy, Planning and Administration at the University of Maryland. Among her many publications are *Regulated Children/Liberated Children: Education in Psycho-Historical Perspective* and *Governing the Young: Teacher Behavior in Popular Primary Schools in Nineteenth-Century United States*.

RONALD K. GOODENOW is Professor (Affiliate) of Education at Clark University in Worcester, Massachusetts. He has published extensively on urban, international and reform issues. Previous books on urban education include *Schools in Cities: Consensus and Conflict in American Educational History* and *Educating an Urban People: The New York City Experience*, both co-edited with Diane Ravitch.

CHRISTINE M. HEWARD is a lecturer in the Department of Education at the University of Warwick. Her research interests are in the history of childhoods, masculinities and equal opportunities policies. Her publications include *Making a Man of Him: Parents and their Sons – Education at an English Public School. 1929–1950.*

CARL F. KAESTLE is William F. Vilas Professor of Educational Policy Studies and History at the University of Wisconsin–Madison. Among his books are *Pillars of the Republic: Common Schools and American Society, 1780–1860, Literacy in the United States: Readers and Reading since 1880, The Evolution of an Urban School System: New York City, 1750–1850* and, with Maris Vinovskis, *Education and Social Change in Nineteenth-Century Massachusetts.*

WILLIAM E. MARSDEN is Reader in Education at the University of Liverpool and was formerly Dean of its Faculty of Education and Extension Studies. He has published extensively in the history of urban education, in the history of the curriculum and in geographical education. Books include *Unequal Educational Provision in England and Wales: The Nineteenth-Century Roots* and *Educating the Respectable: A Study of Fleet Road Board School, Hampstead, 1879–1903.*

DAVID A. REEDER was formerly Senior Lecturer in Education and Urban Studies at the University of Leicester and Deputy Director of the Centre for Urban History, where he is now a Research Consultant. He is editorial associate of the *Urban History Yearbook*, and co-general editor of the series in which *The City and Education in Four Nations* appears. He has written widely on urban history and the history of urban education, and edited *Urban Education in the Nineteenth Century*, and co-edited, with D. Cannadine, *Exploring the Urban Past: Essays in Urban History by H. J. Dyes*

WILLIAM J. REESE is editor of the *History of Education Quarterly* and Associate Professor of Education, History and American Studies at Indiana University at Bloomington. He is the author of *Power and the Promise of School Reform: Grass-Roots Movements during the Progressive Era,* and co-editor of *The Social History of American Education.*

NEIL SUTHERLAND teaches the history of education at the University of British Columbia and directed the Canadian Childhood History Project. He is author of *Children in English–Canadian Society: Shaping the Twentieth-Century Consensus* and *Growing up in Modern Canada: The Children's Perspective.*

KERRY WIMSHURST teaches in the School of Justice Administration in the Division of Education at Griffith University in Queensland. He has published a range of articles on school attendance and school reform around the turn of the century, on reformatory school girls in the nineteenth century and on the part-time employment and work patterns of students in higher education. He is currently researching the careers and experiences of women police officers in Queensland over the past twenty years.

Series editorial preface

The launch of this series rides on the wave of exciting new developments in the study of cities and their history. Particularly important is the growth of international contacts and awareness among historians. In Britain, the ambition to internationalise urban history has been evident since the 1960s and exemplified in the holding of several international interdisciplinary conferences, the international coverage of the *Urban History Yearbook* (now *Urban History*) and the visits of scholars from many overseas countries to the main urban history centres. But in recent years the pace of international collaboration and exchange has quickened, especially in relation to Europe, where the establishment of the European Association of Urban Historians (1989), the holding of regular European colloquia and the teaching and student exchanges under the European community ERASMUS and TEMPUS programmes have provided a powerful new impetus. The simultaneous development of similar contacts among urban historical geographers has also contributed to the new international dimension of city studies.

The intensification of international contacts is only one aspect of the vitality recently injected into the study of urban history by innovative developments and organisational initiatives in many countries of the advanced world, ranging from the formation of the Urban History Association in the United States to the establishment of national research institutes and working groups in Western Europe and the success of the Japanese Tokyo Study Group in Comparative Urban History. From this has stemmed an increasing interest in the varied styles of approach to urban history in different countries, and a growing recognition that an international perspective may help diversify the study of the city and its past, broaden perspectives, resolve some of the major epistemological issues of disciplinary scope and definition, as well as expose the strengths and limitations of particular national methodologies. Such ambitions are not the exclusive prerogative of urban historians, of course. In the historical community generally, a distinctive feature of recent scholarship has been the growth of collaborative international seminars, conferences and publications. These reflect a widespread concern to combat the tendency to parochialism and specialist fragmentation in historical study and a determination to overcome the theoretical, cultural and linguistic problems that beset attempts at international comparisons.

As early as 1974 H. J. Dyos expressed the view that the future of urban history must surely lie in comparative study, by which he meant that the comparisons should not only be of different places, 'but also comparisons between different elements, institutions and phenomena abstracted from different types of society'. The present series of **Studies in International Urban History** has been conceived in this eclectic spirit. It will be principally but by no means exclusively concerned with the European city, with the main emphasis on the early modern and modern periods. The series will include studies by individual authors on urban systems, structures and processes, but it will also embrace collections of essays organised around key themes in the historical development of the city, bringing together whenever possible scholars from different disciplines and countries.

This volume on the **city and education** falls into the second of the two categories. It is a collection of eleven essays, plus an introduction by the American co-editor, dealing with the history of urban education and written by educational historians from Britain and three other English-speaking countries, namely Australia, the USA and Canada. It is mainly concerned with the evolution of urban school systems in the modern period, and sets out to reconstruct, illustrate and assess the way that educational historians have represented this process in each of the four countries.

These collected essays bring out the significance of the history of educational developments to understanding the extent of the social transformation that modern urban growth has entailed. But they do so in a reflective and self-critical way. There is no attempt at arguing for a distinct genre of urban educational study. On the contrary, the essays reflect a range of attitudes towards the impact of urbanisation on educational development and differing opinions about the advantages and drawbacks of making the city a focus of study in educational history. Taken as a whole, the intention of this collection is to stimulate thinking about the potential of different methodological approaches rather than to put forward a concerted view of how the history of urban education should be undertaken.

The four essays in Part 1 survey trends in the history of urban education in the four nations being considered. Whilst they make clear why urban needs and problems have been so prominent in the historical evolution of education, they also show how differing attitudes to educational studies based on city developments are related to national differences in the historiographical evolution of the subject. Each country represented in the volume has been subject to similar intellectual influences, but the timing of these and how far they have given a priority to the urban influence have differed from one country to another. In the North American countries, the impact of a critical social history concerned with the relations between schooling and capitalist development – and the controversy this aroused – was largely responsible for the proliferation of city studies and ambitious attempts to elaborate a general history of urban education. On the other hand, in Britain city studies have gained more from the work of educational historians interested in the demographic and geographical contexts of educational change, although this emphasis is also evident recently in American and Canadian studies. On the whole, these studies make strong claims for the significance of urbanisation in the historical evolution of school systems. However, exponents of a social history of mass education in Australia, as the Australian contributors to this volume argue, are critical of what they regard as a misleading urban–rural dichotomy in the history of education in that country.

What can be said, from these surveys, is that educational history is evidently much less narrowly institutional than was formerly the case and much more concerned with the inter-relationships between schooling, work, residential development, family life and the experience of growing up in different environments. Part 2 of the volume provides four essays to illustrate these themes. The first of these is a general essay by the British co-editor which seeks to make links between urban growth, social stratification and the development of schooling in Britain. It shows precisely why it is so important in this country to take account of the late nineteenth-century urban revolution in assessing the relations between education and social change. A further two essays are illustrative of recent trends in the social history of working-class education in providing case studies which investigate the significance of family life, particularly the family economy, to school attendance in the late nineteenth century. Both of these essays are based on detailed quantitative analysis, with one case study located in Birmingham, England, and the other covering two districts in South Australia. The fourth essay, by an American contributor, presents a survey of how the history of urban education should be extended to take into account many more aspects of the city experience than hitherto with more emphasis on the cultural and psychological aspects of city life. In effect, this essay urges educational historians to take a more all-embracing view of urbanisation as a kind of training that society has had to undergo.

Finally, in Part 3, there are three essays which move away from purely historical concerns to discuss broader methodological issues. These are introduced by an American educational historian who reflects on the relations between theory and history, from the experience of his own studies. The British contribution, written from the point of view of a social scientist, introduces aspects of contemporary debate on the role of history and theory in urban educational study and the implications this has for educational policy-making. The third essay, by an American educationalist, concentrates on the making of comparisons in the historical study of urban educational developments. It reviews the modes of comparative analysis available to urban historians, and, in the light of this, discusses the potential of the various methodological approaches characteristic of urban educational history.

These three concluding essays complement a volume which is exceptional in combining national and local case studies to engage in wide-ranging methodological discussion. As such, it represents a distinctive addition to the literature of educational history. Moreover, in commenting on the intellectual cross-currents which have pushed the study of urban educational history in different directions, the contributors introduce issues of significance to all historians concerned with the city as a reference point or context for studying institutional, social and cultural change. The status of the urban in historical study, the relations between urban history and social theory and the need for comparative study are among the more fundamental of these. Thus, in bringing to the fore recent work on the history of urban educational development, this volume advances debates which are of central importance to the methodological development of urban history more generally.

DAVID A. REEDER
PETER CLARK

Introduction: problematics and domains: thinking internationally about urban education

Ronald K. Goodenow

Cumulatively, the essays in *The city and education in four nations* address a set of needs which have not been considered adequately by historical or comparative educational literature. The book is intended to be read in terms of its inherent value to students of schooling in cities and to those who would wish to see a more cosmopolitan literature on education. Although most of the individual essays dwell on national scholarly trends and traditions, several of them address the international transfer of ideas on cities, policies and historical research, and how, when viewed comparatively, they affected schooling. This requires attention to problematic and domain issues associated with theory, practice and the venues in which historians work.

A foremost problematic revealed in the volume is the relationship between research and practice, one that points to a need to strengthen the theory base upon which historians write. Without a good theoretical foundation, historical inquiry in education can, and often has been, driven normatively by the imperatives of developing and reforming public schooling or fostering social change. As Kaestle notes in his chapter, 'Even if we put the committed Marxists, modernisers, Annalists, Weberians and Parsonians all together (an interesting thought), they are not numerous.' There is, he suggests of historians, 'little in their training, their favourite historical writing, or in their intellectual instincts that inclines them to the sustained use of theory'. Kaestle also writes that unfortunately the exceptions to this rule tend either to be theory-bound, lost in grand world views that give a reductionist character to their work, or mired in overt attempts to be eclectic. While this book is not exactly a call to his own 'middle-ground position', it does put the issue of theory in the foreground, where it belongs.

Theoretical, and other problems noted in *The city and education in four nations*, require attention to the relationship between how schooling in cities has evolved and how historians of 'urban education' and related topics have studied it in the United States, Great Britain, Australia and Canada. As a relatively new aspect of the modern historiography of education the debate is characterised not only by a weak theoretical foundation, but by ambiguous differences over perspective which overshadow agreement over what Angus describes in his chapter as 'the bases on which valid and cumulative generalisation can be built'. The 'field of study' is one which is still seeking common definitions and consensus about basic issues, including, as many of the essays in this book attest, the nature of the boundaries within which scholarship takes place, the relationship between scholarship and policy and whether such terms as 'urban' are appropriate ones.

This condition has several causes. The relationship between urban educational history and mainstream social history is not always well defined. One intellectual problem – and I will elaborate on others below – is stated here by Reeder, who identifies a critical boundary issue when he writes that, 'As more social historians located their studies in towns and cities, the ambiguity of what constituted the field increased and a great variety of studies, many with a society-wide context, were welcomed as contributing grist to the urban historical mill.'

The problem situation is exacerbated to some degree by constraints which transcend those of boundary or theory. Many educational historians work in schools of education, where scholarly and professional objectives must be balanced upon constantly shifting ground. All too often, educational historians are isolated, physically and intellectually, from their more 'academic' counterparts, many of whom but infrequently interact with the city, its populations and the many policy dilemmas inherent in modern urban education.

Professional status and perspective, of course, raise a problem that nags at many educational historians: relations between scholarship and practice. As Reeder also suggests,

The problems of inner city schooling gave rise from the 1960s to a plethora of sociological and educational publications, and these concerns may have influenced almost imperceptibly a renewed interest in the history of mass schooling, but there was no attempt self-consciously to develop an historical perspective on the contemporary debate. Urban educational policies were formulated 'without any adequate awareness of past endeavours to solve problems which may have been exacerbated or may have assumed new dimensions in our own times'. The historians of education are not alone responsible for this neglect of history; it is also the case that urban educational study and debate was conducted in such a way as virtually to exclude them.

If striking a balance between theory, practice and the problems inherent in urban education is a difficult one, integrating them is a delicate proposition, for as Coulby warns in his chapter, 'an exclusively historical approach to urban education may be perceived as a retreat from politics, indeed from policy. Historical approaches may be seen to permit urban educationists the leeway of distancing themselves from the struggles of the present.'

Coulby's essay is a reminder that the sands of theory and practice are shifting ones, best understood in the national domain. Accordingly, Cohen and Reese note in their contribution that national tradition affects matters of emphasis profoundly. Debates about scholarship in the USA, they write, are likely to be framed around questions about the nature and role of public schooling, which occupies a special place in American life. In this context, argument about 'urbanisation' or even the relationship between schools and cities pales by comparison. Each nation, as the essays presented here demonstrate, has its broad historiographical traditions and it is incumbent that they be recognised as affecting any relationship between history and practice, theory and practice and a wide range of research interests. Beyond this, they and their scholarly traditions exist in an international domain.

The liberal democracies included here share much in terms of dominant modes of educational, economic and political ideas and practices, many of which have been transferred between them. They have all partaken in a great twentieth-century phenomenon: the wholesale institutionalisation, systematisation and transfer of mass education. There has been a persistent belief everywhere that schooling is essential to good citizenship, that it rescues nations from economic malaise, and that it serves as creator of 'progress' and 'reform'. Indeed, virtually all nations, regardless of political ideology, share these beliefs. Finkelstein writes in this book, 'The popularisation of schooling, is, by definition, an aspect of modernisation processes all over the world. It has proved to be an irresistible, and apparently irreversible, invention of social and political planners throughout the world.'

Though, as Finkelstein also suggests, the 'relationship of cities or urban settings to all of this is not at all clearly joined', this explosion of mass education has been accompanied by the notion that the consequences of urbanisation may be controlled by educational means. Reinforced by stereotypes which arose around nineteenth-century industrial cities as well as by modern social science, it has become an axiom, particularly among the middle classes in the Western industrialised nations, that cities are cauldrons of immigrants and displaced rural dwellers especially prone to alienation, rootlessness and, as often as not, the more sinful enticements of materialism. Here is a setting of opportunity, fear, conflict and individual and group survival strategies, crowding and movement. It is a domain in which, as Finkelstein writes, myths arise easily about schooling as panacea to cure many social ills. This condition of mass education, as well as underlying beliefs about cities and their dwellers, is a concern of many contributors to *The city and education in four nations*. As several of them suggest, theories on urbanisation are linked inexorably to others on 'urbanisation' and 'development', some of which are embedded in a widely diffused Western social science that has often legitimated dominant and sometimes exploitive patterns of social and economic relations in industrialised and non-industrialised nations – a prime area for new research.

There is, then, a complex set of issues surrounding the evolution of constructions and associated terminologies for defining 'urban' or 'urban education' internationally. There is a need for scholarship on how policy has developed in nations which, if they do share much in the way of political ideology, class structure and economic production, also have significant cultural differences and patterns of intergroup relations. Bureaucracy, centralisation and professionalism seem to be important features of all modern educational systems, as well as the subjects of much scholarly discussion, and their relation to social control and stratification has been elaborated upon by revisionists, as noted by Cohen and Reese in this book. Their relative significance and consequences in various national systems have not, however, received analysis adequate to determine the degree to which they are affected by or are responses to such things as the degree of racial or ethnic pluralism in the population, religious diversity, tradition and loci of political and educational control. Very little thought has been given to the subtle issues of individual choice and consciousness noted by Finkelstein and Marsden in their contributions. The role of social science over and against social and political pressures needs attention.

If historiographic tradition, in the United States at least, has emphasised the extent to which there has been social consensus on the goals and purposes of schooling, and radicals have recently brought to light many of the class and other conflicts which defy and deny consensus, there is another side of the coin yet to be explored comparatively. This is the fluidity and transformational character of the urban experience – as opposed to its many dislocations – as it has affected the family, the neighbourhood and those new aggregates of identification and meaning which may arise only in urban circumstances. Indeed, the significance of these oversights is not to be underestimated, for in Marsden's words, 'Much of the misunderstanding which has permeated academic debates about social class and school provision has resulted from the failure to take account of the disjunction between the official intent and not so much the aggregate response as the tangible individual family and group adjustments at the grass-roots.' As Heward's research on Birmingham reminds us, moreover, the choices made across the lifespan and the degree to which people have had to choose between formal education and other things of importance, including the maintenance of the family or obtaining work, have received far too little attention in the literature – an issue of growing significance as educators address increasingly the needs of the 'non-traditional' adult learner.

Most scholars of educational history are aware of the relationship between social demography, geography, aspiration and the evolution of educational practice and policy. The United States, for example, has historically been 'a nation on the move'. From its very beginnings, as Bailyn, Cremin and many other scholars have documented, immigration and the perpetual internal movement of Americans have influenced deeply the character of all the nation's informal and formal educational agencies, including the family, the church, the neighbourhood and the school and university. There is a literature which argues the need for demographic understanding to affect contemporary education policy.[1] The migration of blacks to the North since the Civil War and the outmigration of urban dwellers to the suburbs in the years after the Second World War have had a profound impact on American life. In the 1970s and 1980s migration to the 'Sun Belt' and the immigration of people from Asia, the Caribbean and Latin America have had significant political and economic consequences.

Relatively few historians of education in the United States have, however, taken into consideration the character of population clusters and when, where, why, how and by whom education policy decisions have been affected by them. This is a great unknown in the historiography. The problem, particularly as it concerns the city, it not unique to the literature of educational history. As stated by Dublin in a recent *Journal of American History* essay, altogether too much research has been narrowly focused and uncomparative. He writes that historical research regarding the nineteenth-century decline of America's rural population and the growth of its cities had 'been limited by the conceptual framework within which it has been carried out'. The rural and urban halves of the process of transformation have rarely been brought together and the problem is particularly evident among scholars of social and geographical mobility who have studied urban population movements and occupational change but who have almost invariably restricted their research to a single community, be it rural or urban. Within that context, generalisations about social mobility, in turn, have been limited to persistent residents in a given community. On occasion, the characteristics of migrants are compared with those of persisters, but rarely is there any analysis of the previous or subsequent experiences of migrants beyond the boundaries of the community under study.[2]

Other scholarship, namely that of one of this volume's editors, has helped set the stage for understanding these issues. Over a decade ago, in 1977, Marsden wrote that 'a "geography of education" is still in its infancy, and an "historical geography of education" hardly yet conceived. Similarly, the geographical component has been neglected by historians of education.'[3]

Shortly after these comments were made, several historians, including Marsden, contributed to Reeder's very useful volume, *Urban Education in the Nineteenth Century*. Homage to the Chicago School of ecological studies, which has dominated much study of the city throughout this century, was given. But *Urban Education in the Nineteenth Century* was also to argue for a more sophisticated approach. The various essays linked structural, hierarchical, cultural and other phenomena and did so in a manner alert to relations between city and town. A case for comparative studies of various kinds was demonstrated and sensitivity to location, space and geography was a feature of several essays. Reeder, the volume's editor, wrote modestly that 'These are early days yet for pronouncing on the range of approaches or judging the priorities for research, whether they should be the development of urban school systems, or the content and processes of urban schooling, or the study of social perceptions and school–community links.'[4] This said, Reeder's book stands as an excellent example of how social and cultural history is informed by social demography. What Katznelson in 1981 described as 'power networks, sets of solitary institutions, distinctive social groupings, psychic territories, loci or primary interactions, symbolic units, territories, market places, and "natural habitats" among other things', have, then, proved to be of increased attraction to historians.[5] The United States, Canada, Australia and, increasingly, Britain are nations of highly mobile immigrants and so they need to be explored by historians of the city in international context.

The contributors to this book were not asked to address issues of comparison and educational transfer between nations specifically. That is, they were not requested to write 'comparative' studies or dwell on the transfer internationally of ideas on education, historical research and cities. What emerges, however, from many of the following essays is a requirement that core questions for comparative historical study be identified and that cross-national influences be taken into consideration appropriately.

A problem which blocks such study, as pointed out by several authors, has been a failure in the United States and other nations to develop a 'comparative' history capable of comprehending the enormous diversity of cities, regions and cultures *within* individual nations. 'The deliberate use of comparison in urban educational history', Angus writes in this book, 'remains rare.' Though some historians, including Kaestle, who contributes to this volume, have broken important ground in the application of comparative methodology (in both domestic American and international settings), it may be argued that the main problem persists: much of what is known about urban education is derived from studies conducted in too few cities on too few segments of the population. The overall situation is not helped by the degree to which there are national traditions of comparative study which vary considerably. As Coulby argues in his essay, the condition of comparative education has kept it from becoming serious about schooling in cities. In some nations, the field of comparative education is wracked by debate on methodology, emphasis and whether historical analysis has any role to play. This, of course, limits its influence on historical inquiry substantially and serves to isolate historians from comparative insights on historical development and policy. We do not have, in Angus' terminology, a historiography that is necessarily 'cumulative', one that offers a steadily increasing knowledge, in his words, 'about the social systems of cities'.

As the essays in this volume reveal, scholars are paying more attention to schooling in cities. When seen in national context, however, the pattern of response has varied. Britain, for example, has only recently developed sophisticated scholarly cognisance of the urban educational condition, and this is largely as the result of the crises which have afflicted cities which themselves have undergone cycles of post-war prosperity and decline. Policy-making mechanisms and the uses of social science vary differently in America and Britain. Yet, as Reeder and Coulby point out here, the British have occasionally turned to the USA for ideas as they struggle with many of the racial and other problems American social scientists began to address well before the Second World War. In America, it is believed, links between scholarship and the addressing of social problems seem natural and progressive. Unfortunately, this borrowing has been highly fragmented, with much work on urban education being entirely devoid of historical context.

Elsewhere, it is possible to argue that Canada and perhaps Australia have suffered from a slightly more 'dependent' condition. As Sutherland and Barman contend, as early as the 1950s new scholarship on the dominant impact of cities in Canadian life suggested that 'Canada's very small number of cities were, in turn, vassals of such external metropolitan centres as London, New York and San Francisco.' There has been a paradoxical reaction to this dependence – brought about in part, as they note, by the influence of radical American social historians of education and their students who turned to Canadian topics. But whatever its ideological content, scholars in Canada, Australia and other nations have tried to develop perspectives to counter the influence of the United States and Britain, nations which have had greater intellectual and institutional capital and which, until recently, dominated graduate training, publishing and the funding of research. While some of these may take the form of enhanced national or domestic outlooks, there can be little doubt that those represented in *The city and education in four nations* are also cognisant of the need to develop a far more international and comparative approach to the enterprise and to use it as a means of reexamining old assumptions and methods.

Unfortunately, however, historians of education in cities must do their work in something of a vacuum, for scholars in the field have neither addressed issues of comparative methodology nor developed a sophisticated perspective on the transfer of ideas as part of an overall pattern of international scholarly relations.[6] Modes for transferring scholarship and policy on urban education and history have not been a major subject for study even in those countries (e.g., the United States) where a new generation of scholarship on the history or urban schooling has served to inspire considerable debate and methodologically sophisticated inquiry. Even radical proponents of 'the new urban social history' critical of mainstream modes of historical analysis – and prone to locate it within the context of international monopoly capitalism – have generally neglected to develop a comparative perspective or comment upon appropriate comparative methodologies even though their influence, as in the case of the American Michael B. Katz's work in Canada, has been powerful. In this regard, the transfer of influences between nations, and the outcomes of transfer, need far more work.

The reader of this volume will see, then, that domain issues are paradigmatic and that several writers are perplexed by the normative character of how urban education and its historiography have evolved over and against national traditions and competing modes of interpretation, including those, which as Sutherland and Barman point out, may be tipping the balance against 'urban' and 'urbanisation' as modes of classification. This, as Davey and Wimshurst suggest here, is not out of confusion about the nature of urban history, but is instead a reflection of the degree to which the sub-disciplinary boundaries of social history are changing.

The city and education in four nations should be read, therefore, not as a definitive statement on the state of research in the United States, Britain, Australia and Canada, though the information presented should be helpful in this regard. Nor does it seek closure. It is intended primarily as a volume which questions boundaries – between theory and practice, between categories and definitions, between fields of study and between nations – so as to encourage the location of work on schooling in cities in a more cosmopolitan context.

NOTES

1 See, especially, Bernard Bailyn, *Education in the Forming of American Society* (New York: Vintage Press, 1960); Lawrence A. Cremin, *American Education: The Colonial Experience, 1607–1783* (New York: Harper and Row, 1970); and

Lawrence A. Cremin, *American Education: The National Experience, 1783–1876* (New York: Harper and Row, 1980). For a useful argument which looks at contemporary urban demography and education policy, see Sheldon Marcus and Thomas A. Mulkeen, 'The new urban demography: implications for the schools', *Education and Urban Society*, Vol. 16 (1984), 395–6.

2 Thomas Dublin, 'Rural–urban migrants in industrial New England: the case of Lynn, Massachusetts, in the mid-nineteenth century', *Journal of American History*, Vol. 73 (December 1986), 623.

3 W. E. Marsden, 'Historical geography and the history of education', *History of Education*, Vol. 6, No. 6 (1977), 21.

4 David A. Reeder (ed.), *Urban Education in the Nineteenth Century* (New York: St Martin's Press, 1978), 10.

5 Ira Katznelson, *City Trenches, Urban Politics and the Patterning of Class in the United States* (Chicago, IL: University of Chicago Press, 1981), 196. See also Ira Katznelson and Margaret Weir, *Schooling for All: Class, Race, and the Decline of the Democratic Ideal* (New York: Basic Books, 1985).

6 For further elaboration upon the author's perspective on educational transfer issues, see Ronald K. Goodenow, 'The progressive educator and the third world: a first look at John Dewey', *History of Education*, Vol. 10, No. 1 (1990), 23–40.

Part 1

Research in national contexts

1 History, education and the city: a review of trends in Britain

David A. Reeder

Despite numerous accounts of the history of urban schools and schooling, there is no distinct genre of urban educational history in Britain. The preoccupation of educational historians with tracing the evolution of institutions in an urban context is primarily a reflection of the timing and extent of urbanisation in a country where half the population was living in urban districts just after the mid-nineteenth century and almost four-fifths of the population were classified as urban by 1914. The industrial-urban transformation has seemed so manifestly a force for change that educational historians have tended to take the urban emphasis in their studies for granted. This has left them vulnerable to the charge of exaggerating the role of the urban factor in educational change.[1]

Since urban-based studies have proliferated in an almost adventitious way, there has been no concerted effort to elucidate the significance of urbanisation, and, for the most part, the city has entered into the educational story mainly as a backdrop, with few questions asked about the interconnections between educational development and processes of urban or social change. In recent years, however, this situation has begun to alter with changes in the methodological scope of educational history in Britain and the development of a new thematic agenda. This essay will indicate how a more sophisticated and analytical approach to the history of schooling in the city (and to an associated range of social and cultural activities) has been contributing to a greater awareness of the relations between education and the city. An important historiographical development has been the application of what might be described very broadly as ecological and structuralist modes of analysis to educational and cultural activities in towns and cities in the past. Before tracing out the implications of these approaches, it may be helpful to put the new trends into broader perspective, with some comments on the changing orientations of historians and educationalists to the modern city more generally.

A vogue for urban analysis became prominent in Britain, as other advanced capitalist societies, during the 1960s. It was related to growing public anxiety about a set of social problems which had seemingly congealed into becoming 'the problem of the city'. Developments in urban studies, including the growth of new sub-disciplines, were a feature of a milieu in which the urban problem had become a matter of public debate and political concern to an extent not known since the 1880s. During this phase, urban policy was increasingly taken up with the idea of regenerating the inner city by drawing on the resources of welfare state capitalism, an outlook which led to new policies for inner city schools.

The emergence of urban history as a self-conscious academic pursuit was itself an aspect of the awakening of contemporary interest in the urban scene. As H. J. Dyos, the outstanding influence amongst the first generation of urban historians, pointed out in 1969, the city 'is now history's looking glass and what it reflects are the conflicts of race, class and ideology that are the products in our time of historical processes far transcending it'.[2] Nevertheless, for Dyos, the city was perceived as having a history in its own right. British historians were neglecting a major part of their cultural tradition by not exploiting it. Moreover, urban history was to be developed as the key urban study, a forum for interdisciplinary research and writing, as well as a way of providing a much-needed perspective on the problems of the urban present.[3] In practice, such large ambitions proved difficult to realise, and much of the impetus for urban history came from changes within historical studies.

British urban history was initially a by-product of economic history; but it was strongly influenced by a tradition of local and municipal history whose approaches it sought to transcend by taking in new methodologies and new historical interests as they arose. This eclecticism helped to maintain a momentum, but left urban history vulnerable to charges of becoming a 'portmanteau' subject. As more social historians located their studies in towns and cities, the ambiguity of what constituted the field increased and a great variety of studies, many with a society-wide context, were welcomed as contributing grist to the urban historical mill. The proliferation of new types of social history undoubtedly made for difficulties in maintaining the identity of modern urban history in Britain, although, paradoxically, there has been a renewed interest in urban themes particularly on the part of historians in the pre-modern period whose leading scholars have imparted a new impetus to urban historical study.

At the same time, changes in the economic and intellectual climate in the 1970s have undoubtedly affected perceptions of urban problems and of the city itself. In the more critical intellectual climate of the early 1980s, the independent status of urban history became more uncertain. It was no longer fashionable to conceive of the city as an independent or even a partially autonomous variable. Criticisms were made of a kind of a history which abstracts the urban from national, regional or local phenomena: this leads, so it was argued, to the reification of a spatial category which can no longer be understood as playing a discreet role within the historical process. Rather, the activities and development of urban institutions should be seen as functional to fundamental relations within complex social systems. The focus on urbanism served only to conceal a variety of more crucial explanatory mechanisms.[4]

However, contrary positions have been adopted on the definition of the urban by social theorists. The argument that the latter should 'renounce any connection between particular spatial locations (cities and towns) and urban studies' can be matched by the argument that 'the city cannot be regarded as merely incidental to social theory but belongs to its very core'.[5] These positions have been further complicated by developments in neo-Marxist analysis, as represented for example by the political economy of continental neo-Marxists such as Manuel Castells. The ideas of French critics of the 'urban question' have been drawn on by British writers to formulate a critique of urban policies, including urban educational policies, which have seemed to create more problems than they have solved with the ending of the long boom.[6] The point about recent Marxist theory, however, is that it not only offers a critique of older definitions of the urban question but restates the urban problematic in a new form. This may have implications for an urban history of the nineteenth century whose future direction, one leading proponent has argued, should lie in becoming increasingly reorientated towards the study of urbanism and in a way that addresses topics which are central to modern political debate, such as the effectiveness of market mechanisms in allocating the costs and benefits of urban growth.[7]

So the negative impact of structuralism, in the sense in which that term is used here, on the pursuit of urban history should not be exaggerated. Nor is structuralism, broadly defined, necessarily incompatible with well-established ecological interests and modes of inquiry as the work of the Marxist historical geographer David Harvey has shown. In recent years, urban historical geographers, as well as social historians, have become interested in the ideological and normative aspects of city development; and, as one geographer has remarked, if this means making necessary reference to the underlying economic system, or even regarding the city as but one element in a larger structural situation, 'then so be it'.[8] More positively, several geographers have sought to combine Marxist socioeconomic interpretations of urban change with inherently ecological perspectives, viewing the city as an 'ecological complex' that is historically produced and changing through time.[9] During the same period, a number of social historians have drawn attention to the nineteenth-century city as a locus or site of power struggles and of the formation of new social hierarchies.[10]

How far are these changing orientations being reflected in urban educational study? The first point to note is the lack of any interconnection between modern policy debates and urban educational history in Britain. The problems of inner city schooling gave rise from the 1960s to a plethora of sociological and educational publications, and these concerns may have influenced almost imperceptibly a renewed interest in the history of mass schooling, but there was no attempt self-consciously to develop an historical perspective on the contemporary debate. Urban educational policies were formulated 'without any adequate awareness of past endeavours to solve problems which may have been exacerbated or may have assumed new dimensions in our own times'.[11] The historians of education are not alone responsible for this neglect of history; it is also the case that urban educational study and debate was conducted in such a way as virtually to exclude them. The point was made in a powerful critique by Gerald Grace, a sociologist of education, of the literature of urban education which he argued was too 'present crisis orientated' and lacking in theory and an adequate sense of history. This critique formed part of a symposium in which Grace argued for what he called a 'critical scholarship' of the urban, based on the application of neo-Marxist analysis. A key notion is the idea of 'urban contradictions', the phrase suggesting that the experience of urban schooling is indicative of the dilemmas created by the wider structural contradictions of a capitalist society. The history-forming part of the critical scholarship should have these dilemmas very much in mind. The plea which Grace makes for a more critical history of the urban school as an agency of cultural transmission reflects his own interests in the cultural dilemmas of teachers in schools in urban working-class neighbourhoods in the 1970s.[12]

Relatively few historians of education have been interested in raising consciousness about an urban focus in educational history and the showpiece conference organised for the History of Education Society in 1976, and published as *Urban Education in the Nineteenth Century* (1977) showed little overt concern for the contemporary situation. This conference was, nevertheless, a first attempt at stimulating interest in urbanisation as an explanatory variable in the history of education. One aim was to bring urban historians and historians of education together so as to start making good the neglect of schooling within urban history – an endeavour which has continued since.[13] From the point of view of the history of education, the conference was one of several initiatives to broaden the scope of research, and as such it became an incident in a more complex historiographical story.

The mid-1970s seem to have been a watershed in British educational history. The sense of change, of new themes, more ambitious methodologies, was conveyed in several 'state of the art' reviews, notably an edition of the *Oxford Review of Education* on history and education whose commissioned editor discerned 'a new vitality, spontaneity and creativity in the field'.[14] An influential contribution was made by Harold Silver who highlighted the need to escape from an unthinking administrative bias in the history of popular education to make reference to differing viewpoints and opinions and the experience of schooling.[15]

One stimulus to broadening out was the new interest of economic and social historians in education. This had not only generated some controversies over substantive issues, but was helping to extend the agenda of educational history, connecting it with the history of childhood and of popular culture, literacy studies and developments in social recruitment and social control, as illustrated for example by articles published in the mainstream social history journal, *Past and Present*.[16] A contributory element here was the incursion of American historians on the English educational scene, several of whom were interested in educational history as revealing aspects of British life and culture. The external influences notwithstanding, the impetus for change also came from within the History of Education Society (founded in 1968), some of whose leading members sought to promote a broader vision of the study and engaged in large-scale reassessments of the educational past that took into account social and political contexts.[17] Two aspects of this broadening out, characteristic of the 1970s, was the interest in the relations between sociology and history in educational studies, mainly in regard to upper-class schooling, and, in contrast, the promotion of new work on labour history in relation to working-class education. But the main concern, as it had been since the 1950s, continued to be the history of state education, studied mainly in administrative terms, and with regard to the role of government, and also increasingly in relation to national politics. But from the mid-70s and extending to the present day, the impact of the so-called new social history was affecting the scope of history of education in publications, documentary texts and annual conferences. Such topics as literacy, 'informal education', middle-class education, education and the working class and the education of women and girls were placed firmly on the historical agenda. There was a new and sociologically informed interest in the emergence and consolidation of educational ideology, whether of the public school or of popular education.

However, it is not easy to gain an overall view of the state of British educational history: it is a diffuse study which caters for a variety of professional and academic interests, and reflects not only historiographical developments but changing priorities and concerns in teacher education.[18] The change in the educational system represented by comprehensive reorganisation and the attempts by a Conservative government to introduce widespread changes in the educational system in the later 1980s have stimulated a resurgence of critical interest in the recent history of educational policy-making and the history of curriculum developments, much of this work drawing on the insights afforded by social and cultural history. Despite this responsiveness to developments in mainstream history, some educational historians concerned with the interrelations between education and society in the past have relayed from time to time a sense of having to overcome much inertia. As late as 1980, for example, John Hurt was suggesting that a bifurcation still existed in the outlook and interests of historians of education associated on the one side with a college teaching situation which tends to be insulated still from mainstream history.[19]

Perhaps the most important division in the literature is that persistent division between writings in which educational change is assumed to be generally progressive in character and those in which change is presented as complex and problematical in intentions and outcomes. Whilst there cannot be said to be a school of radical revisionists comparable to that which has emerged in America, the critical edge of British historical writing on education had been strengthened by contributions from historians influenced by Marxist and neo-Marxist intellectual standpoints. The focus of attention initially in the new critical history was on industrialisation, the proletarianisation of workers and the dislocation of family structures. Such developments were seen as contradictory in their impact on popular education: undermining traditional education, inhibiting new forms of mass schooling on the one hand whilst on the other encouraging perceptions of crisis and the need for reform. But whereas in the USA this focus was associated with urbanisation as an important explanatory variable, the interconnections in English work were not made very explicit. In Britain, Marxist revisionists in the history of education have tended to be on their guard against urban bias and exaggerating the urban factor in educational change.[20] Furthermore, an early emphasis on the way that educational reform was functional to industrial capitalism has been challenged by post-structuralist revisionist accounts and the development of feminist perspectives, the latter appearing to offer a challenge to the dominance of class analysis in the history of educational reform. These are trends which tend to play down the importance of both urbanisation and industrialisation as the crucial variables in explanatory models of educational change.

On the other hand, the distrust of grand theory amongst British educational historians and the continuing emphasis on the importance of historical specificity on the part of critical historians has meant that much new work tends to be based still on case studies in urban contexts – a trend that is reinforced by a move away from interpretations of change at the national level to more detailed local case studies which can take account of how schooling is experienced as well as provided. So far as the development of the school system is concerned, there has always been a strong case for taking into account local conditions, but in addition to this older emphasis on the sub-national scale in English educational development, there is now a much more explicit concern to take account of variations over space as well as over time – in school systems and in the family and social structures associated with them. This sensitivity to spatial variations can be said to be the hallmark of those who have been most prominent in the development of urban educational history in Britain, as the following more detailed account of methodological trends will seek to show. The question to be examined, then, is how far recent changes in methods and emphasis have been contributing in quite specific ways to the evolution of urban educational history?

Let us begin with the long-standing concern with the provision and administration of schools and school systems, a concern that has produced a variety of case studies of urban schooling as teachers and students turned from the national picture to chart progress on the ground. Take first, the proliferation of studies on the logistics of provision. What is noticeable here is the effort being made to explain variations in provision as between different types of community, and over time, and by reference to the distribution of schooling within towns and cities as well as between them. Institutional history is being transformed by an approach that is, in part, a by-product of the rise of quantitative demographic history but which reflects also the application of ecological concepts and thinking. As such, this approach has the potential to illuminate the significance of urban environmental factors in the history of schooling.

A starting point for the development of a demographic cum ecological approach in the history of urban education was the replication of local studies of educational provision on the part of post-graduate students. As early as 1973, W. B. Stephens signalled the need for a more analytical way of undertaking these studies in an argument for investigating regional variations in educational provision during the industrial revolution. Stephens made a plea for a comparative approach making use of statistics of school provision and school enrolments in published returns. He went on subsequently to explore the relations between schooling and the growth of literacy, extending the earlier argument to explore variations in standards of literacy and to bring out the diversity in the cultural experience of provincial England in the early and mid-Victorian period. He has also been concerned to show that such variations existed not only as between town and country but town and town within these different regions.[21]

As is well known, the signatories of marriage registers (which had to be signed either with a name or a cross) have provided data for compiling statistical indices of literacy (or illiteracy) for the eighteenth and nineteenth centuries. Research based on this data was undertaken against the background of an ongoing debate about the relations between industrialisation, school provision and the growth of literacy. This had the advantage for urban educational history of focusing attention on the northern industrial towns. The view was advanced that industrial take-off was not assisted by a growing level of literacy, and several studies tended to confirm a picture of northern industrial towns as suffering from a collapse in standards of literacy in the later eighteenth and nineteenth centuries.[22] A second wave of studies, beginning in the 1970s, was more broadly based and concerned with wider issues of modernisation. W. B. Stephens chose a representative selection in a publication of 1983. The emphasis was on studying factors influencing literacy, including relationships and attitudes to the provision and use of schooling in districts that illustrated different types of economic activity and population structure, including small country towns as well as industrial and commercial centres. This variety was important to the editor and brought out the need for 'a more sophisticated differentiation of community types'. A similar conclusion was reached by Harvey Graff in reviewing American studies for this symposium: as he said, '"urbanity" is too gross a measure for variations in types of communities'.[23] This is not to imply that the concept should be abandoned, only to recognise the diversity of the urban experience, especially in Britain.

Thematic local studies continue to be a way of exploring the significance of that diversity. With regard to literacy, they are providing a context for increasingly sophisticated work using methods of record linkage which offers the possibility of establishing more precise relationships by linking data from different data sources with the aid of the computer.[24] Local studies of urban schooling are also more sophisticated in techniques and methodology, despite the persistence of an older descriptive tradition. New work seeks systematically to elucidate the interconnections between school provision, school enrolments and local social systems evaluating such factors as the strengths of rival religious denominations, the role of local elites, the availability and character of local employment, as well as the overall social and demographic character of populations.[25]

A key theme in recent locally based investigation has been the quantitative analysis of the incidence of school enrolments and school attendance. This work can help to throw light on basic issues in the nineteenth-century history of schooling. It is necessary in order to decide, for example, how far the problems of elementary schooling in attracting and holding working-class pupils in the major cities, as implied in contemporary investigations, was less a failure of overall provision than of the maldistribution of provision. How far can the criticisms of contemporary observers of working-class families be supported? Was there really a stratum of the population in the poorer districts unwilling to send children to school? And to what extent was the effective demand of working-class parents undermined by economic and domestic pressures leading to irregular school attendance? Or, to move up the social scale, what was the impact of the emergence of a lower middle class in the larger cities on the demand for schooling and the emergence of a new 'modern' sector of post-elementary education? Central to all these issues is the question of who went to school and for how long. The systematic collection and analysis of data on school enrolments and attendance can help to establish this and test hypotheses about the socio-economic factors and relationships involved. No great claims can be made about the technical sophistication of this work so far, and it has been hampered by the poor rate of survival of attendance registers in many cities. Nevertheless, useful studies have been made of such matters as the incidence of schooling in Leeds, patterns of school attendance in London and Preston, social recruitment to an organised science school in Birmingham, the provision of schooling at the margins of the lower middle and skilled working class in Southport, the relationships between environment, social attitudes and educational provision and achievement (as measured by elementary school 'standards') in the Merseyside town of Bootle, and the relationships between home, school and work in the Birmingham jewellery quarter.[26]

Many of these studies make use of information in the census enumerators' schedules of households from which the aggregated published returns for the census districts were compiled. The value of these schedules as containing direct evidence on the incidence of schooling from the designation of scholar in the return of child occupations was first argued in 1972, but has since turned out to be more problematical than was first thought. A characteristic of more recent work is the use of 'indirect' evidence: the details of household composition, parental occupations and birthplaces, from which it is possible to construct socio-economic profiles of the catchment areas of schools at ten yearly intervals, 1841–81. Thus, schooling can be brought into connection with the morphological development of the city, linking into an established genre of urban history concerned with the social dynamics of residential development by means of the utilisation of social area analysis.

Amongst educational historians, W. E. Marsden has been most influenced by socio-geographical or ecological approaches. His pioneering forays into previously uncharted urban territory form part of a series of studies of spatial inequalities in educational provision and take-up at national, regional, metropolitan and local urban levels, which throw light on the origins of the contemporary 'distribution' problematic in the allocation of resources in urban education.[27] A central contention is that territorial segregation, social stratification and educational gradation interacted to reproduce inequality. By the late nineteenth century, as his contribution to this volume argues, schooling provisions reflected distinctions in status, income levels and parental choice; and, more than that, they reinforced social distinctions, even at the level of elementary education where Marsden points to the development of a hierarchy of elementary schooling in the metropolis. The mechanism of gradation was the school fee. Another researcher has provided confirmatory evidence of the relations between the catchment areas of elementary schools and social differentiation amongst the working classes in a study of late Victorian and Edwardian Birmingham.[28]

This is not the only theme to be explored: an important aspect of the process of social polarisation was the declining middle-class support for the voluntary schools in those cities subject to suburbanisation on a large scale. As one study of the London Kentish suburbs in the early and mid-Victorian period put it, the effect of middle-class migration away from the old core districts was to 'pull the rug from under the voluntary schools'.[29] The rise of suburbs was also important to middle-class schooling, of course, affecting the fortunes of old-established endowed and proprietory schools beached in or near city centres whilst leading to a proliferation of new private schools and academies in the suburbs, a process that still goes on. There are some descriptions but few systematic investigations of these relationships.[30] However, the issue of how far schooling was able to respond to new aspirations for social mobility, especially on the part of the lower middle class, is a matter that is beginning to receive more attention.[31] Yet it has to be said that amongst recent general accounts of twentieth-century educational development very little prominence is given to evaluating the impact of ecological change (as embodied in the growth of suburban housing estates, for example) on the social distribution of urban populations and its implications for school catchment areas in the interwar years. For the post-war period, however, Roy Lowe has made a point of highlighting the significance of the impact of suburban change on the school policies of local educational authorities.[32]

The ecological approach still remains to be further exploited. But work in this field so far is sufficient to raise fundamental questions about the relevance of size and scale as factors in educational change, since much of the evidence on the impact of urban social change comes from the history of schooling in the big cities. It also raises questions about the scope of urban educational history. W. E. Marsden looks on a socio-ecological approach, when separated from its earlier association with a philosophy of urbanism, as forming the basis for an interdisciplinary pursuit of urban educational history. But the framework he proposes is based on taking account mainly of demography, changes in urban social structure and in the urban experience as expressed in modes of behaviour and thought characteristic of urbanites.[33] The problem here is to avoid a too deterministic model of urban educational change by incorporating politics and the decision-making of administrative bodies into the explanatory analysis of what was happening in particular urban locations. But how far can matters related to decision-making be combined with an ecological approach? And should we regard political cum administrative studies as representative of a distinct alternative mode of explanation?

The political and administrative history of urban education takes various forms, some of which seem more capable than others of contributing to urban themes. There are several straightforward accounts of city schooling which set out in effect to trace the development of educational sub-systems. These vary considerably in the extent to which they link up educational development with local social systems.[34] Then there are thematic studies of the urban administrative process, as, for example, the study of administrative agencies and of the growth of expertise, from the lowly school attendance officers to the powerfully influential directors of education in the inter-war years and beyond. The value of most of these studies, however, lies more in the illumination of administrative than urban themes.[35] On the other hand the broader conceptual framework of recent administrative history has encouraged a new emphasis on the dynamics of change as evidenced in such matters as the interplay of local politics and the impact of pressure groups on educational movements and educational decision-making. Recent administrative studies have dealt with the interplay of central–local relations, as in the conflicts over the ambitions of late Victorian urban school boards; and others have examined the history of comprehensive reorganisation in the 1960s to elucidate the role of local politics and community interests in educational change.[36] There are now many studies of the politics of urban education which are concerned to link the national and local in a way that makes urban educational history a kind of borehole able to penetrate various layers of the political system.[37] These studies include descriptions of party political attitudes and activities at the local level, as, for example, the role of Labour in the formation of educational policy in northern industrial towns.

But the more significant contributions to urban educational history have come from studies concerned with an altogether broader approach to the politics of educational reform and new institutional developments. Some of them succeed in throwing light on how urban energies and needs generated new demands for educational reform; others more directly and explicitly show how urban educational institutions functioned in relation to the process of class formation. These two approaches will be treated as separate categories in illustrating the way they contribute to urban themes, but there is much overlap, and many of the educational and cultural historians in the first of the categories represent their accounts of new initiatives as manifestations of the social and cultural ambitions of the urban middle class. To that extent, all these studies can be regarded as contributing to a socio-economic perspective on urban educational history, even when they offer descriptive accounts as distinct from a thorough-going structuralist analysis.

Historians of educational ideas or reform movements have frequently made links between the intellectual milieu of radical groups, the representatives of a middling class, in London and other cities in the early nineteenth century, and the formulation of novel educational ideas – the ideas, for example, that lay behind the distinctively British conception of the infant school or those associated with the self-consciously utilitarian conception of the ideal middle-class school. Others have paid attention to groups of predominantly middle-class citizens in northern and midland industrial towns who were prominent in new educational campaigns from the 1840s – the campaign for national elementary education, for example, which originated from the interrelated political, social and religious ambitions of Manchester businessmen. The optimistic rationalism of some radical leaders in the cities was reflected in the advocacy of new forms of government – the provincial board of regional administration by the Manchester reformers, a more full-blown democratic localism on the part of Sheffield reformers. It was also reflected in the endorsement which reforming groups gave to the idea of a new-style secular curriculum for the people whose rationale was shaped by intellectual influences that flowed along an Edinburgh–London–Manchester axis. The subsequent, well-researched campaign of the 1860s, based on Birmingham, further illustrates the interconnections between local dissent and radical politics; whilst an interest in the quintessentially urban communities of middle-class Unitarians has revealed their pervasive influence in defining the constituents of an emergent urban culture in which education (including that of girls) had a central place.[38] The considerable body of descriptive institutional studies undertaken by educational and local historians on the various voluntary associations concerned with the promotion of science and art in the cities amply demonstrates the cultural energies of the Victorian urban middle class. A more significant contribution to urban educational history, however, has been made by those historians concerned with institutional developments as a study in the politics of culture.[39]

A paradox in the cultural life of Britain is the apparent failure of the urban middle class to develop a systematic provision of schooling for their own children on the basis of an urban utilitarian model. The reasons are complex but of crucial social importance to claims made by cultural historians about the way that upper-class norms continued to be diffused throughout urban industrialised England. Educational historians have contributed to this debate about cultural diffusion in various ways. They have argued for the role of the public school as a source of cultural diffusion showing how these high-status boarding establishments became increasingly important to the family ambitions of urban leaders. They have shown that these schools played a key role in the symbiosis, or fusion, of the commercial, financial and industrial (to a lesser extent) bourgeoisie and the aristocracy together with leading elements from the leading professions, into what is called the Victorian upper middle class.[40] But they have also shown how these schools transformed older upper-class values in the interests of an elite defending its privileges but inspired by the motivations and concepts of evangelical religion. And, as the most recent social historian of the culture of the urban middle class has pointed out, the 'family ideals' of the evangelical and respectable were not aristocratic in origin: 'they were transmitted to the aristocracy as part of the bargaining with the powerful culture created in places like Leeds, Birmingham and Manchester'.[41] Evidently, there is no simple relationship between the rise of an industrial urban society and cultural developments.

Other contributions to the history of middle-class education provide information that throws light on the divisions within the urban middle class over the schooling of their own children and their failure to organise a systematic provision of middle-class schools. There is much evidence in local histories of bitter conflicts and divisions over the ambitions of many of the town grammar schools and endowments – ambitions that were frequently in conflict with the needs of a petty bourgeoisie who were so reliant on these schools and the free place provisions they offered. There is also much descriptive evidence available on how distortions in local provision were created because of the patronage of the middle class of private and proprietary schools whose various curricula were governed by market forces rather than educational principle.[42]

All these matters are brought together and put in chronological context in Margaret Bryant's comprehensive account of the metropolitan contribution to the evolution of a concept and system of secondary education.[43] In dealing with the London experience in the nineteenth century, this account gives proper attention to the variety and extent of private and proprietary schools in the capital showing how responsive middle-class education was to the social and topographical complexity of the metropolis. It also shows how curricular change and experiments on the part of many notable London schools reflected the intellectual as well as the practical challenges posed by a large modernising city. But the author concedes that despite the success of such endowed grammar schools as the City of London school, the 'heroic ingenuity' of private adventure schools and the advantages of those 'brilliant improvisations', the London proprietary schools, none of these institutions proved capable of forming the basis for an organised and coherent system. New initiatives in middle-class education were sporadic and piecemeal, and in the absence of any agreed model of what middle-class education should be, London schooling continued to be influenced by localist interests and sectarian differences whilst powerful conservative interests obstructed adaptations to change, especially those imposed from above in the form of the recommendations of the Endowed Schools Commissioners. Nor was London exceptional in these respects. Even in the provincial cities where one would have expected middle-class initiatives in the provision of schooling to have counted for more, there was no co-ordinated urban attempt to develop plans for the organisation of middle-class schooling before the 1860s, either within these cities or on a national scale.

What, then, did influence the attempted reorganisation of middle-class schooling as embodied in the plans of the Endowed Schools Commission? The conclusion reached by David Allsobrook after a detailed study of the background to this commission is that the more significant influences came from the rural counties; and he argues persuasively that ideas evolved in a rural context and representative of what he calls a 'Georgic model' of education had great potency in the plans that were developed at the time and in the development of a concept of secondary education more generally.[44] This model reflected a conjunction between the representatives of upper-class gentry society in the counties and the academic liberals based in the Universities of Oxford and Cambridge. Hence, the effort to reorganise and establish new principles for middle-class education can be regarded as an attempt at social retrenchment, restoring the stabilising influences of the countryside as against the mercurial politics of the town, and in the interests of what the cultural theorists regarded as the organic unity of the state.

Historians of urban institutional developments in the late Victorian city have carried further this ongoing debate about the social politics of culture. They have seen in this period a resurgence of urban energies as manifested in new initiatives in higher elementary, technical and higher education in association with a meritocratic and utilitarian outlook on the need for educational change. The outcome of this energetic upthrust within the centres of urban culture in the main provincial cities was the beginnings of the development of an 'alternative system' which had a quite different ethos and different objectives to traditional institutions.[45] On the other hand, the late nineteenth century was notable for the way that liberal academics broadened the concept of liberal culture and associated it with a doctrine of collective responsibility based on social citizenship. These values were carried into the city in a cultural mission which ranged from the kindergarten to the adult tutorial class and the university college. It was a mission that overlapped with new religiously inspired initiatives amongst working-class youth which can be seen as underpinned by the concept of Christ's duty to the city, revitalising its religious and educational life.[46] Some historians have shown how vulnerable such pre-eminently city institutions as the new university colleges were to cultural infiltration on the part of Oxbridge representatives of liberal culture; and in the world of adult education it seems that the academic aggrandisers triumphed eventually over those who had genuinely sought to open up new opportunities in the industrial cities.[47] Yet it would be a mistake to represent local urban elites as merely giving way to these outside influences: on the contrary, they were themselves more coherently organised, much less functional in outlook, than in earlier times, able systematically to develop such civic strategies as Birmingham's 'civic gospel' or Bristol's social citizenship. And they were capable of holding idealistic concerns in tension with a sense of the practical requirements of city life, as is evident in the way that school boards in many cities were encouraged to develop a modern sector of higher elementary education to the consternation of the officials of the central government's Department of Education. The government-led reconstruction of secondary education that occurred in the first decade of the twentieth century was undertaken once again by those who were concerned to preserve social stability and maintain cultural uniformity. The implications of this reorganisation for the role of technical and vocational education in the inter-war city is only just beginning to receive thorough evaluation and illustration.[48] But the general point to make is that the English experience of educational development in the view of Brian Simon tends to the conclusion 'that the forces primarily involved in the restructuring and systematisation of English education were political and social rather than economic' and 'the struggle of subordinate classes for hegemony in a capitalist society may conflict with the role of "established culture"'.[49]

Historians of class formation and cultural developments have begun to offer systematic analysis, based on the experience of particular cities, of how urban educational institutions became a site of struggle and negotiation as between classes and as between class fractions with different objectives. The most thorough-going non-Marxist structural interpretation of urban educational development in these terms is a study by a sociological historian, Dennis Smith, of social relations in Birmingham and Sheffield in the nineteenth century.[50] Smith contends that the institutional history of the Victorian cities had a strategic importance in the evolution of English society. The role of city educational institutions was not merely to provide an index of social differentiation but to become a means by which various social groups actively participated in the shaping of new social configurations. A complex form of structural analysis is used to make sense of the precise connections from this point of view between social and educational change which provides a valuable perspective for understanding the character, government and use of educational institutions. One feature of this account is that it embraces all the main educational agencies from the Sunday school to the civic college. Another is that it succeeds in highlighting the nature of variations between the two cities. Differences of urban context really did imply differing patterns of formal education, the great city furnishing a repertoire of institutional arrangements, the nature of which has to be understood in terms of the development and configuration of local elites and their relationships not only with a local petty bourgeoisie and the working class but also with county society, and, increasingly, the state. What is particularly interesting about this structuralist analysis is the attempt at relating developments to different levels or scales of activity from the national level to the local community.

The coming together of a structuralist with an ecological perspective is also evident in recent studies of urban cultural institutions. It can be observed, for example, in the work of those historians of science prominent recently as intermediaries between urban history and education in the study of adult institutions as urban cultural phenomena. This has begun to involve a more pointed analysis of these institutions in terms of the cultural and social geography of the early Victorian city: who actually financed and provided institutions, the social recruitment of members, relations of the scientific community to county and metropolitan society on the one hand and on the other to emergent social networks in the city. Deciphering the connections between culture, class and community is seen as a legitimate interest on the part of urban historical geographers as well as social historians.[51]

The popularity of science in the urban culture of early Victorian England is no longer in doubt, but there are various interpretations of its significance to debates about the relations between class and cultural development to which this survey has already referred. One issue is whether science institutes reflected an autonomous cultural development on the part of the urban middle class or whether this development was subverted from the outset by the cultural imprint of county and metropolitan society. Arnold Thackray, an American historian, threw down the gauntlet on the basis of work on early Victorian Manchester in claiming that science activists and audiences were significantly representative of an alternative value system and their success as urbanites was an element in the social transformation of Britain in the period of the industrial revolution. The key to understanding, Thackray argued, may lie in 'the social legitimation of marginal men', through membership of a science institute.[52] Since then, other historians have tended to put more emphasis on the importance of these institutes to the public role of emergent urban elites. Indeed, the combined effect of several local studies, as one symposium makes clear, is to point to the need to 'recognise and accommodate contingent variations in the specific contexts of an early Victorian science culture'. This is important in taking account of provincial responses to the cultural influence and authority of London, one of the themes of the symposium, as well as in looking at the relations between science and local social networks. Manchester was by no means all of urban England: the situation in Bristol, for instance, was quite different in that science played a dominant role within already established elites, and was conservative in emphasis, whilst science in Edinburgh, to take another case, was much affected by tensions arising from the status of a city that was a provincial capital. The editors of this symposium, Ian Inkster and Jack Morrell, pay attention in their introduction to both demographic and structural aspects of urbanisation in what amounts to a discussion of Louis Wirth's proposition that voluntary associations developed as 'intrinsic structural concomitants of a process of urbanization'.[53]

Another issue to concern historians of science institutions in the Victorian city has been how they functioned as agencies of popular education. Here, the starting point for structuralist analysis has been the claims made by Shapin and Barnes on the basis of researches in Edinburgh that these institutes were a form of class cultural domination. This kind of argument has been challenged with regard to the experience of other cities, notably by Ian Inkster in a study of Sheffield which claims that the institutes provided a vehicle for the social elevation of a clearly identifiable sub-group. Garner and Jenkins, on the other hand, in a study of the Leeds Mechanics' Institutes are more concerned to relate the type of social control to educational effectiveness: they argue that in Leeds, a patrician class controlled the Institute, co-ordinated instruction and established clearly defined 'spheres of influence' for this and other adult institutes in the town. Again, what this underlines is the importance of taking cognisance of different local conditions.[54]

Indeed, the problem with many of the early structuralist interpretations of the history of popular education, for urbanists, is that they made scant reference to the local (mainly urban) context in which these studies were located. Nevertheless, the emergence of this critical perspective, whether based on a concept of social control or utilising the more radical and theoretically based concept of class cultural control, has opened up a range of new topics in urban educational history, as well as raising controversial issues. The initial impact of this perspective was to promote a series of studies concerned with the intentions and motives of the founders of schools and, more broadly, the relations between new educational developments and what Richard Johnson called a 'crisis in hegemony' on the part of the Anglican church, factory owners and coal owners in the industrial and mining districts affected by working-class political and educational movements.[55] Some of these writings proved very controversial; and others prompted leading educational and social historians to criticise the unilateral nature of social control theory and express considerable scepticism as to whether the intentions of the providers can ever be said to have been effective in practice. A variety of studies emerged to pose awkward questions about the cruder versions of social control theory. Some of these were concerned with asking why such provided agencies as the Sunday schools appeared so rapidly to become integral to working-class community life. Others were more concerned to challenge the idea of schooling and other educational institutions as effective disseminators of values. In the sphere of adult education, it has been argued that depicting situations in terms of social control denies or glosses over a range of reactions to middle-class intellectual and cultural initiatives. Recent studies of such new initiatives as the urban settlement movement have been more sensitive to these reactions.[56]

What the social control approach did succeed in doing was to foster a more general interest in the ideological influences on the history of popular education, although not necessarily in the context of exposing the authority relations of capitalist society. One of the new topics opened up in recent years is the relations between education and urban poverty as represented by a growing historical literature on the provision and experience of workhouse schools, ragged, reformatory and industrial schools, and philanthropic orphanages; but each of these subjects has tended to be dealt with in a largely unconnected way and many studies are merely descriptive and lacking any theoretical perspective.[57] Nor has there been much attention paid to the relevance of European neo-Marxist and Foucaultian theories on the role of the penitentiary, and an asylum concept of reform, to the definition and treatment of 'deviancy' in capitalist societies. One reason for this, perhaps, is the very abstract way that links are made in the theoretical and historical literature between what one French historian has called the 'social technology' implicit in making educational provision for poor children and the rise of an industrial-urban society.[58]

One way of making these links is through exploring contemporary perceptions of the sub-culture of poverty and street life that lay behind many new schemes and policy recommendations. Social historians have traced the relations between poverty and juvenile delinquency in contemporary perceptions: at one level tracing out how a concept of delinquency emerged in the writings of urban investigators and philanthropic workers, and, at another level, showing how 'destitute juveniles were frequently classified as delinquent juveniles and treated accordingly' (by the London police).[59] This way of making sense of new initiatives in the cities has been most in evidence in the history of education and childhood for the period of the late nineteenth and early twentieth centuries, a period identified as reflecting a distinct cycle of anxiety about growing up in the city.[60] This work reflects a desire to take account of the urban experience – at least as refracted through contemporary perceptions – and link this up with the evolution of concepts of adolescence. It has come to fruition in several investigations of an ideology of youth in late Victorian and Edwardian England.[61] A related approach is that dealing with ideological influences affecting the education of girls. One writer succeeds in demonstrating the symbolic power of dualistic notions of the urban and the domestic in the rhetoric of educational reformers. And late Victorian perceptions of the urban experience have been incorporated into studies that are concerned with the development of an ideology of motherhood and its implications for the education of working-class girls.[62] There is, indeed, a whole range of interconnections that can be made in studying the climate of social and educational opinion in the late nineteenth and early twentieth centuries as between the urban historian's concern with elucidating attitudes towards city life, the social historian's concern with an ideology of childhood and the educationalist's concern with progressive movements of reform.[63] In the last respect, it is necessary to recognise the ambivalence of progressive educational ideas towards city life. In this ideological outlook, there was a conservative tradition of ideas deeply pessimistic about the implications of industrialism for the quality of life in modern urban society, but on the other hand, from Owen onwards, there was a radical tradition of communitarianism in which a reformed system of education would become the spiritual hub of planned communities. In the early twentieth century, as recent work has shown, this tradition took a new turn when the model of the new education as implemented by independent progressive schools was taken up and promoted in connection with the ideology of the garden city planning movement.[64]

But to return to the question of ideology and the urban experience, it might be argued that we have had enough now of exploring climates of opinion and that the more important task is to research how far contemporary perceptions reflected real changes in the condition and lifestyle of the urban working class. Indeed, one reason why a social control approach has gone out of fashion in the history of popular education is not only its ambiguity as a theoretical concept but the way it tends both to exaggerate the consistency of purpose amongst the middle-class sponsors of education and to underestimate the independence and autonomy of the working class.[65] The radical critique has gone through various phases, moving away from cruder versions of theories of social reproduction to lay stress on social theories that emphasise contradictions, resistance and human agency; and a new critical view has emerged of the direction in which a structuralist history of popular culture should be going.[66] These movements within social history coincided with a renewed emphasis in the history of education on studying the attitudes of working-class people to educational reform and their use of provided institutions.[67]

One theme explored by historians of popular culture is the activities of a stratum of artisans in the nineteenth century who actively co-operated in attempts at the moral reformation of their fellow workers. An artisan reforming tradition seems to have existed in several cities, Birmingham notably, broader than but overlapping with the social politics of Owenite radicalism.[68] Exponents of this view have been careful, however, to avoid merely reinforcing nineteenth-century distinctions between the 'respectable' and the 'rough'. What the argument illustrates is a general trend in the history of popular culture whereby a model of 'hegemony' is giving way to one that emphasises 'negotiation' within and between classes. The implications for the historian of popular education is to seek a better understanding of the ambiguities and tensions surrounding the attitudes of working-class people towards education and schooling, and, to that end, develop a more interactive methodology in local studies of urban schooling.

The need for a new perspective is further underlined in other research on the attitudes of working-class people to education, as reflected, for example, in studies of local Chartist and labour branch activity, an aspect of what A. E. Dobbs once called an 'education by collision'. Then there are the studies of worker educational efforts – the Mutual Improvement Societies, for example, a prime case of how workers were effective in raising standards of literacy and shaping new leisure activities.[69] Nor can we ignore the ubiquity and role of private schooling in the repertoire of working-class parents in urban communities before the 1870s, thanks to the efforts made in recovering so many of what Phil Gardner calls the 'lost elementary schools' of England.[70] If there really was, as Gardner suggests, 'a powerful identifiable working-class educational culture', we need to know more about how this influenced and fitted in with attitudes towards the whole range of educational facilities at the local level for adults and children. This may entail some kind of socio-ethnological approach, focusing on working-class people as social actors in a local (community) world.

This is where the ecological approach should lead, Marsden has suggested, in pointing to ways of recreating aspects of schooling in late Victorian slum neighbourhoods. The local study, whether of a town or neighbourhood, also provides an opportunity for relating schooling to basic processes of family formation and life strategies, as Christine Heward indicates in her contribution to this volume. How did the conflicting pressures on working-class parents work out in practice? Heward's work is based on the premiss that school attendance was a family decision, and that schooling, paid work and home help were systematically interconnected, the strategies adopted being affected by structural developments in the economy.[71] A similar premiss underpins a new wave of post-graduate studies on the late Victorian elementary schools, all of which make use of methodological developments in family history, particularly the family strategies approach, to help elucidate attitudes and relationships in different types of community settings.[72] There is a new incentive to reexamine relationships between home, school and work; and also to look again at how bureaucratic structures associated with the development of schooling in the later nineteenth century affected family decision-making. From this point of view, for example, the enforcement of school attendance can become a significant index of community relations. An earlier picture of this enforcement, based on a pioneering study of the London School Board's attempts to enforce strict policies, has been subsequently modified. In the small Essex textile towns, it seems that school boards were primarily institutions of negotiation and facilitation, remitting school fees where they could and bending the regulations in the effort to meet the problems of parents. Nor was it only the poor who were adversely affected by the introduction of compulsory schooling.[73]

The attempt to reconstruct the normative attitudes of the working class towards education is very much dependent on the development of particular school studies in which schooling is related to the work and life situations of children and parents. This is a claim which echoes the emphasis of Raphael Samuel, a leading exponent of 'history from below' in seeking to promote a new type of local history to which he has contributed himself in reconstructing some of the more fugitive aspects of the life of poor children in late Victorian London.[74] An ethno-historical approach becomes more possible with the proliferation of published reminiscences of childhood and a more evocative style of local history in which there is more information about the lives of children and teachers in the past. A start has been made also on the systematic use of personal reminiscences, and of oral testimony, to evaluate the experience of schooling in the early twentieth century, the oral 'data' being gathered first hand or derived from archive collections that are being created.

Some of the new work tends to view the working-class school critically, as a site of conflict. An example is the use made of the Bristol archive to reconstruct and analyse recalled behaviour which teachers and social investigators were all too ready to depict as 'hooliganism' but which, it is argued, should be regarded as a manifestation of hostility to the brutality and impositions of an authoritarian school system.[75] The history of school strikes – whether by children or teachers – has also been looked at from this point of view. The subject of parent–school relationships has also been pursued through research on school logbooks and local authority archives, the minutes of school attendance committees and school medical services revealing frequent conflicts between parents and bureaucratic officials with responsibilities for working-class children.[76]

But it is important also to explore the origins of the consensual relationships that existed between parents and schooling. An early attempt to do so based on the oral testimony of the inhabitants of a working-class district of Sheffield showed how some teachers and schools gained respect, even affection, over the inter-war years.[77] Recently, W. E. Marsden has made a more ambitious attempt to explore this subject in relation to a London school patronised by upper working-class to lower middle-class parents. This also incorporates oral history. But the aim of his study is to explore the complex interfaces in what Harold Silver has described as 'the total social relationships' of schooling: the 'ways in which schools, pupils, teachers, educational activities in general, related to wider social experience'.[78] What is needed now is to take this kind of work further into the twentieth century, so as to trace out the impact of social and ecological change on school–community relationships over a long time span. Crucial themes demanding historical reconstruction are the effects of urban decentralisation and of the settlement of different immigrant ethnic groups on schools that were formerly situated in the older and more settled working-class neighbourhoods. Whilst there is some historical work on the schooling of earlier immigrant groups, such as the Irish and the Jews, the historian has so far made little contribution to reconstructing the history of school–community relations in those cities particularly affected by the post-war immigration of different ethnic groups.[79]

The socio-ethnology of school–community relations is still in its infancy as an approach but it should be evident that, taken as a whole, new methodological developments have been considerably extending the scope of urban educational history in Britain. This is not to deny the existence of tensions as between different approaches – between an approach conceived in terms of ideology and politics and an approach that is concerned with such aspects of urbanisation as the massing of population in towns and cities, social and economic differentiation and the variety of social and family relationships embedded in city life. The contention of this review, however, is that such approaches can be reconciled, and that studies based on the city as a site for the working out of social conflict and negotiations, as well as those studies that relate more explicitly to urban processes, have contributions to make towards the evolution of urban educational history.

But defining such a field and advancing its study in a coherent way is complicated in Britain by the fragmentary nature of much research and writing on urban topics, although there is now a growing body of signpost books. The most promising work in urban educational history, as we have seen, has been undertaken by means of thematic case studies. Many of these studies reveal significant variations in the urban educational experience in the past, with the research suggesting that scale and type of settlement really does matter. If one trend is towards the fleshing out of these differences by recovering more fully the historical texture of local educational life, another trend is towards the more sustained analysis of differences based on deliberate comparisons between places which can be categorised in terms of types or families of towns and urban localities. These comparisons might include neighbourhoods in large cities, small market towns and rural villages, and they are capable of being extended to take in comparable places in other countries. This thematic and comparative mode of proceeding seems to offer the best possibility of determining what elements in localised urban developments in the past were common to all capitalist societies.

NOTES

1 For example, R. D. Gidney, 'Making nineteenth-century school systems: the Upper Canadian experience and its relevance to English historiography', *History of Education*, Vol. 9 (1980).
2 H. J. Dyos, 'Some historical reflections on the quality of urban life', reprinted in D. Cannadine and D. Reeder (eds.), *Exploring the Urban Past: Essays in Urban History by H. J. Dyos* (London and New York: Cambridge University Press, 1982), 65.
3 For Dyos and his influence, see David Cannadine, 'Urban history in the United Kingdom: the "Dyos phenomenon" and after', *ibid.*, 191–203.
4 Criticisms came mainly from sociologists, as, for example, the late Philip Abrams in the introduction to Philip Abrams and E. A. Wrigley (eds.), *Towns in Societies* (London and New York: Cambridge University Press, 1978), and R. E. Pahl, 'Concepts in context: pursuing the urban of "urban" sociology', in D. Fraser and A. Sutcliffe (eds.), *The Pursuit of Urban History* (London: Edward Arnold, 1983).
5 The comments come from P. Dunleavy and A. Blowers respectively as cited and discussed in Peter Williams, 'Theory and process in Urban Studies', in *Urban Studies Yearbook*, Vol. 1 (Sydney, London and Boston: George Allen and Unwin, 1983).
6 See Anthony Sutcliffe, 'In search of the urban variable: Britain in the later nineteenth century', in Fraser and Sutcliffe (eds.), *The Pursuit of Urban History*. For a critique of inner city school policies, see Rachel Sharp, *Knowledge, Ideology and the Politics of Schooling* (London: Routledge and Kegan Paul, 1980), and 'Urban education in the current crisis', in Gerald Grace (ed.), *Education and the City: Theory, History and Contemporary Practice* (London and Boston: Routledge and Kegan Paul, 1984).

7 R. J. Morris, 'Externalities, the market, power structures and the urban agenda', *Urban History Yearbook* (Leicester: Leicester University Press, 1990), 99–109.
8 Harold Carter, *Social Areas in Cities: Past and Future* (University of Maryland, Institute for Urban Studies, 1984), 15. However, Carter regards structuralist approaches as eroding the differences between historical geography and socio-economic history: see *An Introduction to Urban Historical Geography* (London; Cambridge University Press, 1983), xiii–xv.
9 See the valuable summary of structuralism in urban historical geography by Richard Dennis and Hugh Prince, 'Research in British urban historical geography', in Dietrich Denecke and Gareth Shaw (eds.), *Urban Historical Geography: Recent Progress in Britain and Germany* (Cambridge and New York: Cambridge University Press, 1988). For a study that is a methodological landmark in combining neo-Marxist (Gramscian) approaches with ecological perspectives, see the most recent contribution to the Cambridge Human Geography series, Lila Leontidou, *The Mediterranean City in Transition: Social Change and Urban Development* (Cambridge and New York: Cambridge University Press, 1990).
10 See the contribution to the Themes in the Urban History series by R. J. Morris (ed.), *Class, Power and Social Structure in British Nineteenth Century Towns* (Leicester: Leicester University Press, 1986).
11 Gordon Batho reviewing D. A. Reeder (ed.), *Urban Education in the Nineteenth Century* (London: Taylor and Francis, 1977), in *Journal of Educational Administration and History*, Vol. 11 (1979).
12 Grace (ed.), *Education and the City*.
13 See the report in *Urban History Yearbook* (Leicester: Leicester University Press, 1986), on the session of the 1985 annual conference of the Urban History Group on urban schooling in the nineteenth century. The *Yearbook* carries references to urban educational history in reviews and bibliography.
14 Charles Webster, 'Changing perspectives on the history of education', *Oxford Review of Education*, Vol. 2 (1976), 202.
15 Harold Silver, 'Aspects of neglect: the strange case of Victorian popular education', *ibid.*, 57–70.
16 See Joan Simon, 'The history of education in *Past and Present*', *Oxford Review of Education*, Vol. 3 (1977).
17 As, for example, K. Charlton, W. H. G. Armytage, Brian Simon and Joan Simon.
18 Articles submitted to *History of Education*, 1972–85 inclusive, were distributed amongst the five categories in the following way: institutional studies 49; the system 50; ideas 36; curricula and teaching 53; social and political movements 25.
19 In the introduction to J. Hurt (ed.), *Childhood, Youth and Education in the Late Nineteenth Century* (Leicester: History of Education Society, 1981), x. On the other hand, this narrow tradition in so far as it still exists is being squeezed out along with much that is valuable by the decline in the role of history of education in initial teacher training courses – see Gordon Batho and Keith Dent, *Trends in the Study and Teaching of the History of Education* (Leicester: History of Education Society, Occasional Publications No. 7, 1983).
20 See the discussion of the relations between urbanisation, proletarianisation and family life by the critical historian, Andy Green, *Education and State Formation: The Rise of Education Systems in England, France and the USA* (London: Macmillan, 1990), 48–66.

21 See W. B. Stephens, *Regional Variations in Education during the Industrial Revolution, 1780–1870: The Task of the Local Historian* (Leeds: Museum of the History of Education, University of Leeds, 1973); 'Illiteracy and schooling in the provincial towns, 1640–1870: a comparative approach', in Reeder (ed.), *Urban Education in the Nineteenth Century*, 27–47; *Education, Literacy and Society, 1830–1870: The Geography of Diversity in Provincial England* (Manchester: Manchester University Press, 1987).

22 M. Sanderson, 'Literacy and social mobility in the Industrial Revolution in England', *Past and Present*, Vol. 56 (1972); W. B. Stephens, 'Elementary education and literacy 1770–1870', in D. Fraser (ed.), *A History of Modern Leeds* (Manchester: Manchester University Press, 1980).

23 W. B. Stephens (ed.), *Studies in the History of Literacy: England and North America* (Leeds: Museum of the History of Education, University of Leeds, 1983), 96. This symposium had contributions covering the Erewash Valley coalfield, Bristol and Gloucestershire, Worcestershire and north-east Cheshire.

24 For example, J. M. Gratton, 'Aspects of literacy and 19th century society: the environs of Liverpool', *Journal of Educational Administration and History*, Vol. 13 (1985).

25 A useful guide is Peter Cunningham (ed.), *Local History of Education in England and Wales: A Bibliography* (Leeds: University of Leeds, 1976). The pioneer of systematic analysis in the local history of schooling was W. B. Stephens – see 'Early-Victorian Coventry: education in an industrial community, 1830–1851', in Alan Everitt (ed.), *Perspectives in Urban History* (London: Macmillan, 1973). The Leeds tradition of local history is still in evidence, as, for example, Robert W. Unwin, 'Alternative educational establishments in an English market town, 1830–1870', *Journal of Educational Administration and History*, Vol. 17 (1985). This journal carries several local thematic studies of this kind.

26 The pioneer was the social historian B. I. Coleman, 'The incidence of education in mid-century', in E. A. Wrigley (ed.), *Nineteenth Century Society: Essays in the Use of Quantitative Methods for the Study of Social Data* (London: Cambridge University Press, 1972). Contributions to quantitative study from the educational historians are to be found in P. McCann (ed.), *Popular Education and Socialisation in the Nineteenth Century* (London: Methuen, 1977); R. Lowe (ed.), *New Approaches to the Study of Popular Education, 1851–1902* (Leicester: History of Education Society, Occasional Publications No. 4, 1979); and P. Searby (ed.), *Educating the Victorian Middle Class* (Leicester: History of Education Society, 1982). Christine Heward's contribution to this volume provides another example. Most of these studies attempt correlations along two or at the most three dimensions. The only multivariate analysis known to me is in an unpublished thesis: W. B. Nixon, '"Scholars not schools": an evaluation of the success of the Voluntary Agencies in encouraging the development of schooling in the borough of Hanley prior to the establishment of the first School Board' (PhD thesis, University of Keele, 1982).

27 W. E. Marsden, *Unequal Education Provision in England and Wales: The Nineteenth-Century Roots* (London: Woburn Press, 1991).

28 Carl Chinn, 'Was separate schooling a means of class segregation in late-Victorian and Edwardian Birmingham?', *Midland History*, Vol. 13 (1988).

29 K. P. Stannard, 'Ideology, education, and social structure: elementary education

in mid-Victorian England', *History of Education*, Vol. 19 (1990), 116. This article is concerned primarily with the methodology of local studies arguing for a study of education in terms of an interaction between social processes and local conditions of schooling and social structure.

30 An exception is the unpublished thesis of H. J. Foster, 'Variations in the provision of secondary education in the 19th century: a regional study' (PhD thesis, University of Liverpool, 1988). A small part of this systematic investigation of the impact of residential change is reproduced in his contribution to Peter Searby's volume on the education of the Victorian middle-class cited above.

31 For example, I. D. Roberts, 'Social mobility and the school: St Michaels' College, Leeds, 1905–15', *Journal of Educational Administration and History*, Vol. 21 (1989). For a study of a London suburban school that embodied meritocratic values, see W. E. Marsden, *Educating the Respectable: A Study of Fleet Road Board School, Hampstead, 1879–1903* (London: Woburn Press, 1991).

32 R. Lowe, *Education in the Post-War Years* (London: Routledge, 1988).

33 W. E. Marsden, 'Education and urbanization in nineteenth century Britain', *Paedagogica Historica*, Vol. 23 (1983), 85–124.

34 Examples are: David Wardle, *Education and Society in Nineteenth Century Nottingham* (London and Cambridge: Cambridge University Press, 1971), and Gerald T. Rimmington, *Education, Politics and Society in Leicester 1833–1903* (Hantsport: Lancelot Press, 1978). The connections made with the local context are not systematically pursued in either of these studies. See also J. S. Maclure, *One Hundred Years of London Education, 1870–1970* (London: Allen and Unwin, 1970).

35 As, for example, D. W. Thoms, *Policy Making in Education: Robert Blair and the London County Council 1904–24* (Leeds: University of Leeds, 1980).

36 Examples are E. Fearn, 'The local politics of comprehensive secondary reorganisation', in E. Fearn and B. Simon (eds.), *Education in the Sixties* (Leicester: History of Education Society, 1980), and R. Saran, *Policy Making in Secondary Education: A Case Study* (London: Oxford University Press, 1974).

37 See the summary by D. Fraser, 'Education and urban politics c. 1832–85', in Reeder (ed.), *Urban Education in the 19th Century*. Examples of more recent work by Geoffrey Fidler and others can be found in Roy Lowe (ed.), *Labour and Education: Some Twentieth Century Studies* (Leicester: History of Education Society, Occasional Publications No. 6, 1981). An example of the type of study concerned with central-local relations is A. Elliott, 'The Bradford School Board and the Department of Education', *Journal of Educational Administration and History* Vol. 13 (1981). This journal carries numerous articles on local administrative and political developments in the nineteenth and twentieth centuries too numerous to cite individually.

38 There are suggestive implications on these several matters in the work of P. McCann on the importance of the metropolitan milieu to the ideologues of the infant school, *Samuel Wilderspin and the Origins of the Infant School Movement in Britain* (London: Allen and Unwin, 1982); Donald K. Jones on the role of Manchester in the movement for national elementary education, summarised in his book *The Making of the Education System 1851–81* (London: Routledge, 1977), and 'The movement for secular elementary education in Great Britain', in William Frijhoff (ed.), *The Supply of Schooling: Contributions to the Comparative*

Study of Educational Policies in the XIX Century (Paris: Service d'Histoire de l'Education, 1982); R. E. Watts on 'The Unitarian contribution to the development of female education 1790–1850', *History of Education*, Vol. 9 (1980). The relations between liberalism, education and the city ethos have been illuminated by social historians such as John Seed on Unitarianism, 'Unitarianism, political economy and the antimonies of liberal culture in Manchester', *Social History*, Vol. 7 (1982), and for the Birmingham reformers, E. P. Hennock, *Fit and Proper Persons: Idea and Reality in Nineteenth Century Urban Government* (London: Edward Arnold, 1973). For an attempt at relating the ideas of Liberal intellectuals on education to urbanisation, see David A. Reeder (ed.), *Educating Our Masters* (Leicester: Leicester University Press, 1980).

39 A pioneering book in this respect is Janet Wolff and John Seed (eds.), *The Culture of Capital: Art, Power and the Nineteenth Century Middle Class* (Manchester: Manchester University Press, 1988).

40 See the summary of Brian Simon in 'Systematisation and segmentation in education: the case of England', in D. Muller, F. Ringer and B. Simon (eds.), *The Rise of the Modern Educational System, 1870–1920* (London: Cambridge University Press, 1987). For the influence of the public school as a 'defining institution' in the process whereby social hierarchies were converted into academic hierarchies so affecting the fortunes of many town grammar schools, see the contribution in the same volume of Hilary Steedman at 111–34.

41 R. J. Morris, *Class, Sect and Party: The Making of the British Middle Class: Leeds, 1820–50* (Manchester and New York: Manchester University Press, 1990). This study offers a valuable corrective to some of the assumptions of Martin J. Weiner, *English Culture and the Decline of the Industrial Spirit, 1850–1980* (Cambridge: Cambridge University Press, 1981). The best contributions to the history of the late Victorian public school as a socio-cultural phenomenon have been made by John Honey and J. A. Mangan in various writings.

42 For example, Paul Simpson, 'Education for profit: the proprietorial schools of Bath in the 19th and 20th centuries', *Journal of Educational Administration and History*, Vol. 18 (1986).

43 Margaret Bryant, *The London Experience of Secondary Education* (London: Athlone Press, 1986).

44 David Allsobrook, *Schools for the Shires: The Reform of Middle Class Education in Mid-Victorian England* (Manchester: Manchester University Press, 1986).

45 For this concept and the references to the descriptive studies, see David Reeder, 'The reconstruction of secondary education in England, 1869–1920', in Muller, Ringer and Simon (eds.), *The Rise of the Modern Educational System*.

46 A good account of this cultural offensive in Bristol by a social historian is Helen Meller, *Leisure and the Changing City* (London: Routledge, 1976). For intellectual aspects of liberal culture, see Sheldon Rothblatt, *Tradition and Change in English Liberal Education* (London: Cambridge University Press, 1976).

47 On Oxbridge and the city university colleges, see Roy Lowe, 'Structural change in English higher education', in Muller, Ringer and Simon (eds.), *The Rise of the Modern Educational System*, 163–80; on Oxbridge, the city and adult education, see Stuart Marriott, *A Backstairs to a Degree: Demands for an Open University in Late Victorian England* (Leeds: University of Leeds, 1981).

48 See the contributions of Meriel Vlaeminke, 'The subordination of technical education in secondary schooling, 1870–1914', David Thoms, 'Technical education and the transformation of Coventry's industrial economy, 1900–1939', and Sarah King, 'Technical and vocational education for girls. A study of the central schools of London, 1918–1939', in Penny Summerfield and Eric J. Evans (eds.), *Technical Education and the State since 1850: Historical and Contemporary Perspectives* (Manchester: Manchester University Press, 1990).
49 Simon, 'Systematisation and segmentation in education', 160.
50 Dennis Smith, *Conflict and Compromise. Class Formation in English Society 1830–1914. A Comparative Study of Birmingham and Sheffield* (London: Routledge and Kegan Paul, 1982).
51 See M. Billinge, 'Hegemony, class and power in late Georgian and early Victorian England: towards a cultural geography', in A. R. H. Baker and D. Gregory (eds.), *Explorations in Historical Geography: Interpretive Essays* (Cambridge: Cambridge University Press, 1984). Compare the approach of the social historian as in A. J. Kidd and D. Roberts (eds.), *City, Class and Culture* (Manchester: Manchester University Press, 1985).
52 Arnold Thackray, 'Natural knowledge in a cultural context: the Manchester model', *American Historical Review*, Vol. 79 (1974).
53 Louis Wirth, 'Urbanism as a way of life', *American Journal of Sociology*, Vol. 44 (1938), 22. For the symposium on local developments in science institutions, see Ian Inkster and Jack Morrell (eds.), *Metropolis and Province: Science in British Culture, 1780–1850* (London and Melbourne: Hutchinson, 1983).
54 Steven Shapin and Barry Barnes, 'Science, nature and control: interpreting Mechanics' Institutes', in Roger Dale *et al.* (eds.), *Schooling and Capitalism: A Sociological Reader* (London: Routledge and Kegan Paul and the Open University Press, 1976); I. Inkster, 'The social context of an educational movement: a revisionist approach to the English Mechanics' Institutes, 1800–1850', *Oxford Review of Education*, Vol. 2 (1976); A. D. Garner and E. W. Jenkins, 'The English Mechanics' Institutes: the case of Leeds 1824–42', *History of Education*, Vol. 13 (1984).
55 Richard Johnson introduced the concept of social control into the interpretation of educational history in England in 1970, and developed the argument along Gramscian lines in 'Notes on the schooling of the English working class, 1780–1850', in Dale *et al.* (eds.), *Schooling and Capitalism*. For controversy, see the debate between R. Colls and A. J. Heeson and B. Duffy, 'Coal, class and education', *Past and Present*, Vol. 90 (1981). Even non-structuralist historians began to present accounts of educational initiatives as responses to labour movements, for example, M. A. Cruickshank, 'The Anglican revival and education: a study of school expansion in the cotton manufacturing areas of north west England 1840–50', *Northern History*, Vol. 15 (1979).
56 T. W. Laqueur has questioned social control interpretations of the Sunday schools in *Religion and Respectability: Sunday Schools and Working Class Culture* (New Haven, CT, and London: Yale University Press, 1979). But see Malcolm Dick, 'The myth of the working-class Sunday school', *History of Education*, Vol. 9 (1980), and 'Urban growth and the social role of the Stockport Sunday school c. 1784–1833', in John Fergusson (ed.), *Christianity, Society and Education* (London: SPCK, 1981). For other critiques, see Stephen Humphries,

'"Hurrah for England": schooling and the working class in Bristol, 1870–1914', *Southern History*, Vol. 1 (1979), and the contribution of Tony Evans, 'The University settlements, class relations and the city' in Grace (ed.), *Education and the City*.

57 The descriptive writings are too numerous to list here. E. A. G. Clarke was writing about schools in 1969, for example, and is still doing so: see 'The diffusion of educational ideas: ragged and industrial schools, 1841–57', *Journal of Educational Administration and History*, Vol. 20 (1988). For work on reformatory and industrial schools, see the survey by John Hurt, 'Reformatory and industrial schools before 1933', *History of Education*, Vol. 14 (1985). (There are also studies of Mary Carpenter and Barnardo available.) In this field, the published work of educational historians seems relatively untouched by the interest which social historians have shown in the way that a middle-class ideology of childhood developed and informed such philanthropic agencies as the National Society for the Prevention of Cruelty to Children (M. Behlmer, *Child Abuse and Moral Reform in England 1870–1908* (New York: Stanford University Press, 1983)).

58 J. J. H. Dekker, 'The birth of social technology as a new possibility of re-education of dangerous and difficult children in nineteenth-century Europe, c. 1800–1850', *International Standing Conference for the History of Education*, Vol. 58 (1983).

59 For example, Margaret May, 'The concept of juvenile delinquency in early Victorian England', *Victorian Studies*, Vol. 12 (1973); J. M. Feheney, 'Delinquency among Irish Catholic children in Victorian London', *Irish Historical Studies*, Vol. 23 (1983).

60 John Gillis, 'The evolution of juvenile delinquency in England 1890–1914', *Past and Present*, Vol. 67 (1975), a study based on Oxford.

61 For example, M. J. Childs, 'Boy labour in late Victorian and Edwardian England and the remaking of the working class', *Journal of Social History*, Vol. 23 (1990); H. Hendrick, *Images of Youth: Age, Class, and the Male Youth Problem, 1880–1920* (Oxford: Clarendon Press, 1990).

62 Mica Niva, 'The urban, the domestic and education for girls', in Grace (ed.), *Education and the City*. For related approaches, see Carol Dyhouse, '"Good wives and little mothers": social anxieties and the schoolgirls' curricula, 1890–1920', *Oxford Review of Education*, Vol. 3 (1981), and Anna Davin, 'Child labour: the working-class family and domestic ideology in 19th century Britain', *Development and Change*, Vol. 13 (1982).

63 See my attempt to make these interconnections in D. A. Reeder, 'Predicaments of city children: late Victorian and Edwardian perspectives on education and urban society', in Reeder (ed.), *Urban Education in the 19th Century*.

64 As explained by Ron Brooks, 'Professor J. J. Findlay, The King Alfred School Society, Hampstead and Letchworth Garden City Education, 1897–1913', *History of Education* (forthcoming).

65 For the development of this kind of left critique generally, see G. Stedman Jones, 'Social expression versus social control', *History Workshop*, Vol. 4 (1977), and Richard Johnson's introduction to J. Clarke *et al.* (eds.), *Working Class Culture: Studies in History and Theory* (London: Hutchinson, 1979).

66 See, for example, Peter Bailey, *Leisure and Class in Victorian England* (London: Routledge, 1978), and Eileen and Stephen Yeo (eds.), *Popular Culture and Class*

Conflict 1590–1914: Explorations in the History of Labour and Leisure (London: Harvester Press, 1983).
67 As, for example, J. S. Hurt, *Elementary Schooling and the Working Classes 1860–1918* (London: Routledge, 1979).
68 For an example of this approach based on Birmingham, see D. A. Reid, 'The decline of Saint Monday 1766–1876', in P. Thane and A. Sutcliffe (eds.), *Essays in Social History*, Vol. II (Oxford: Oxford University Press, 1986).
69 S. A. Harrop, 'Adult education and literacy: the importance of post-school education for literacy levels in the 18th and 19th centuries', *History of Education*, Vol. 13 (1984), 191–205. There is quite an extensive literature now on Improvement Societies, but the work on the educative role of political meetings and labour branch activity is restricted mainly to unpublished theses – an example is Alyson Andrew, 'The working class and education in Preston 1830–1870: a study in social relations' (PhD thesis, University of Leicester, 1987). Richard Johnson has some reflections on the problems of discussing labour educational attitudes from the point of view of the leaders only in '"Really useful knowledge": radical education and working class culture', in Clark *et al.* (eds.), *Working Class Culture*.
70 Phil Gardner, *The Lost Elementary Schools of Victorian England* (London: Croom Helm, 1984).
71 See also her remarks in 'Growing up in a Birmingham community, 1851–1871', in Hurt (ed.), *Childhood, Youth and Education in the Late Nineteenth Century*.
72 Regrettably, very little of this new work has been published as yet. An example with an interesting comparative dimension is Catherine G. Elliott, 'The school and the family: patterns of educational interaction in four communities, 1861–1891' (D Phil thesis, University of Oxford, 1986).
73 The classic study is D. Rubinstein, *School Attendance in London 1870–1914: A Social History*. (Hull: University of Hull, 1969). But there has been stimulating new work since, as, for example, Grace Belfiore, 'Family strategies in Essex textile towns 1860–1895: the challenge of compulsory elementary schooling' (D Phil, University of Oxford, 1986), and 'Compulsion and community in Essex textile districts' (unpublished paper reported in *Urban History Yearbook* (Leicester: Leicester University Press, 1986)). See also Janet Lewis, 'Parents, children, school fees and the London School Board', *History of Education*, Vol. 2 (1982), and T. R. Phillips, 'The elementary schools and the migratory habits of the people 1870–90', *British Journal of Educational Studies*, Vol. 26 (1978).
74 Raphael Samuel, 'Local history and oral history', *History Workshop*, Vol. 1 (1976). The best-known reconstruction of childhood in the classic slum is Robert Roberts, *A Ragged Schooling* (Manchester: Manchester University Press, 1968).
75 Stephen Humphries, *Hooligans or Rebels? An Oral History of Working-Class Childhood and Youth 1889–1939* (Oxford: Basil Blackwell, 1981).
76 For example, W. R. Meyer, 'School vs parents in Leeds, 1902–44', *Journal of Educational Administration and History*, Vol. 22 (1990).
77 Cheryl Parsons, *Schools in an Urban Community: A Study of Carsbrook, 1870–1965* (London: Routledge and Kegan Paul, 1975).
78 Harold Silver, *Education as History: Interpreting Nineteenth and Twentieth Century Education* (London: Methuen, 1983). Marsden's study is *Educating the Respectable*.

79 There is interesting work on the Jews as, for example, L. Osborne, 'Achievers of the ghetto: the education of Jewish immigrant children in Tower Hamlets 1870–1914', in A. Newman (ed.), *The Jewish East End* (London: Jewish Historical Society, 1982).

2 Education and America's cities

Ronald D. Cohen and William J. Reese

'I view great cities as pestilential to the morals, the health and the liberties of man', wrote Thomas Jefferson in 1800. Centres of commerce and culture, cities concentrated material and human resources in ways that terrified republicans of the early national period. Nearly two centuries later, Americans' still hold negative or at least ambiguous attitudes toward cities. Many citizens today equate them with evil and moral decay, economic segregation and racial apartheid. More sanguine observers, however, emphasise the high culture: theatre, libraries, newspapers, magazines, book publishers and colleges and universities, located or produced in cities that enrich the lives of local residents as well as the nation. Whether a cancer or symbol of human diversity and creativity, cities remain vital to the nation's public life. Their histories can provide a unique window on America's educational past.[1]

Samuel P. Hays, a leading social historian, offers some useful observations on the historical dimensions of urban life. He identifies several interrelated aspects of cities that help organise one's understanding of many rich and varied human experiences. According to Hays, heterogeneity (shaped by ethnicity, religion, race and social class) has often especially characterised American cities. A second definite feature has been inequality, which has assumed different guises for various groups since the early days of the Republic. A third interrelated feature is the continual tension in cities between parochial and more cosmopolitan lifestyles and ideals. And, finally, Hays argues that leaders have usually responded to heterogeneity, inequality, and cultural tensions by inventing 'administrative and technical systems' to impose order and to shape the lives of urban residents.[2]

I

Towns and cities were sparse and rudimentary before 1776, when the story of urban education must nevertheless begin. Recently, historians have devoted little attention to the early development of urban education, particularly schooling, seeing little connection between formal education and colonial life. An older literature, of course, analysed how town Latin grammar schools and the handful of colonial colleges prepared male leaders for state and church. Historians now more typically focus not on schools *per se* but on the broader forms of education and socialisation that introduced the young to reading, writing and the values most prized by adults. Gary Nash therefore notes that 'learning – whether religious, vocational, or concerned with the socialization of the young – was conducted typically through human interchange, the mark of all oral societies preceding the modern era'.[3]

The most ambitious historical analysis of colonial education is Lawrence A. Cremin's *American Education: The Colonial Experience, 1607–1783*. Cremin defined education as 'the deliberate, systematic, and sustained effort to transmit or evoke knowledge, attitudes, values, skills, and sensibilities'. He thus examined the role of families, apprenticeships, churches, communities and other sources of education. Describing an overwhelmingly rural and agrarian world, he more briefly examined urban influences upon education, though he noted the large number of teachers and various types of schools in Philadelphia and New York City by the 1770s. Despite the lack of widespread schooling, high literacy rates (especially for white males) already characterised American social development. Indeed, something as fundamental as learning to read still did not depend upon formal schools, as Carl F. Kaestle noted in his study of the New York City schools between 1750 and 1850. Reading was largely learned at home, certainly strengthened at school for those who attended, and reinforced in many sections of the country through increased exposure to an expanding world of print. William J. Gilmore demonstrates how even rural sections of New England were increasingly awash in a sea of written words.[4]

Independence did not suddenly transform educational configurations along the Eastern seaboard. Major changes were nevertheless slowly refashioning the world of urban education. Nash, for example, highlights the rising importance of urban commerce in the eighteenth century, which led to 'the restructuring of social groups, the redistribution of wealth, the alteration of labor relations, the emergence of states of consciousness that cut horizontally through society, and the mobilization into political life of the lower ranks of laboring people'. All this reshaped the city and the nature of education. Private venture, tuition pay schools had existed since the late seventeenth century, and they still flourished for middle- and upper-class white families in cities in the 1790s. Protestant reformers also opened free charity schools for some of the unchurched poor whose lives were so altered by commercial expansion and economic inequality. Boston was unique since it opened a fairly comprehensive public system in 1789. But even that centre of learning did not include everyone in its schools, and the Boston 'system' supplemented the informal learning of the home, church and neighbourhood.[5]

School reformers throughout the first half of the nineteenth century struggled to eliminate the influence of various schools with diverse origins and purposes in favour of a universal system of tax-supported, free, public education with common goals. They attempted to make careful distinctions unknown to previous generations between 'private' and 'public' schools. In many cities in the early 1800s, for example, the union of tax dollars and private funds often made the education of the poor in charity schools possible. New York's Free School Society, a voluntary organisation of philanthropic Protestants formed in 1805, operated numerous Lancasterian schools for the unchurched poor by the early 1820s. Critical of the home life of the poor, these schools performed a public function, however repugnant their aims appeared to later historians. The poor were drilled in basic literacy laced with heavy moral, Protestant values, all aimed at separating children from their parents. While some poor children attended these pauper schools, many white middle- and upper-class children continued to attend tuition schools. These schools catered to different intellectual and moral needs and also separated the favoured classes from the heterogeneous mass.[6]

How to break the power of academies, pay schools and other rival educational institutions utilised by the middle and upper classes dominated much political debate after the 1820s. The line between private and public in educational matters became more precise over time. Central to the campaign for a single system of public schools was the creation of the free high school, whose appeal to important sectors of the middle classes proved irresistible. Reformers such as Horace Mann of Massachusetts realised that public primary schools might receive greater financial support if wealthier citizens were attracted to the system. Expensive, academically respectable and open to merit, the free high school became known as the 'people's college' even though the poor were severely underrepresented within its walls. Cities had the concentrated wealth and population size and density that made graded classrooms and high schools possible, and these specialised institutions often proved essential to middle-class life by the middle of the nineteenth century.[7]

As commercial and then industrial capitalism altered the urban economy, public high schools became integral to class formation. Mary Ryan offers an important analysis of social change and educational development in *Cradle of the Middle Class*, a case study of Oneida County, New York, which included the city of Utica. When surplus farmlands for the old Yankee-stock middle class disappeared, and when commerce and industry in Utica transformed economic relations and opportunity, middle-class parents increasingly lacked the wherewithal to transmit their skills or much property to their children, whose class advantages were thus imperilled. Changes in the economy produced more jobs for clerks, managers and other specialised workers, and attending the high school enabled a small percentage of children to avoid lives as proletarians and prepare them for membership in a 'new' middle class. Poorer children, who earlier attended charity schools, and who now attended the emerging public schools, but only through the grammar grades, were often destined to become unskilled labourers and factory hands. In contrast, high schools offered boys a semblance of mobility, reinforcing the larger economic inequality that characterised the city.[8]

Ryan's careful reconstruction of family life during a time of rapid change reflects the wide-ranging interests of social historians studying the nineteenth century. Schools are a small part of her analysis, even though they became an increasingly important part of middle-class family strategies as the century progressed. Numerous writers continue to focus on the diverse sources of 'education' in urban areas in the last century. They draw upon different intellectual interests, political agendas and methodological styles. While not especially interested in urban education, Lawrence Cremin continued a broad analysis of his subject in *American Education: The National Experience, 1783–1876*. Like other writers, he emphasised the breadth of educational experiences gained from not only schools but especially newspapers, magazines, work, churches, neighbourhoods, wars and families.[9]

Women's historians have especially enriched scholarly understanding of urban history. Schooling for girls was widespread in common, public schools by the ante-bellum period, and the lack of equal job opportunities and the availability of elementary teaching positions made women's enrolments in high school swell. Scholars still debate the meaning of a rising 'domesticity' in middle-class worlds. As broad-scale social changes altered family life, as work, home and school became more sociologically distinct, women assumed new roles in society. Expanded opportunities for formal education led to controversies over coeducation, curriculum and work. Increasingly seen as the best natural child nurturers and the moral guardians of society, middle- and upper-class women also constituted a cheap labour pool of teachers as reformers tried to expand local school systems as rapidly and inexpensively as possible.[10]

The image of the moral mother and dutiful teacher contrasted sharply with the crisis of youth perceived by countless social commentators before mid-century. Many school reformers painted a picture of an ideal family life that many poor, especially immigrant, parents never attained. The child's natural place was in the home, at the mother's side, but what of the thousands of poor children in many cities whose home life was scarred by intemperate parents of questionable morals? Children who were scavengers on the street or adolescents who joined raucous youth groups like voluntary fire departments contradicted life as it should be, and the mode of living which schools hoped to produce. Public schools continued to try to produce literate, cleanly scrubbed children despite the odds. When the schools and society vividly failed, cities by the 1820s even built separate institutions for orphans, delinquents and otherwise dependent youth. 'Houses of Refuge' became the substitute for 'bad' homes and the street, and state reform schools of various types by mid-century arose to demonstrate that victory was elusive.[11]

While disagreeing about the precise connections between the rise of juvenile asylums and urban change, scholars agree that many urban leaders assumed that the traditional sources of social order and discipline had seriously eroded in their lifetime. Families, churches and other sources of education and control seemed insufficient to meet the possibilities and crises of the growing city. Institutions funded almost exclusively by tax dollars, whether local public schools or state-operated industrial schools, arose throughout the North by mid-century as an expression of both hopefulness and despair.

Understanding the full dimensions of these changes has been central to the work of Michael B. Katz. Unlike Cremin, whose broad definition of education excludes very little, Katz focused on public schools as they evolved, expanded and became more bureaucratic in the nineteenth century. While Cremin applauded the rich diversity and various strands of education in the period, Katz offered a more critical and more tightly defined assessment of education. The rise of capitalism led to more landless, unskilled workers, drove all citizens into a more competitive economic system, deepened poverty and despair for many and even forced bourgeois women into a state of 'enforced repression inherent in contemporary ideals of domesticity'. Children without productive uses 'were swept into massive brick structures' called schools and taught 'sensual restraint, dependability, willingness to work, acquiescence in the legitimacy of the social order, and acceptance of one's place within it – [which] were all serviceable traits in early capitalist America'.[12]

Katz's *The Irony of Early School Reform* (1968) early identified many of the issues debated so strenuously then and now by historians of urban education. Based on case studies of educational change in Beverly, Lawrence and other Massachusetts communities, his study concluded that schools had been imposed upon the working classes, who were sometimes hostile to and often sceptical of educational reform. Katz saw the reformers as self-interested, anxious elites 'who founded schools with a sense of superiority, not compassion'. In the early 1970s, though with different emphases, Stanley K. Schultz and Carl F. Kaestle published studies on Boston and New York City respectively that added further critical words to an emerging debate about the origins and meaning of urban education. Schultz among other things said that Boston's elites hoped to make the poor more 'harmless' to society and unthreatening in the 'urban order'. Kaestle also argued that the elite values of the schools led to their estrangement from the very populations they claimed to serve. Linking 'crime, vagrancy, and immorality with cultural traits', reformers deepened the chasm between the schools and the lower classes.[13]

Katz expanded his critique of public schools in 1971 by asserting that they had assumed their modern form by the 1880s. They were 'universal, tax-supported, free, compulsory, bureaucratic, racist, and class-biased'. Most importantly, he extended his analysis by emphasising the import of the rise of school bureaucracy. The system emphasised order, efficiency and uniformity, and it reflected the interests of the favoured classes as well as budding professionals at the top of the school system, who issued directives from above to everyone below. Other scholars independently highlighted the growing influence of bureaucratic organisations that often became more insular and distant from popular control. In New York between 1805 and 1853, for example, schooling was 'consolidated, coordinated, and standardized in a process that one is tempted to call a bureaucratic revolution'. In Boston, too, 'a new breed of professional managers began to emerge' who promised efficiency but also sought to insulate themselves from public scrutiny or criticism. David B. Tyack reminded everyone in *The One Best System* that the bureaucratic revolution did not triumph completely anywhere, and certainly nowhere before the Civil War. Still, numerous scholars by the early 1970s now agreed that urban schools had increasingly embraced bureaucracy.[14]

The logic of common schools and bureaucratic uniformity collapsed when racial questions surfaced in nineteenth-century cities. Understanding racial politics and racism, however, remains complicated. As early as 1800, Boston's free blacks requested separate schools, which were granted by the School Committee. By the 1830s, however, blatant inequalities in school facilities and education led the black community to demand integrated schools. Finally, in 1855, with abolitionist support and new state legislation, Boston's schools became legally integrated. But New York's schools, whether private or public, remained segregated. Philadelphia had eight separate, underfunded black schools by 1850. As Carl F. Kaestle concluded in *Pillars of the Republic*, free Northern blacks remained outside the supposedly inclusive common school, which led to understandable ambivalence among black parents and leaders about the desirability of integrated education in such a racist atmosphere. Blacks often opened their own private schools when white supremacists prevented sympathetic whites from doing so.¹⁵

Urban diversity and inequality led to further social conflicts. Native Protestant elites often rose to positions of dominance in the emerging urban school systems, both as members of school committees and as administrators. The heavy influx of German and Irish immigrants in some cities after the 1830s led to tense debates about the Protestant character of the curriculum and religious instruction in 'public' institutions. Nativists attacked Catholic efforts to divide the school fund in the 1830s and 1840s, and they assailed early efforts thereafter to establish separate parochial schools. This tension between a cosmopolitan and parochial culture (school reformers smugly assumed they were the former) often boiled over in Cincinnati, Philadelphia and other cities with sizeable immigrant populations. Scholars still know very little about the role that parochial schools played in different cities, including their relationship over time with public schools and why these private schools later grew dramatically in some places but not in others with large numbers of Catholics. In his model study of Chicago, James W. Sanders reminds us that Catholics often led two-pronged battles, against certain public school practices and for expanding the parochial system, and that local contexts often had powerful class and ethnic overtones.[16]

While scholars continue to debate these various aspects of the social history of nineteenth-century schooling, Carl F. Kaestle has provided a comprehensive and sophisticated interpretation of the founding and expansion of common schools before the Civil War. Drawing on his own research and that of Maris A. Vinovskis and many other scholars, Kaestle offers a sweeping reanalysis in *Pillars of the Republic*. Here, he makes an important distinction between enrolment increases, which 'were the dynamic feature of rural schooling in the early national period', and changes in 'organisation and funding [which] were the key developments in urban schooling'. The concentrated populations of cities, which were increasingly often segregated along racial, ethnic and social class lines, also offered the opportunity to create hierarchical systems, a sequenced and uniform curriculum and innovations such as graded classrooms, high schools and the hiring of women as elementary teachers. Cities remain central to the rise of the public schools, but Kaestle more clearly than any other writer identifies the precise influence of cities versus the countryside upon various aspects of schooling.[17]

Scholars will continue to debate important questions about the origins and establishment of schools in the nineteenth century. Issues so divisive in their own time – the rise of capitalism and changing economic realities, the place of women, blacks and poor people in the Republic and the evolution and expansion of schools and other sources of education and socialisation – will no doubt give rise to competing interpretations among historians trying to understand the relationship between social change and education in its many forms. Scholars have still not produced many studies on urban education in Southern towns and cities, or charted the role that working-men's associations played in school politics in the North after the 1830s. Revisionists such as Katz offered stinging criticisms of the origins of public schools, and even scholars who dissent from his interpretations benefited from the exciting questions raised about such basic social institutions.[18]

By the Civil War, public schools in the North began to assume their modern shape. They proclaimed themselves to be universal, despite widely varying practices. They were locally controlled, with women teachers in the lowest grades, offering an increasingly standardised curriculum. They were governed by men who faced a sometimes hostile urban world, one that was characterised by cultural and racial diversity and various forms of inequality. Urban leaders constructed new organisational forms that attempted to offer opportunity to some and order for everyone. Successive generations would continue to ask schools to teach moral values and academic subjects but also to address a whole host of contentious social, political and economic issues.

II

By the late nineteenth century, urban school systems had demonstrated their staying power and their ability to gather widespread political support. Public schools everywhere received exclusive control over tax dollars and formed an educational monopoly. Catholics and some smaller religious groups still refused to send their children to the state system. At the same time, the transformation of the city after 1900 brought new challenges to urban education. Older problems such as diversity, inequality, the tensions between cosmopolitan and parochial viewpoints and the administrative character of schools continued to affect city life. Now influenced by a new phase of economic development, where corporate capitalism loomed large, urban schools revealed a remarkable ability to bend in new directions and to adapt to the coming of a new social order. Schools assumed additional responsibilities that were once the province of families, churches, neighbourhoods and the work-place.[19]

Between 1870 and 1920, the urban population increased from 9.9 million to 54.3 million. The number of cities with populations over 100,000 expanded from fifteen to sixty-eight, and those with more than 500,000 climbed from two to twelve. This movement to the city included ex-slaves and their children, whites displaced from the farms or seeking a new way of life and millions of Eastern and Central Europeans who migrated to America after the turn of the century. These immigrants, often Catholic or Jewish, contributed substantially to the diversity of the American city, especially in the Northeast and Midwest. Urban areas served as a magnet of opportunity, allowed newcomers to join kinsmen and friends in somewhat self-contained, expanding ethnic neighbourhoods, and became once again the centre of a national debate about the nature of America and its destiny. How to educate, control and socialise the young fuelled a national debate and became a practical problem for urban reformers.[20]

Public schools expanded enormously during the early twentieth century. A few examples highlight the change. San Francisco's school population swelled from over 46,000 in 1876 to over 98,000 in 1905. During the same period, the numbers jumped from over 69,000 to over 96,000 in New Orleans, from over 43,000 to over 114,000 in Cleveland, from over 110,000 to over 489,000 in Chicago and from over 375,000 to about 1 million pupils in New York City. Children often attended half-day sessions in some cities; in others, they were literally turned away because of lack of space. By the turn of the century, moreover, schools were different from what they had been in 1850, gradually assuming novel social and economic functions as the political economy shifted in new directions.[21]

The period between 1890 and 1920, commonly called the 'progressive era', was rich in efforts to reform the public schools. In his seminal work, *The Transformation of the School*, Lawrence A. Cremin offered the liberal interpretation of progressive era school reform. The reformers, he argued, were largely benevolent men and women who wanted to extend the promise of American life to all the people. They embraced ideas of child study, scientific experimentation and whatever else might enable schools to solve social ills such as poverty or personal problems such as maintaining healthy teeth. This largely uncritical view of the reformers quickly fell from favour among 'revisionist' writers in the late 1960s and early 1970s. This eclectic group of educators and historians shared the perspective of Samuel P. Hays, whose seminal articles in the early 1960s urged scholars to link educational reform with larger political and structural changes of the progressive era. Hays and subsequent educational historians adjusted their sights from the intellectual history of reform to the social dynamics of educational change.[22]

In particular, Hays argued that municipal government by the early twentieth century shifted from ward-based, often ethnic, leadership to a more centralised, professionalised, and business-dominated structure. Ethnic and ward politicians were squeezed from power, whether on the city council or on the school board, producing a revolution in urban governance. Experts and non-elected officials soon dominated in many branches of government, including the schools. Who would control the schools, and for what purposes and for whose benefit, would now dominate critical studies of urban education.[23]

David B. Tyack's *The One Best System*, the most widely read work on progressive reform, drew upon much original research and a growing number of monographs, many of which sustained Hays' earlier conclusions. Tyack's description and analysis of the 'adminstrative progressives' undermined the earlier notion that reformers promoted democracy and justice for the masses. Largely middle- and upper-class, native-born, well-educated white men, the administrative reformers constituted a powerful political bloc in many towns and cities in the early 1900s. Attorneys, physicians, business leaders and educational administrators joined with elite club women and professional associations to streamline school boards, to centralise decision-making in the hands of 'disinterested' experts and to destroy ethnic and working-class power. A small band of non-elected, professionally trained school administrators now hired teachers, organised the curriculum and headed the growing bureaucracies without traditional lay interference. In *Managers of Virtue*, Tyack and Elisabeth Hansot reaffirmed the power of these reformers, who empowered 'a new breed of professional managers who made education a lifelong career', thereby replacing the 'part-time evangelists' of the common school era.[24]

Nearly every scholar of school reform in some way links educational change with the rise of a corporate economy. The rise of the corporation was central to Joel H. Spring's *Education and the Rise of the Corporate State*. In an era of newly formed trusts and corporations, educational reformers preached the gospel of efficiency, specialisation, scientific planning, centralisation and expertise, leading to a host of specific reforms to serve 'an increasingly complex society'. Urban innovations that later appeared in the country schools included school lunches, vocational programmes, student government, medical inspection and other reforms that, in Spring's view, challenged the traditional authority of the family, church and other time-tested institutions.[25]

The extensiveness of the reforms clearly demonstrated that public education had entered a new phase. Did these programmes aim to extend the promise of America to everyone, or were they class-based attempts to control the masses as many historians contended? A more complex, more highly industrialised, city seemed to elicit numerous efforts to alter radically the schools.

Vocational education programmes, buttressed by the increased use of tests and guidance procedures, appeared in many schools and were common by the 1920s. Many scholars labelled them class-biased and destructive of democratic education. Did workers play a role in their establishment, or were poorer citizens the victims of social control? In *The Politics of School*

Reform, 1870–1940, Paul E. Peterson attacked the 'revisionist' position by asserting that workers as well as capitalists influenced the shape of these reforms. Ira Katznelson and Margaret Weir, in *Schooling for All*, nevertheless examined the same cities and discovered a very divided working class, whose ethnic and racial divisions prevented the existence of any single labour voice. They thus rejected Peterson's pluralistic interpretation while reemphasising the centrality of class and racial politics.[26]

The idea that the elite classes ran roughshod over everyone else nevertheless has fallen on hard times in the educational historiography on progressivism. Both Julia Wrigley and David J. Hogan, in conceptually diverse books on the nature of class and school politics in Chicago, see a host of competing forces at work, shaped but never completely controlled by narrowly defined class interests. In *Power and the Promise of School Reform: Grass-Roots Movements during the Progressive Era*, William J. Reese analysed school politics in four divers cities. He stressed the role of trade unionists, socialists, women's organisations, parent and neighbourhood groups and other reformers who wanted to mitigate the negative influences of corporate capitalism in children's lives. By supporting free breakfasts and lunches for the needy, vacation schools, medical and dental care, playgrounds and the use of the schools as social centres, these reformers wanted to challenge centralised power and to advance educational democracy. These reformers never gained more power than the bankers on the school board or professionals in the superintendent's office, but they formed alliances at different moments to lessen their impact. Ronald D. Cohen and Raymond A. Mohl have in another context called this alliance of normally antagonistic groups part of the 'paradox' of progressive educational movements.[27]

The interplay between efficiency, expertise, reform and social class formation was highlighted in the changing nature of the urban high school. Nearly one high school per day was built in America between 1890 and 1920, an amazing index of social change. In his encyclopaedic but invaluable volume, *The Shaping of the American High School, 1880–1920*, Edward Krug observed that the progressive era was 'an age in which many more young people than ever before decided to go to high school – or had it decided for them', as schools adjusted to the impact of broad social changes. By the 1880s, at least in the North in most towns and cities, high schools were familiar institutions whose enrolments surpassed those of the rival academies. But what would happen now that children from different family backgrounds were forced to attend school to survive in a more competitive economic environment? How would school reformers respond to the increased demand for schooling, to the needs of corporate America and to traditional ideals of equal opportunity and common education? Could the needs of business prove compatible with the demands of democracy?[28]

Heady debates raged over such questions after 1900. In the end, vocational and general courses of study expanded to meet the swelling enrolments of teenagers in the high school. The middle classes predominated in the more academic, college preparatory tracks, while poorer youth were overrepresented in the less academic courses. As Marvin Lazerson explains, the idea of the 'common curriculum' confronted the realities of an unequal, increasingly specialised economic system. Children from the more modest homes were labelled 'hand-minded', and working-class youth filled the vocational classes and thereby lowered their own status and market worth. All the talk about meeting the individual needs of pupils seemed to translate into unequal education. The irony is that schoolmen offered shop classes and leather craft, not the skill training actually needed for the industrial workplace. More important, perhaps, was the isolation of many working-class pupils from wealthier social groups and their exclusion from the most difficult academic courses. Trade unions did shape the educational process in many communities, fighting with intellectuals such as John Dewey against the separation of vocational schools from the comprehensive high school.[29]

The expansion of high schools therefore led to greater specialisation in courses of study and thus in teaching. According to Janice Weiss, many teachers in Chicago, Philadelphia and other cities feared that the addition of the commercial classes would dilute the academic character of the high school. By the late nineteenth century, social promotion had replaced entrance exams to the high school, and fears about quality continued to grip school debates throughout the century. After 1905, the junior high school also appeared as a product of more bureaucratic specialisation. Whereas the grammar level grades in the late nineteenth century had served as the end of most children's schooling, this innovation separated the elementary grades and the high school, offering schoolmen with a way to engage in pre-vocational testing and guidance. The common school ideal retreated even further from view.[30]

The majority of teenagers still did not enrol in high school even in 1920, but these secondary schools could not be confused with nineteenth-century high schools. As cities swelled and the demands of urban life grew, high schools added a wide variety of services and programmes that would have puzzled Horace Mann's generation. Dieticians, nurses, counsellors, teachers of specialised subjects and new layers of educational administration stood between pupils and their last day in school. Pupils enrolled in special interest clubs, served on student government, wrote for the school newspaper or joined athletic teams. They appeared in school assemblies no matter what course of study they pursued. Did some common experiences outside of the classroom substitute for the unequal opportunities of different groups to learn academic subjects? Were schools structured to maintain the distance between various social classes and races?[31]

Understanding the motivation of the reformers and the actual social functions of schools remains difficult. There was clearly never any monolithic victory by the administrative reformers, who nevertheless did set the terms of the debate over how to reshape and redefine the school. The idea that most reformers were simply humanitarian seems untenable, though some studies emphasise that many men and women of good will struggled to apply democratic procedures and to establish humane reforms in the schools. Every part of the reform agenda is open to charges of elitism or, on the contrary, applause for their democratic potential. Kindergartens increasingly appeared in some urban schools, even though as late as 1915 they reached only 12 per cent of the eligible population. Some historians see the kindergartens as an example of the humane side of progressivism, since they offered relaxed, sometimes experimental learning environments for the poor. Other scholars more critically note that, once established, kindergartens simply tried to discipline, shape and prepare otherwise unruly children for the more rule-driven elementary grades.[32]

Happily, scholars have increasingly favoured more complex, dialectical interpretations of urban school reform. More simple theories of how elites control the poor have given way to attempts to understand the wide gaps between intent and outcome, and especially to see that children and workers are active agents who spoil the best laid plans. Interpreting the social history of urban play highlights this point. In *Choosing Sides*, Cary Goodman argued that New York's reformers wanted to impose bourgeois notions of play upon a wide range of immigrant groups. Yet it has become clear that working-class groups often actively lobbied for safe playgrounds for neighbourhood children in the early twentieth century. Parks were often located far from grimy industrial neighbourhoods, and contemporaries wanted not manicured areas but safe playgrounds where children could romp and enjoy themselves. Milwaukee's socialist trade unionists numbered in the tens of thousands and strongly endorsed the playground movement. Studies of urban leisure in Worcester, Massachusetts and Pittsburgh, Pennsylvania, ably demonstrate that the history of recreation cannot be understood well by references to theories of social control.[33]

Studying one segment of the working class – newly arrived immigrants – reveals complicated patterns of accommodation and resistance, harmony and discord, mobility and continued inequality. Largely poor and Catholic, Orthodox or Jewish, often untutored in English, the new ethnics changed the face of urban life and inevitably altered the schools. Cities had long been the home of immigrants, but nothing matched their numbers and diversity at the turn of the century. Educators tried to treat them as a uniform mass, who needed to embrace a narrow Americanisation, the English language, spread-eagle patriotism, and capitalism. But there proved to be no single immigrant experience or uniform response to the schools.[34]

John Bodnar and other historians argue that schoolmen were often unsympathetic to the cultural and economic demands many immigrant parents made on their children. Families from Eastern and Central Europe expected their children to contribute to the family economy, so extended schooling was a luxury many could ill afford. Much of the curriculum beyond basic literacy seemed 'irrelevant to the requirements of the industrial workplace', and public schools taught secular as well as pan-Protestant values. Thus, many Slavic families embraced parochial schools as a way to maintain cultural values and religious faith. James Sanders notes, too, that Catholics built parochial schools at different rates in various cities, as ethnics interacted in complex ways with the local political and educational environments.[35]

Calling all the diverse newcomers 'immigrants' disguised the diversity between various groups, as the most perceptive schoolmen realised. Poles and southern Italians valued child labour for family survival and doubted the value of extended schooling; Jews and Romanians, on the other hand, often valued more high school education for their children. Financial necessity and the desire to purchase a home propelled Chicago's Polish youth into the workplace early. When Jews in New York and other cities started to climb into the middle class, they drew upon traditions that emphasised the value of education but also no longer needed their children's income to survive. As Selma C. Berrol writes, 'widespread utilization of secondary and higher education *followed* improvements in economic status and was as much a result as a cause of upward mobility'.[36]

A richer literature also now exists concerning immigrant aspirations, cultural legacies, Americanisation efforts, gender differences, generational conflicts and economic conditions. All of this influenced family decisions about whether children should receive an extended education. Yet we still need more knowledge about the intersection of home, school and work. How different were the experiences of German and Russian Jews, northern and southern Italians, or different generations within particular groups? How did different groups interact with native culture? How did parents reconcile the desire for their children to enjoy economic mobility in the new land while simultaneously demanding respect for traditional values?[37]

Studies on racial politics have similarly sharpened our comprehension of the role of schools in the progressive era. Immigrants often faced ugly ethnocentrism, but African-Americans suffered graver forms of discrimination. While immigrants varied greatly in their enthusiasm for the public school, black Americans usually supported public education. They did not generally form separate, non-public schools but rather attempted to enjoy equal treatment and equal access to basic American institutions. The bitter irony was that their faith in the power of education was often crushed by racist practices in the schools and in the labour market. Vincent Franklin has remarked that native blacks were as enthusiastic about the potential of education as many East European Jews but by 1915 remained on the bottom of the occupational ladder.[38]

African-American children in the South attended legally segregated, underfunded schools. That contrasted with some glimmers of success in the North, since before the First World War many black children in Chicago and Philadelphia attended some integrated schools. That did not prevent racist practices, of course, and the general annihilation of black civil rights in the Progressive era resulted from widespread white support for a strong colour line. Blacks who mastered Cicero became janitors anyway, destroying the dream of mobility through schooling. IQ tests and counselling and guidance procedures discriminated severely against African-American children, who were urged to avoid academic subjects. As the colour line appeared more boldly in many Northern cities after 1900, blacks boycotted schools, rallied in favour of integration and yet found themselves in very ambiguous situations. Whenever segregated schools closed, black teachers were usually fired. Scholars will no doubt continue to examine the history of racism in the schools, but understanding the place of churches, voluntary organisations and other sources of learning and socialisation will enrich our understanding of America's most oppressed people.[39]

The history of women's education has also enlivened the study of urban education. Generalisations about class, race and ethnicity that do not address women's place in history increasingly lack credibility. For example, vocationalism differed greatly for boys and girls, parents often made different decisions about formal instruction based on gender, and the belief that girls were mostly future wives and mothers remained powerful in many sectors of society. Young working-class women, like their brothers, often supplemented the family income by working, dropping out of school to help their parents. According to Miriam Cohen, Italian girls seldom finished high school in New York City, partly due to family values, but also because enough unskilled jobs still existed there in the 1920s to make further education unnecessary. When clerical jobs increased, they remained in school longer in response to the market demand for language skills and proficiency in arithmetic. Jewish girls, Cohen points out, stayed in high school longer in New York, as parents drew upon different cultural traditions and employed different strategies for success in the urban economy.[40]

Attempts to generalise about the diverse experiences of immigrants, African-Americans and women remain challenging. Theories of social control hardly capture the rich texture of human existence and the dialectical interplay between school and society. In the attempt to understand the lives of those who left few written records, historians also confront the perennial problem of inferring beliefs from actions. One can more easily cite school enrolment figures than explain what young people and their families hoped schools might offer.

Moreover, the heavy reliance on single case studies, though hardly a problem unique to historians of education, makes framing sound generalisations difficult. John L. Rury writes that many scholars study a host of educational issues in cities, but that the subjects they examine are hardly unique to cities. Racism, sexism, ethnocentrism and class bias are not limited to metropolitan areas. Rury also believes that scholars should be more attentive to regional differences in urban history. Generalisations about 'urban' schools are usually based on large Northeastern or Midwestern systems that may have had little in common, for example, with the South.[41]

The practical difficulties of capturing all the human drama, diversity and complexity of urban education at the turn of the century will mean in all likelihood that case studies will continue to flow from the presses. Swept along by the onrushing ride of monopoly capitalism, schools became highly specialised, more bureaucratic, stratified institutions that attempted to prepare and adjust young people to an unequal social order. High schools opened their doors to young people but did not offer everyone the same academic opportunity. School boards were centralised under the banner of disinterested leadership but met resistance from various opponents who sought more democratic decision-making. Schools taught materialism, secularism and a narrow brand of patriotism, even though cities were rich and diverse in the types of ethnic, racial and economic groups found in many neighbourhoods. Diversity of values persisted despite the attempts of schools to homogenise culture; inequality of access to job opportunities and to goods and services persisted as schools buttressed the new corporate order.

III

Urban citizens first became the majority of the nation in 1920. Familiarity sometimes bred contempt, as rural and urban conflict characterised the coming decade. Moreover, many urban dwellers who could afford it moved to the suburbs – to safer streets and cleaner air and more homogeneous neighbourhoods. Urban schools serving those left behind remained embedded in a world of contradictory forces that led to spectacular wealth and abysmal poverty, to pressure for cultural diversity and the melting-pot ideal. Bureaucratic in form and now quite centralised, schools nevertheless remained locally controlled. Only when local citizens lobbied for more financial assistance from state government in the 1930s, or for federal aid to help solve racial and economic problems in the 1960s, did local control not appear completely absolute. From the 1920s to the present, urban schools have continued to be tugged by contradictory forces and tensions.[42]

Even though the majority of Americans after 1920 lived in towns or cities, most studies of urban education cover the ante-bellum period or the progressive era. Only a handful of detailed case studies even exist on urban schools after the First World War, and most only deal with a single important subject such as race. Yet the outlines of the history of urban schools seem clear. By the 1920s, the business-inspired administrative progressives of the previous decades seemed fairly victorious. Pillars of the business community, professionals and society women dominated on school 'boards' and experts with advanced professional degrees became superintendents and lower-level functionaries within the entrenched bureaucracy. The corporate nature of business appealed to the school managers, who sometimes likened children to raw materials on the assembly line.[43]

The efficiency promoters, as David B. Tyack and Elisabeth Hansot note, remained enthralled by business practices and often wanted to operate schools like a machine. This was never completely achieved, and protests by discontented groups forced concessions even during the difficult days of the great depression. Moreover, civil rights groups and teacher unions decades later also forced the normally insular school bureaucrats to emerge from their shell and alter certain educational practices. Advocates for children with special needs, and who spoke languages other than English, also often successfully pressured reluctant legislators in the 1970s to expand the mission of public education to include new children and new programmes.[44]

The social role of urban schools continued to expand in the twentieth century. Some cities in recent decades have even offered free birth control counselling in extremely poor neighbourhoods. Geraldine J. Clifford has noted that citizens often pressured urban schools to increase services even though the tax base of central cities continued to erode and business support for education declined. The cost of operating urban schools escalated in the twentieth century for many reasons. Teacher unions fought for a living wage, not the going wage, and teachers in cities were often older, more experienced and hence more expensive. More specialised services in some urban as compared with rural areas, necessitated by the consequences of such concentrated poverty in some neighbourhoods, also inflated local budgets.[45]

Teacher unions emerged as potential players in school politics by the 1930s, though research in this area remains sketchy. The early Chicago

Teachers Union successfully wielded some power, but by the 1920s along with other affiliates of the American Federation of Teachers (AFT) quickly lost influence. Soon the New York City local union comprised half of the national membership. Much has been written on the role of Communists in splintering the New York group in the 1930s. Little is known about the activities of other urban teachers, whether organised or unorganised. Only spectacular events, such as the central role of New York's unions in the controversy over community control in the late 1960s, has thus far attracted the interests of researchers.[46]

The starting place for understanding these and related research issues is *Public Schools in Hard Times*, by David B. Tyack, Robert Lowe and Elisabeth Hansot. In their discussion of the 1930s, they conclude that rural schools suffered more economically because they began with fewer resources and programmes. Country school terms were already shorter, teacher salaries were lower, and so forth; urban schools could at least cut social services or ancillary programmes. Many cities slashed budgets by 1935, but many programmes and basic academic programmes remained intact. Protection for the urban school often depended upon an alliance of teachers and various civic groups. In Chicago, cuts were deep; in Detroit, pro-school coalitions banded together to preserve much of the system. Given the local nature of school politics, such coalitions made all the difference in the world. Budgets still depended overwhelmingly on local taxes, and the New Deal did not fundamentally alter that reality.[47]

Hard times nevertheless produced significant changes, moulding political and economic beliefs that still inform school politics. For example, business leaders, once strong advocates for increased spending in the progressive era, now fought against more increases, often locking horns with teachers and their allies. Business values still dominated the school structure and the curriculum, but businessmen worked to reduce revenues to the minimum. As a result, many educators, liberal reformers and progressive labour leaders pushed with some success then and in subsequent decades for more state assistance for local schools. Teacher unions sometimes became more politically active. Moreover, as more young people were displaced from the market place and attended high school, local educators fought for the expansion of non-academic courses, foreshadowing the Life Adjustment movement of the 1940s. The dark days of the depression did not mean the collapse of the urban schools.[48]

The Second World War quite naturally influenced the nation's schools, though the subject demands further investigation. Wartime production and manpower needs led to shortages of teachers and material. High school enrolment decreased as employment opportunities increased. Female students predominated in the classroom, and curricula seemed more sensitive to world issues than ever before. Many pupils, such as those in Indianapolis, apparently remained apathetic or indifferent toward the war. In Gary, Indiana, fears increased of uncontrolled youth and radical demands for integrated schools. The Steel City's heterogeneous population and industrial character perhaps produced extreme fears shared to a lesser degree in other places.[49]

Diane Ravitch offers a broad survey of education across the nation after the war in *The Troubled Crusade*. She examines economic problems, progressive education, racial issues, anti-Communism, student protest, and more. These topics animated policy discussions about schools everywhere, not just in urban areas. Like many writers, however, Ravitch recognises the poverty and despair that characterised many urban school systems by the 1960s. Poor black and Hispanic children living in segregated ghettos attended underfunded schools, as wealthier whites left the inner city for safer suburbs. Ravitch does not address the broad economic and social forces that made this economic and racial segregation possible. Many 'revisionist' writers, on the other hand, link the 'crisis' of schools with the 'progress' of American capitalism, which stretched its arms to many parts of the globe after the Second World War.[50]

Many monographs on urban education after 1920 deal with racial problems, exacerbated by the movement of more whites to the suburbs. Black migration from the rural South to local and Northern cities after 1900 forever altered the nature of the public schools. Indeed, case studies of Northern cities document the hardening of the colour line after 1920. By 1945, for example, Chicago had shifted from a city system with considerable integration to one that was largely segregated by race. Black protests proved futile. In Philadelphia, Gary and many other cities, the percentage of black children in inner cities continued to rise until nearly complete segregation existed within a few decades. *De facto* segregation in the North and *de jure* segregation in the South was the rule when the *Brown* decision declared legally segregated schools unconstitutional in 1954. Only 2 per cent of black children in the South, however, attended mixed schools two years later. Soon the federal government, pressured by a growing civil rights movement, was forced to address racial segregation through legislation and more activist enforcement of the law, always with ambiguous results.[51]

Initial interest in racial questions in the South soon shifted to the North by the mid-1960s. The Second Reconstruction would include cities outside of Dixie. White hostility to *Brown*, however, fuelled black nationalist sentiments, understandable given the increasing racial segregation and negligible progress of the integrationist movement. Many middle- and upper-class whites supported integration but not the busing of their own children. They had, after all, moved to the suburbs to escape the city and enjoyed schools with a stronger tax base. In the inner city, black power confronted white teacher power in cities like New York in the late 1960s. Community control advocates found themselves endorsing segregation, and blacks grew angry and then tired of white reluctance to form a racially integrated system. In Gotham, as elsewhere, controversies focused on urban heterogeneity, cultural diversity, inequality, parochialism versus cosmopolitanism and the effectiveness of the administrative structure and alleged racism of the school managers.[52]

In 1971, the US Supreme Court in *Swann* v. *Charlotte Mecklenburg* ordered cities to use virtually all means, including busing, to integrate the public schools. The large increase in non-white enrolment in the cities, however, made busing more difficult than ever. White pupils were a shrinking minority in New York, Chicago, Cleveland, Gary and Washington, DC. When the Court in 1974 balked at the forced integration of suburban and inner city districts, one possible avenue to building racially inclusive schools closed. Housing segregation in the North continued to make neighbourhood schools not common but racially segregated. When the civil rights movement enabled some blacks to climb out of the ghetto and into the suburbs, the inner cities became not only more racially segregated but also more segregated by income.[53]

More studies of the history of race and urban education will help clarify the outlines of the subject. David Kirp's *Just Schools*, an analysis of five San Francisco Bay communities, will hopefully be supplemented by a growing literature on racial politics in many parts of the nation. The rich texture of local politics and cultural conflict forms the backdrop to the prize-winning work of J. Anthony Lukas on the Boston schools. Boston's experience proved more violent than most, but Lukas provides a compelling portrait of families caught in the grip of history and modern struggles for social justice. Future studies will doubtless address how well blacks and other working-class Americans compete economically and educationally with a new wave of immigrants now transforming the city.[54]

Indeed, urban schools continue to address not only the struggle between whites and blacks for racial understanding, but also the struggle of other groups for quality, culturally sensitive schools. Many large cities have sizeable neighbourhoods of Mexican-Americans, Native-Americans, Puerto Ricans and other minorities. Often living in poor, segregated neighbourhoods, they offer yet another challenge to urban schools. Japanese- and Chinese-Americans, often portrayed as the model of academic overachievement, comprise a strikingly different example of ethnic distinctiveness and of academic success. As early as 1934, the Service Bureau for Intercultural Education was created to counter ethnocentrism and to promote the value of cultural pluralism. The revival of the idea of bilingual and bicultural education, and the appearance of English Only opponents, testify to the reality of diversity and the dream of homogeneity.[55]

Catholic schools, too, helped promote religious and cultural diversity, but the decline in the teaching orders and shifts in their clientele have produced considerable change. Chicago's parochial school enrolments grew in the 1940s and 1950s, then declined in the 1970s, and have recently attracted black Protestants escaping from the deteriorating public schools. How parochial schools fared in many places will continue to fascinate historians. So will the proliferation of fundamentalist Christian day schools in many towns and cities after the 1960s; they constitute a tiny percentage of private education but represent another challenge to the idea of a common public school. We do not have as many rich histories of non-public education as we have on race, and sociologists rather than historians have published the most prominent interpretations of modern private schools.[56]

Whether studying race, ethnicity, religion or other sources of human diversity, scholars interested in urban schools must necessarily examine social change in the light of broad economic changes that have defined the parameters of urban education. Instead of providing hope and opportunity, urban schools by the 1950s were confirming inequality. Suburban schools became the model systems, in contrast with the underfunded, increasingly racially segregated central city schools. James B. Conant predicted in *Slums and Suburbs* that 'social dynamite' existed in the nation's metropolitan areas, and it exploded in the late 1960s in many places. Moreover, the connections between the spread of international capitalism and the national search for markets ultimately shaped the overall urban economy. The decline of industry, the movement of businesses to the suburbs, the rise of the service economy: all this has led to further deterioration of the economic infrastructure of the inner city. The collapse of job opportunities, filled partially by the illicit drug trade, has made more effective public schools more important and less likely.[57]

The social history of life within schools, especially studies of teachers and students, is surprisingly thin given the abundance of primary source materials generated since 1920. More is known about court cases, school boycotts, teacher strikes and other well-publicised incidents than about everyday experiences in the classroom. In both the 1930s and 1960s in particular, critics attacked the conservative nature of teaching and instruction, accusing teachers of authoritarianism, didactic teaching methods and so forth. Larry Cuban has been a pioneer in studying teaching practices, and he contends that teaching styles remained quite uniform throughout the modern period despite all the complaints.[58]

Ronald D. Cohen's study, *Children of the Mill*, remains unique since it examines in great detail the fate of one famous school system in Gary,

Indiana, from the progressive era through the 1950s. For Cohen, 'the Gary schools exemplified the rise of a system of mass education in a multiracial, multiethnic, class-structured urban setting'. First, they 'did not just offer curricular and extracurricular choices to children, but also provided medical care, baby sitting, social welfare services, recreation for the entire family, adult programs (particularly during the early decades), facilities for the handicapped, and employment opportunities, and served as an anchor for the community'. Moreover, 'because of their important and visible public role, [the Gary] schools have served as a magnet for the views and interests of a complex of organizations, interest groups, and individuals, whether local, state, or national'. The long-time superintendent William A. Wirt (1907–38), while moulding the schools to confront a multitude of urban problems, was, like his fellow superintendents, never comfortable living in a city. Indeed, influenced by the dream of an homogenised, small-town America, perhaps most city superintendents (until recently) have been essentially anti-urban.[59]

The history of recent urban schooling in the United States has not produced any consensus of interpretation. Like studies of the ante-bellum period and the progressive era, analyses of the schools after the 1920s are ideologically diverse, address different questions and offer conflicting conclusions. Yet broad outlines of the history of urban education emerge from this literature. Urban schools were fundamentally shaped by the contrary forces influencing city life since the First World War. Everywhere, citizens felt the tensions between centralised authority and demands for decentralised control, between human diversity and pleas for assimilation and between experts and lay people. America's corporate economic state, emerging so visibly before the First World War, grew more powerful still as multi-national corporations expanded their reach into markets throughout the world by the early 1950s. As central cities lost their economic vitality, growing poorer and more non-white, the challenges of urban educators increased at the very time resources and public will declined.

The stark contrast between urban and rural schools in the nineteenth century somewhat faded after the 1920s as reforms such as graded classrooms, a uniform curriculum, centralised school boards, professional administrators and the like spread outside the urban borders. Still, city schools remain distinctive forms of educational life, as comparisons with neighbouring suburbs always make clear. City schools are unique for their complex racial and ethnic mixes, vast bureaucracies and specialised functions and services. As inner city families continue to suffer from a collapsing local economy, more pressure will undoubtedly arise to make schools more effective, whether by taming the children, educating them or separating them from their parents, peers or the streets.[60]

Many citizens in the 1990s still wonder if Thomas Jefferson's early assessment of cities was accurate. Weakened by serious economic and social ills, cities often seem to represent the worst side of American life, and their school systems quite naturally appear to some as lesions on the body politic. Those who hate the public school monopoly demand more market solutions to the educational needs of the inner city, even though the market has not provided the poor and people of colour with reasonable access to quality food, affordable and safe housing or well-paying jobs. Given the complex ills of our society, reforming urban schools will remain difficult, and writing their history remains a daunting task.

NOTES

1 Thomas Jefferson, quoted in Charles N. Glaab and A. Theodore Brown, *A History of Urban America* (3rd edn, New York: Macmillan, 1983), 54.
2 Samuel P. Hays, *American Political History as Social Analysis* (Knoxville, TN: University of Tennessee Press, 1980), 327. On urban education, see also James Sanders, 'Education and the city: urban community study', in John Hardin Best (ed.), *Historical Inquiry in Education: A Research Agenda* (Washington, DC: American Educational Research Association, 1983), 211–29; Selwyn K. Troen, 'Education in the city', in Raymond A. Mohl and James F. Richardson (eds.), *The Urban Experience: Themes in American History* (Belmont, CA: Wadsworth, 1973), 127–43; and Robert Church and Michael Sedlak, *Education in the United States: An Interpretive History* (New York: The Free Press, 1976).
3 Gary Nash, *The Urban Crucible: Social Change, Political Consciousness, and the Origins of the American Revolution* (Cambridge, MA: Harvard University Press, 1979), 5.
4 Lawrence A. Cremin, *American Education: The Colonial Experience, 1607–1783* (New York: Harper and Row, 1970), xiii, and 535–41; Carl F. Kaestle, *The Evolution of an Urban School System: New York City, 1750–1850* (Cambridge, MA: Harvard University Press, 1973), 5. See also Carl Bridenbaugh, *Cities in the Wilderness: The First Century of Urban Life in America, 1625–1742* (New York: Alfred A. Knopf, 1960), 121–7, 280–9, 442–51); Carl Bridenbaugh, *Cities in Revolt: Urban Life in America, 1743–1776* (New York: Alfred A. Knopf, 1955), 172–9, 373–80; James Axtell, *The School Upon a Hill: Education and Society in Colonial New England* (New Haven, CT: Yale University Press, 1974); Stanley Schultz, *The Culture Factory: Boston Public Schools, 1789–1860* (New York: Oxford University Press, 1973); and William J. Gilmore, *Reading Becomes a Necessity of Life: Material Culture in Rural New England* (Knoxville, TN: University of Tennessee Press, 1989).
5 Nash, *The Urban Crucible*, 382–3. For New York see Kaestle, *Evolution of an Urban School System*, 28–74; for Boston, Schultz, *Culture Factory*, 14–21.
6 On the Lancasterian schools, see Carl F. Kaestle (ed.), *Joseph Lancaster and the Monitorial School Movement: A Documentary History* (New York: Teachers College Press, 1973).
7 On high schools, see Maris A. Vinovskis, *The Origins of Public High Schools: A Reexamination of the Beverly High School Controversy* (Madison, WI: University

of Wisconsin Press, 1985); Reed Ueda, *Avenues to Adulthood* (Cambridge: Cambridge University Press, 1987); and David F. Labaree, *The Making of an American High School* (New Haven, CT: Yale University Press, 1988).
8 Mary Ryan, *Cradle of the Middle Class: The Family in Oneida County, New York, 1790–1865* (Cambridge: Cambridge University Press, 1981). For the dispute over the class nature of high schools, see Michael B. Katz, *The Irony of Early School Reform: Educational Innovation in Mid-Nineteenth Century Massachusetts* (paperback, Boston, MA: Beacon Press, 1970); Vinovskis, *The Origins of Public High Schools*.
9 Lawrence A. Cremin, *American Education: The National Experience, 1783–1876* (New York: Harper and Row, 1980).
10 Barbara Berg, *The Remembered Gate: Origins of Feminism, The Woman and The City, 1800–1860* (New York: Oxford University Press, 1978), 7. On women and education, see Carl Degler, *At Odds: Women and the Family in America from the Revolution to the Present* (New York: Oxford University Press, 1980); Nancy F. Cott, *The Bonds of Womanhood: 'Women's Sphere' in New England, 1780–1835* (New Haven, CT: Yale University Press, 1977); Linda Kerber, *Women of the Republic: Intellect and Ideology in Revolutionary America* (Chapel Hill, NC: University of North Carolina Press, 1980); and David B. Tyack and Elisabeth Hansot, *Learning Together: A History of Coeducation in American Public Schools* (New Haven, CT: Yale University Press, 1990).
11 Joseph Kett, *Rites of Passage: Adolescence in America 1790 to the Present* (New York: Basic Books, 1977), 38–108; Robert Mennell, *Thorns and Thistles: Juvenile Delinquents in the United States, 1825–1940* (Hanover, NH: University Press of New England, 1973), 3–77; Steven L. Schlossman, *Love and the American Delinquent: The Theory and Practice of 'Progressive' Juvenile Justice, 1825–1920* (Chicago, IL: University of Chicago Press, 1977), 18–54; Barbara Brenzel, *Daughters of the State* (Cambridge, MA: MIT Press, 1983); Joseph M. Hawes, *Children in Urban Society: Juvenile Delinquency in Nineteenth-Century America* (New York: Oxford University Press, 1971); Christopher Lasch, *The World of Nations: Reflections on American History, Politics and Culture* (paperback, New York: Vintage Books, 1974), 17.
12 Michael B. Katz, 'Origins of the institutional state', *Marxist Perspectives*, Vol. 1 (Winter 1978), 18–20, which reappears in Michael B. Katz, Michael Doucet and Mark Stern, *The Social Organization of Early Industrial Capitalism* (Cambridge, MA: Harvard University Press, 1982), Chap. 9.
13 Katz, *The Irony of Early School Reform*, 112; Schultz, *Culture Factory*, 277; and Kaestle, *Evolution of an Urban School System*, 188.
14 Michael B. Katz, *Class, Bureaucracy, and Schools: The Illusion of Educational Change in America* (expanded edn, paperback, New York: Praeger, 1975), xviii, 70; Kaestle, *Evolution of an Urban School System*, 159; Schultz, *Culture Factory*, 133; David B. Tyack, *The One Best System: A History of American Urban Education* (Cambridge, MA: Harverd University Press, 1974).
15 Schultz, *Culture Factory*, 167; Carl F. Kaestle, *Pillars of the Republic: Common Schools and American Society, 1780–1860* (New York: Hill and Wang, 1983), 174–5, 179; Vincent P. Franklin, *The Education of Black Philadelphia: The Social and Educational History of a Minority Community, 1900–1950* (Philadelphia, PA: University of Pennsylvania Press, 1979), 32–3; Philip Foner and Josephine

Pacheco, *Three Who Dared: Prudence Crandall, Margaret Douglass, Myrtilla Miner – Champions of Antebellum Black Education* (Westport, CT: Greenwood Press, 1984).

16 Diane Ravitch, *The Great School Wars: New York City: A History of Public Schools as Battlefields of Social Change* (New York: Basic Books, 1974), 33; James W. Sanders, 'Roman Catholics and the school question in New York City: some suggestions for research', in Diane Ravitch and Ronald K. Goodenow (eds.), *Educating an Urban People: The New York City Experience* (New York: Teachers College Press, 1981), 122–3; James Sanders, *The Education of an Urban Minority: Catholics in Chicago, 1833–1965* (New York: Oxford University Press, 1977), 23–4, Kaestle, *Pillars of the Republic*, 166–71; Schultz, *Culture Factory*, 306–8.

17 Diane Ravitch, *The Revisionists Revised: A Critique of the Radical Attack on the Schools* (New York: Basic Books, 1978); Carl F. Kaestle and Maris A. Vinovskis, *Education and Social Change in Nineteenth-Century Massachusetts* (Cambridge: Cambridge University Press, 1980), 24, 234; Kaestle, *Pillars of the Republic*, 30, 77.

18 On the South, see David Plank and Rick Ginsberg (eds.), *Southern Cities, Southern Schools: Public Education in the Urban South* (New York: Greenwood Press, 1990).

19 For an overview of the period, see Richard L. McCormick, 'Public life in industrial America, 1877–1917', in Eric Foner (ed.), *The New American History* (Philadelphia, PA: Temple University Press, 1990), 93–117. See also Selwyn K. Troen, *The Public and the Schools: Shaping the St. Louis System 1838–1920* (Columbia, MO: University of Missouri Press, 1975).

20 See Alan I. Marcus, 'The city as social system: the importance of ideas', *American Quarterly*, Vol. 37 (Bibliography 1985), 338–40.

21 For a recent review of the literature on urban history, Raymond A. Mohl, 'New perspectives on American urban history', *International Journal of Social Education*, Vol. 1 (Spring 1986), 69–97.

22 Lawrence A. Cremin, *The Transformation of the School: Progressivism in American Education, 1876–1957*, (New York: Alfred A. Knopf, 1961), viii.

23 Samuel P. Hays, 'The politics of reform in municipal government in the progressive era', *Pacific Northwest Quarterly*, Vol. 55 (Oct. 1964), 157–69. For background, see Jon C. Teaford, *The Unheralded Triumph: City Government in America, 1870–1900* (Baltimore, MD: Johns Hopkins University Press, 1984); Jon C. Teaford, *The Twentieth Century American City: Problem, Promise, and Reality* (Baltimore, MD: Johns Hopkins University Press, 1986); Raymond A. Mohl, *The New City: Urban America in the Industrial Age, 1860–1920* (Arlington Heights, IL: Harlan Davidson, Inc., 1985).

24 Tyack, *One Best System*; David B. Tyack and Elisabeth Hansot, *Managers of Virtue: Public School Leadership in America, 1820–1980* (New York: Basic Books, 1986), 106. See also David C. Hammack, *Power and Society: Greater New York at the Turn of the Century* (New York: Russell Sage Foundation, 1982); Troen, *The Public and the Schools*; William A. Bullough, *Cities and Schools in the Gilded Age: The Evolution of an Urban Institution* (Port Washington, NY: Kennikat Press, 1974); Raymond E. Callahan, *Education and the Cult of Efficiency: A Study of the Social Forces that Have Shaped the Administration of the Public Schools* (Chicago,

IL: University of Chicago Press, 1962). For the effect of administrative reform on rural schools, see Wayne E. Fuller, *The Old Country School: The Story of Rural Education in the Middle West* (Chicago, IL: University of Chicago Press, 1982); William A. Link, *A Hard Country and a Lonely Place: Schooling, Society, and Reform in Rural Virginia, 1870–1920* (Chapel Hill, NC, and London: University of North Carolina Press, 1986).

25 Joel H. Spring, *Education and the Rise of the Corporate State* (Boston, MA: Beacon Press, 1972), xii.

26 Paul E. Peterson, *The Politics of School Reform, 1870–1940* (Chicago, IL: University of Chicago Press, 1985); Ira Katznelson and Margaret Weir, *Schooling for All: Class, Race, and the Decline of the Democratic Ideal* (New York: Basic Books, 1985). For more emphasis on the role of capitalism, see Samuel Bowles and Herbert Gintis, *Schooling in Capitalist America: Educational Reform and the Contradictions of Economic Life* (New York: Basic Books, 1976). See also the essays in Harvey Kantor and David B. Tyack (eds.), *Work, Youth, and Schooling: Historical Perspectives on Vocationalism in American Education* (Stanford, CA: Stanford University Press, 1982).

27 Julia Wrigley, *Class Politics and Public Schools: Chicago, 1990–1950* (New Brunswick, NJ: Rutgers University Press, 1982); David J. Hogan, *Class and Reform: School and Society in Chicago, 1880–1930* (Philadelphia, PA: University of Pennsylvania Press, 1985); William J. Reese, *Power and the Promise of School Reform: Grass-Roots Movements during the Progressive Era* (Boston, MA: and London: Routledge, Kegan Paul, 1986); Ronald D. Cohen and Raymond A. Mohl, *The Paradox of Progressive Education: The Gary Plan and Urban Schooling* (Port Washington, NY: Kennikat Press, 1979), Chap. 1.

28 Edward A. Krug, *The Shaping of the American High School*, Vol. I: *1880–1920* (New York: Harper and Row, 1964), 169. See also Herbert Kliebard, *The Struggle for the American Curriculum, 1893–1958* (Boston, MA, and London: Routledge, Kegan Paul, 1986).

29 Marvin Lazerson, *The Origins of the Urban School: Public Education in Massachusetts, 1870–1915* (Cambridge, MA: Harvard University Press, 1971), 255–6.

30 Janice Weiss, 'The Advent of education for clerical work in the high school: a reconsideration of the historiography of vocationalism', *Teacher College Record*, Vol. 83 (Summer 1982), 613–38; David F. Labaree, 'Setting the standard: alternative policies for student promotion', *Harvard Educational Review*, Vol. 54 (February 1984), 67–87.

31 Spring, *Education and the Rise of the Corporate State*, 108–9. See also Paul Violas, *The Training of the Urban Working Class: A History of Twentieth Century American Education* (Chicago, IL: Rand McNally Pub. Co., 1978).

32 Marvin Lazerson and W. Norton Grubb (eds.), *American Education and Vocationalism: A Documentary History, 1870–1970* (New York: Teachers College Press, 1974), 39; and Lazerson, *Origins of the Urban School*, 72–3. For the most recent positive history, read Michael S. Shapiro, *Child's Garden: The Kindergarten Movement from Froebel to Dewey* (University Park, PA: Pennsylvania State University Press, 1983).

33 Cary Goodman, *Choosing Sides: Playground and Street Life on the Lower East Side* (New York: Schocken Books, 1979); Roy Rosenzweig, *Eight Hours for What we Will: Workers and Leisure in an Industrial City, 1870–1920* (New York:

Cambridge University Press, 1983); Francis G. Couvares, 'The triumph of commerce: class culture and mass culture in Pittsburgh', in Michael Firsch and Daniel Walkowitz (eds.), *Working-Class History* (Urbana, IL: University of Illinois Press, 1983), 123–52.

34 Alan M. Kraut, *The Huddled Masses: The Immigrant in American Society, 1880–1921* (Arlington Heights, IL: Harlan Davidson, 1982).

35 John Bodnar, *The Transplanted: A History of Immigrants in Urban America* (Bloomington, IN: Indiana University Press, 1985), 193; Sanders, 'Roman Catholics and the school question in New York City', 122. See also Bernard J. Weiss (ed.), *American Education and the European Immigrant, 1840–1940* (Urbana, IL: University of Illinois Press, 1982); Michael R. Olneck and Marvin Lazerson, 'The school achievement of immigrant children: 1900–1930', *History of Education Quarterly*, Vol. 14 (Winter 1974), 453–82; Maxine Seller, 'The education of immigrants in the United States', *Immigration History Newsletter*, Vol. 13 (May 1981), 1.

36 David Hogan, 'Education and the making of the Chicago working class, 1880–1930', *History of Education Quarterly*, vol. 18 (1978), 227–70; Selma C. Berrol, 'Education and economic mobility: the Jewish experience in New York City, 1880–1920', *American Jewish Historical Quarterly*, Vol. 65 (March 1976), 271. For an article countering the Hogan argument, see Joel Perlmann, 'Working class homeownership and children's schooling in Providence, Rhode Island, 1880–1925', *History of Education Quarterly*, Vol. 23 (Summer 1983), 175–94.

37 See Raymond A. Mohl and Neil Betten, *Steel City: Urban and Ethnic Patterns in Gary, Indiana, 1906–1950* (New York and London: Holmes and Meier, 1986), Chap. 6; Weiss (ed.), *American Education and the European Immigrant*; Tyack, *One Best System*, 229–55; Paula S. Fass, *Outside In: Minorities and the Transformation of American Education* (New York: Oxford University Press, 1989), part 1; and for a review of the literature, William J. Reese, 'Neither victims nor masters: ethnic and minority study', in Best (ed.), *Historical Inquiry in Education*, 230–50.

38 Vincent Franklin, 'Continuity and discontinuity in black and immigrant minority education in urban America: a historical assessment', in Ravitch and Goodenow (eds.), *Educating an Urban People*, 62.

39 David Ment, 'Patterns of public school segregation, 1900–1940: a comparative study of New York City, New Rochelle, and New Haven', in Ronald K. Goodenow and Diane Ravitch (eds.), *Schools in Cities: Consensus and Conflict in American Educational History* (New York: Holmes and Meier, 1983), 104. See also Michael W. Homel, *Down from Equality: Black Chicagoans and the Public Schools, 1920–41* (Urbana, IL: University of Illinois Press, 1984), Chap. 1; Ronald D. Cohen, *Children of the Mill: Schooling and Society in Gary, Indiana, 1906–1960* (Bloomington, IN: Indiana University Press, 1990), *passim*; Judy Jolley Mohraz, *The Separate Problem: Case Studies of Black Education in the North, 1900–1930* (Westport, CT: Greenwood Press, 1979). Tyack, *One Best System*, 217–29; Louis R. Harlan, *Separate and Unequal: Public School Campaigns and Racism in the Southern Seaboard States, 1901–1915* (Chapel Hill, NC: University of North Carolina Press, 1958); and Franklin, *Education of Black Philadelphia*, Chap. 4.

40 Weiss, 'The advent of education for clerical work in the high schools'; Geraldine

J. Clifford, '"Marry, stitch, die, or do worse": educating women for work', in Kantor and Tyack (eds.), *Work, Youth, and Schooling*, 267–8; John L. Rury, 'Vocationalism for home and work: women's education in the United States, 1880–1930', *History of Education Quarterly*, Vol. 24 (Spring 1984), 21–44. Maxine Seller, 'The education of immigrant women: 1900 to 1935', *Journal of Urban History*, Vol. 4 (May 1978), 307–30; Miriam Cohen, 'Changing education strategies among immigrant generations: New York Italians in comparative perspective', *Journal of Social History*, Vol. 15 (Spring 1982), 457.

41 John L. Rury, 'Urbanisation and education: regional patterns of educational development in American cities, 1900–1910', *Michigan Academician*, Vol. 20 (Summer 1988), 261–80.

42 Tyack, *One Best System*. Also see the final volume of Lawrence A. Cremin's trilogy, *American Education: The Metropolitan Experience, 1876–1980* (New York: Harper and Row, 1988), Part IV.

43 Tyack and Hansot, *Managers of Virtue*, 157, 223, 225.

44 The relevant literature is cited below.

45 Geraldine J. Clifford, *The Shape of American Education* (Englewood Cliffs, NJ: Prentice-Hall, 1975), 42–4.

46 Thomas R. Brooks, 'Teachers divided: teacher unionism, in New York City, 1935–1940', in Ravitch and Goodenow (eds.), *Educating an Urban People*, 206; Lana Muraskin, 'The interests of the teachers union, 1913–1935', in *ibid.*, 219–29; Cohen, *Children of the Mill*, passim; Goodenow and Ravitch (eds.), *Schools in Cities*, 276–7; Ravitch, *The Great School Wars*, 251–398. And on the history of the AFT, see William E. Eaton, *The American Federation of Teachers, 1916–1961*, (Carbondale, PS: Southern Illinois University Press, 1975); Wayne Urban, *Why Teachers Organize* (Detroit, MI: Wayne State University Press, 1982). On the teachers union in Chicago, see the studies of Hogan, Wrigley, Peterson, and Katznelson and Weir listed above.

47 David B. Tyack, Robert Lowe and Elisabeth Hansot, *Public Schools in Hard Times: The Great Depression and Recent Years* (Cambridge, MA: Harvard University Press, 1984), 33–7, 91. See also Edward A. Krug, *The Shaping of the American High School*, Vol. II: *1920–1941* (Madison, WI: University of Wisconsin Press, 1972).

48 Jeffrey Mirel, review of Tyack, Lowe and Hansot, *Public Schools in Hard Times*, in *Educational Studies*, Vol. 16 (Summer 1985), 156–64; Jeffrey Mirel, 'The politics of educational retrenchment in Detroit, 1929–35', *History of Education Quarterly*, Vol. 24 (Fall 1984), 323–58; Cohen, *Children of the Mill*, Chap. 5.

49 Richard Ugland, 'Viewpoints and morale of urban high school students during World War II – Indianapolis as a case study', *Indiana Magazine of History*, Vol. 77 (June 1981), 150–78; Cohen, *Children of the Mill*, Chap. 6.

50 Diane Ravitch, *The Troubled Crusade: American Education, 1945–1980*, (New York: Basic Books, 1983), 326. See also Joel Spring, *The Sorting Machine: National Educational Policy Since 1945* (New York: David McKay, 1976); Guadalup San Miguel, Jr, *'Let All of Them Take Heed': Mexican Americans and the Campaign for Educational Equality in Texas, 1910–1981* (Austin, TX: University of Texas Press, 1987); and Gilbert G. Gonzales, *Chicano Education in the Era of Segregation* (Philadelphia, PA: Balch Institute Press, 1990).

51 Homel, *Down from Equality*, x; Franklin, *Education of Black Philadelphia*, 148–9,

188. On the situation in Gary, Indiana, see Cohen, *Children of the Mill*, Chaps. 7–8.
52 J. Harvie Wilkinson, *From Brown to Bakke: The Supreme Court and School Integration, 1954–1978* (New York: Oxford University Press, 1979); George Metcalf, *From Little Rock to Boston: The History of School Desegregation* (Westport, CT: Greenwood Press, 1983); Richard Kluger, *Simple Justice: The History of Brown v. Board of Education and Black America's Struggle for Equality* (New York: Alfred A. Knopf, 1976). And see in general, Harvard Sitkoff, *The Struggle for Black Equality, 1954–1980* (New York: Hill and Wang, 1981); Jack Bloom, *Class, Race, and the Civil Rights Movement* (Bloomington, IN: Indiana University Press, 1987).
53 Ravitch, *The Great School Wars*, 181, 397; and Bernard Schwartz, *Swann's Way: The School Busing Case and the Supreme Court* (New York: Oxford University Press, 1986).
54 David Kirp, *Just Schools: The Idea of Racial Equality in American Education* (Berkeley, CA: University of California Press, 1982), 80–1; Wilkinson, *From Brown to Bakke*, 213; J. Anthony Lukas, *Common Ground: A Turbulent Decade in the Lives of Three American Families* (New York: Alfred A. Knopf, 1985). See also Richard A. Pride and J. David Woodard, *The Burden of Busing: The Politics of Desegregation in Nashville, Tennessee* (Knoxville, TN: University of Tennessee Press, 1985); and Daniel J. Monti, *A Semblance of Justice: St. Louis School Desegregation and Order in Urban America*, (Columbia, MS: University of Missouri Press, 1985).
55 Meyer Weinberg, *A Chance to Learn: A History of Race and Education in the United States* (Cambridge: Cambridge University Press, 1977), 140–259; Nicholas Montalto, *A History of the Intercultural Education Movement, 1924–1941* (New York: Garland Pub. Inc., 1982).
56 Sanders, *Education of an Urban Minority*, 230: Fass, *Outside In*, Chap. 6. On Pittsburgh, see John Bodnar, Robert Simon and Michael Weber, *Lives of Their Own: Blacks, Italians, and Poles in Pittsburgh, 1900–1960* (Urbana, IL: University of Illinois Press, 1982), 201; and William J. Reese, 'Soldiers for Christ in the Army of God: the Christian school movement in America', *Educational Theory*, Vol. 35 (Spring 1985), 175–94.
57 James B. Conant, *Slums and Suburbs* (New York: McGraw-Hill, 1961).
58 Larry Cuban, *How Teachers Taught: Constancy and Change in American Classrooms, 1890–1980* (New York: Longman, 1984), 136; and Ravitch, *The Troubled Crusade*, 265.
59 Cohen, *Children of the Mill*, x.
60 William B. Thomas and Kevin J. Moran, 'Social stratification of school knowledge in character training programs of South Buffalo, New York, 1918-1932', *Journal of Education*, Vol. 170 (1988), 77–94; William B. Thomas and Kevin J. Moran, 'Centralization and ethnic coalition formation in Buffalo, New York, 1918–1922', *Journal of Social History*, Vol. 23 (Fall 1989), 137–53; William B. Thomas, 'A quantitative study of differentiated school knowledge transmission in Buffalo, 1918–1931', *Journal of Negro Education*, Vol. 57 (1988), 66–80; S. J. Kleinberg, *The Shadow of the Mills: Working-Class Families in Pittsburgh, 1870–1907* (Pittsburgh, PA: University of Pittsburgh Press, 1989); Bryce Nelson, *Good Schools: The Seattle Public School System, 1901–1930* (Seattle, WA: University of Washington Press, 1988).

3 The 'State' of the history of urban education in Australia

Kerry Wimshurst and Ian Davey

Introduction

At first glance, a survey of the historiography of urban education in Australia appears a relatively easy task. From the outset, we can say that little published research has been concerned with this field. For example, there are no Australian equivalents to *Urban Education in the Nineteenth Century* or *The One Best System*, the former a collection of British local urban history studies and the latter a history of American urban education.[1] To explain why this is the case, we commence with a discussion of research trends in the history of education and urban history over the past two decades. We then consider some emerging research concerns which appear to transcend traditional disciplinary boundaries. As we shall demonstrate throughout, there is indeed much innovative research in social history underway in Australia. We argue, however, that a 'leap-frog' situation has emerged whereby some education and urban historians now are exploring key issues in social history by building upon the earlier concerns and methodologies of overseas work in the 1960s and 1970s.

Aspects of social class and gender formation, modes of social control and resistances and the role of the state in the construction of dominant hegemonies have become central to work here within only a few years. It is noteworthy that such a situation has come about without Australia appearing to experience those intervening renaissances observed in America and Britain two decades ago, when the upsurges of interest and activity called the 'new' urban history and the radical revisionist history of education occurred. Much of this earlier overseas work often was impelled by a sense of impending social crisis. Racial tensions and civil liberties movements, regressive education systems and urban decay, all led towards an historical focus upon the origins and processes of urban schooling. While there has always been an element of social criticism informing and linking some of the best scholarly work in Australia in the broad fields of education and urban studies, widespread concern has gathered momentum rather more slowly. For example, interest in educational policy and urban youth only became fuelled during the early 1980s by crises such as high levels of unemployment among school leavers.

Two further contextual points should be noted concerning the development of the historical profession in Australia. First, courses in Australian history have always been taught in the universities but, with few institutional exceptions, such courses were small in number and were usually to be found nestled among numerous offerings in foreign histories. Indeed, even now the number of seminal studies in Australian history and the number of historians prominent in this field remain surprisingly few. When tertiary institutions underwent their massive expansion in the period spanning the late 1950s through to the late 1970s, overseas academics arrived bringing their historical specialities with them. Their post-graduate students often then went on to complete their own formal studies overseas. Thus, until fairly recently there has been little sense of a thriving community of scholars engaged in Australian social history. This generalisation is particularly true of historians in education where there has been relatively little research into the social history of education until the last few years. One further reason for the hesitant beginning of work in the social history of education relates to a methodological matter, the lack of an extant manuscript census in Australia. The absence of this important resource initially limited the possibility of the types of quantitative research which provided such an impetus to the 'new social history' elsewhere.

Second, the role of the Federal government has also been important in developing research activities, directly through project funding and indirectly by the fostering of a supportive ideological climate. The tendency has been for Labor administrations to encourage socially critical research. Those periods where Labor has been in office have traditionally been the times for an increase in the research activities which, for example, usually accompany major changes in the social policy arena. In the face of domestic economic problems and imbalances in foreign trade arrangements, the current Labor administration has from the late 1980s shifted its focus more to those economic, technological and scientific matters identified as 'national priorities'. While such a shift might normally leave scholars in the humanities wondering where they stand in terms of research funding, a number of factors have kept the historical profession quite buoyant in the age of 'high-tech' priorities. The bicentenary of white settlement in Australia that was celebrated in 1988 encouraged an upsurge in historical studies throughout the decade and the resulting impetus and scholarly productivity (some of it by no means celebratory) will continue well into the 1990s.[2] In addition, while science and technology might be high-priority concerns, 'Australian Studies' has also been identified as a national priority. Federal and state authorities are in the process of evaluating and upgrading offerings in Australian Studies in schools and tertiary institutions and historians are playing a major leadership role in these endeavours.[3]

In this sense, there has been a take-off in the last few years with renewed emphasis in teaching and research upon Australian society. Many of the transplanted 'foreign' specialists have directed their skills to things Australian. A generation of students in the 1980s looked to progressive British and American works in the 'new' urban and education histories for ideas and approaches, and these researchers have applied themselves vigorously to the Australian scene. Nor has this upsurge in activity simply been the result of wholesale borrowing from overseas insights, useful though many of these are. In the following sections we briefly describe and assess some of these new directions. There has been no attempt to incorporate all of the published works in either the history of education or urban history over the past two decades. Instead, we identify some major preoccupations and concerns in both fields and note particularly important changes of direction. The final section addresses some theoretical issues which we believe raise doubts about the conceptual usefulness of any attempt to establish a specifically urban research focus in the history of education in Australia.

History of education

Our chapter title stresses the 'state' for two reasons. First, the unit of analysis for much research in the history of education in Australia has been located within the geographical and administrative boundaries of the six states and two territories which make up the Commonwealth of Australia. Second, a corollary of this has been the tendency in much of the published work to conceptualise either explicitly or implicitly the political state within a liberal framework. The state is seen as a neutral arbiter between a plurality of competing interest groups and as a provider, where necessary, of essential public services by way of its bureaucratic machinery. Certainly, some earlier studies looked at the bitter conflict in the nineteenth century between church and state over who would control the education of the people.[4] However, the conception of mass schooling as an arena of contestation where the terrain has been held mostly by ruling-class interests by way of state control of educational provisions has not featured prominently in writing on the history of schooling in Australia. This is an important historiographical point because the absence of a theoretically informed concept of the role of the state, and particularly the social structuring activities of the state, helps to explain the relative paucity of studies which have explored the social history of mass schooling. In fact, it was only as recently as 1980 that the parameters of the debate about state centralisation of education in colonial Australia began to shift away from geographical and administrative interpretations. This intervention was made by a sociologist engaged in a major critique of the historiography of Australian education who called for closer attention to the role of the state in representing ruling-class interests in movements for educational reform in nineteenth-century Australia.[5]

Despite the increasing involvement of the Federal government since the 1940s in the education of all Australians, the provision of public (mass) schooling has remained in the control of individual state authorities and the regional level of administration has been placed at the state level since the 'compulsory, secular and free' Acts of the late nineteenth century. Hence, we have a number of state systems which may differ on minor points but which do share major characteristics. Overall, the unit of organisation has remained centralised in the state Department with local government influence being weak. As a result, historians in the 1960s and 1970s tended to locate their research efforts within a restricted paradigm of state administrative activities. The outcome has been that the sorts of issues they addressed and the questions they have asked over the years about the role(s) of schooling have coalesced with a century of mainstream Education Department rhetoric in each state.

This mainstream rhetoric conformed to certain themes which, in many respects, resemble the traditional 'Whig' interpretations so vigorously attacked elsewhere by revisionist historians over the past two decades. On the Australian scene, the democratic intentions and outcomes claimed of mass schooling were said to have worked successfully for over a hundred years. Important also for our purposes, equality of opportunity was said to characterise children's experiences of compulsory schooling whether they lived in the bush or the city. Swamped by this nineteenth-century 'equality' rhetoric, the urban context of schooling has remained quite simply an issue of no real concern for historians. The occasional article has looked at urban imperatives in educational and childhood reform movements, but no major study specifically dealing with relationships between schooling and urban processes has yet appeared.[6] Instead, research throughout the 1970s and into the early 1980s tended to focus upon issues such as the evolution of enlightened school bureaucracies (triumphant over the 'inefficient' and largely voluntary provisions of the earlier nineteenth century), the absorption of great (foreign) ideas into Australian education and the trials and tribulations of prominent (male) administrators.[7] The ideological impulse for such scholarly work simply reinforced the mythologies of the founders of compulsory schooling without subjecting mainstream folklore to critical scrutiny.

It is puzzling that a significant body of revisionist research in the history of education and critical Marxist and feminist studies did not emerge earlier than the 1980s in Australia. The earlier works of Katz, Lazerson, Spring and Karier were featured in university courses from the mid-1970s. The work of the Birmingham Centre for Contemporary Cultural Studies on resistances and popular culture was widely known and generated considerable sociological inquiry. The work of radical curriculum theorists like Michael Apple and Jean Anyon had been well received and one might have hoped for additional impetus in the historical domain. Perhaps a major reason for the paucity of a readily identifiable and theoretically informed body of critical history is related to the fact that the great majority of higher degree candidates in Education Faculties are usually part-time students engaged in teaching/administrative duties in state departments. These characteristics led to a tendency for research to follow familiar paths along known trails to anticipated destinations.

While we have suggested that the historiography of Australian education reveals a tapestry of disparate works over the past two decades, there are now signs of a critical resurgence in which research activities are beginning to converge upon common issues. It should also be noted that despite the pot-pourri nature of the field, some earlier concerns have established a strong and continuing scholarship. For example, histories dealing with the lives and experiences of teachers and teacher unionism are examples that appear regularly.[8] To take another example, Selleck and Sullivan's *Not So Eminent Victorians*, which traces the lives of several nineteenth-century teachers, illustrates the way biographical studies continue to enrich the history of education.[9] However, the major recent change of direction has followed the lead of social historians in that much more emphasis has been placed upon the lives of the recipients of mass education.

It is over a decade since Cook, Davey and Vick began to map out ways in which Australian historians might examine class conflict in the development of mass schooling in nineteenth-century capitalist societies.[10] A related development has been the work of feminist historians of education who have explored gender issues and, in particular, the relationship between the domestic ideology and educational reform in the late nineteenth and early twentieth centuries. Both of these theoretical perspectives inform Miller's *Long Division: State Schooling in South Australian Society*, a major Marxist–feminist account of the rise of public schooling in one Australian state.[11] This study is an important one because it examines the relationship between mass schooling and transformations in class relations in a state which remained an agricultural and pre-industrial capitalist society until well into the twentieth century. In addition, Miller's analysis explores the impact of the sexual division of labour and patriarchal relations on the development of the institutional forms of schooling, the content of the curriculum and the implications of gender inequities in the experience of schooling for South Australia's social development.

Because the construction of gender relationships in capitalist Australia and the often contradictory dynamics between capitalism, patriarchy and the role of the state are issues which transcend the urban–rural dichotomy, we shall return to these in following sections. Miller and Davey have outlined the types of questions that historians might pursue in the 1990s when they note that changing capitalist formations in the eighteenth and nineteenth centuries not only resulted in prolonged crises in class relations but also led to ruptures in age and gender relationships.[12] The state – and schools in particular – helped to break down and reshape traditional class, gender and age relations both within and outside of families over time. Although their work on patriarchy and the building of the educational state in Australia remains speculative, Theobald's recent writings on nineteenth-century female pupils and teachers in the fledgling state systems are examples of the necessary theoretical and empirical groundwork that has already been done.[13]

While some of the most interesting work has arisen from the history of women's education,[14] there has been a parallel focus upon aspects of the history of family life, childhood and youth. Recent studies have explored historical definitions of deviancy and the efforts that powerful groups have exerted in order to enforce their own constructions of social reality.[15] Most of the researchers mentioned might be labelled educational historians, yet obviously their work has moved to incorporate much wider concerns of social history with emphases upon family and work, childhood and the state and aspects of gender construction and reproduction through schooling and family life. There has been little explicit attention given to the urban aspects of these matters, although there has tended to be some implicit focus upon city and town life.[16] Yet as we demonstrate in a later chapter of this volume, and also show in our following comments on urban historical studies, many of the current concerns clearly transcend both the urban–rural dichotomy and the traditional disciplinary boundaries. In their overt interest in social theory and the work of other social historians and sociologists, these educational historians share the concerns of other groups of researchers and have also begun to explore the implications of Foucault's work and post-structuralist perspectives for the study of schooling. In fact, as elsewhere, perhaps the most significant aspect of recent research in the history of education is the tendency of its practitioners to define themselves as social historians rather than educational historians and to participate in the wider forums of the historical profession.

Urban history

The observation has often been made that for a country so heavily urbanised from the very beginnings of white settlement, the study of our urban history arrived very late. Bate's *Lucky City: The First Generation at Ballarat, 1851–1901* and Davison's *The Rise and Fall of Marvellous Melbourne* are prime examples of urban biographies to emerge in the late 1970s.[17] Biography is used here in the sense that such works examine various dimensions of processes that are said to be identifiably urban in nature. Both of these volumes were written in the Melbourne tradition of historical research, a tradition associated with elegantly crafted writing. Unlike their overseas counterparts of the quantitative 'new' urban history, Australian historians have had little recourse to an earlier generation of commentators who had been proclaiming for many years the importance of researching city life and culture (like Handlin and Schlesinger Snr in the United States). Our urban historians of the 1970s were venturing into unmapped terrain dominated by a popular cultural paradigm which for generations (indeed, since the late 1890s) had sought to locate the true essence of Australianism within an ethos of 'bush' pioneers and 'outback' rural workers.[18]

In the last decade or so, urban history in Australia has continued to thrive and one can point to a more unified body of work in this field than is the case for educational history.[19] The biographical tradition remains strong, encouraged by the resurgent popularity of local history studies. However, during the 1980s there was a tendency to move away from urban biography and, in fact, to move away from the specifically urban vision as a frame of reference. Now, urban and regional histories concentrate more upon issues similar to those already noted as emerging concerns of the educational historians. For example, Kelly's 1978 collection of studies on nineteenth-century Sydney emphasised obvious urban themes with essays on suburban development, transport, slum conditions and provision of amenities.[20] But, two years later, the companion volume on the early twentieth century edited by Roe was subtitled *Studies in Urban and Social History*.[21] This work paid more attention to the social fabric of metropolitan Australia – gender and social class issues, popular culture, grass-roots resistances to oppression, work environments and 'wayward' youth. Davison, already mentioned as one of the founders of urban history here, in his study of city-bred children weaves together the complex historical threads of health and welfare provisions, infant and vocational education, architecture and town planning, eugenics and social control, and this work has been carried forward into a study of Melbourne's 'outcasts'.[22]

We strongly doubt whether this reorientation is simply confirmation of the 'confusion of definition' that Dyos suggested was an occupational hazard for urban historians when he wrote in 1977 that 'there is some sense of confusion and, in particular, some misconception as to what urban history is or might become or had better do'.[23] Rather, this shift in emphasis illustrates our claim throughout that a demolition of disciplinary boundaries in social history in Australia has been set in train. Researchers schooled in different specialities are converging upon common problems, often with common ideological intentions, and producing collaborative works. A good example of collaborative efforts is *What Rough Beast?* from the Sydney Labour History Group. Many of the studies in this collection would neatly fit the requirements and concerns of journals addressing different specialist interests. The research ranges over topics as diverse as immigrant Irish servants, desertion and non-support legislation, and secret armies in Melbourne. The overarching aim of the book is to deal with the nature and function of the Australian state over the period roughly 1840–1940. Although the historical specificity of the relationship between state intervention and the social order remains rather vague in some of the articles, those especially that deal with issues of sexuality, gender relationships and the state again reveal the often contradictory tensions between the demands of patriarchal and capitalist interests in the sphere of state action.[24]

Once again, it seems that some of the most innovative recent work in urban and regional history has arisen from a perspective that addressed gender issues. Two studies, both centred on the state of Victoria, illustrate the point. Reiger's urban-oriented *The Disenchantment of the Home* explores fundamental contradictions in the ideology of the family which arose from the technocratic rationalisation of domestic life in the early twentieth century.[25] By the 1920s, in order to perform their 'natural' functions as wives and mothers, women were being exhorted on all sides to heed the advice of experts: domestic scientists, infant welfare and nursing experts, gynaecologists and obstetricians. The study explores the ways in which the ambiguities, tensions and contradictions of this 'legitimation crisis' impinged upon families throughout the first half of the twentieth century. Yet while much is learnt from this impressive study about what was expected of women (what was being both said and done to them by the experts), little is said about any changing definitions of masculinity over the period. However, there are hints in places that a parallel redefinition of the concept of manhood and maleness in family life was also occurring.

Such complex dynamics in relations between men and women in families are addressed in Lake's study of the hopes and disappointments of soldier settler families in rural Victoria after the First World War.[26] In *The Limits of Hope*, Lake details the exploitation of rural women through their unpaid and often unacknowledged heavy labour on small 'family farms'. Ironically, with the almost hegemonic emergence of concepts of domestic femininity in the late nineteenth century, the ongoing manual labour of women gave rise to male guilt, both public and private, which thus created additional emotional tensions within families. In this study, the household is seen as an arena of struggle in which each family member is shaped by internal and external economic processes, where individuals within and outside of the family struggle to advance their own interests. Taken together, both Reiger and Lake reveal ways in which the best features of the urban and regional biograpahical tradition have moved to incorporate issues and questions central to a better understanding of Australian social history, in this case, the changing expectations of and relations within families over time.

Conclusion: beyond the rural–urban dichotomy

In this essay we have argued that there is a considerable lack of studies devoted specifically to the urban history of Australian education. Further, we suggest that this might not be as detrimental to the state of the profession as one might initially suspect. We believe this to be the case because recent empirical and theoretical work in social history in Australia and elsewhere casts doubt on the utility of the rural–urban dichotomy as an appropriate organising principle for the study of the relationship between schooling and social structure. Conceptually, the apparent correlation of educational reform and urbanisation and industrialisation early on led overseas historians to focus more carefully on the politics of the rise of the public school systems in the cities. Methodologically, the enthusiasm for quantitative analysis saw the proliferation of single city and suburban studies in which the data-bank could be kept to a manageable size. However, while this research was exceptionally important during the 1970s in redefining the field and exploring a range of new questions about the impact of schooling on the lives of children and their families, by the early 1980s doubts were beginning to be expressed about the validity and usefulness of conclusions. Scholars began to question both the generalisability of conclusions based on single cities and the adequacy of theories of urbanisation and industrialisation as explanations for the rise of mass schooling.

Some of these criticisms were encapsulated in Vinovskis' review of quantitative approaches in the United States. As he points out, the focus on single urban communities resulted in a failure to distinguish between different types of urban and industrial developments which made it impossible to separate analytically the effects of urban development from more general changes in society.[27] This is precisely what the major study by Kaestle and Vinovskis of nineteenth-century Massachusetts attempts to rectify, and their findings cast doubt on earlier formulations of the relationship between industrialisation and educational reform.[28] Importantly, though, even with the vast expansion of the empirical base to take account of different developments within Massachusetts over that time, the rural–urban distinction remains central to the conceptualisation of the problem.

This is because the authors are primarily concerned with addressing the critical question of the relationship between public schooling and industrialisation, a question which had been brought into sharper relief by Marxist critiques of the initial revisionist projects.

From the late 1970s, in economistic and cultural analyses on both sides of the Atlantic, Marxist scholars mounted an assault on theories based on urbanisation and industrialisation, stressing the relationship between the transition to industrial capitalism and the rise of mass schooling.[29] This stimulated a far more theoretically informed discussion of schooling and social change but the focus overseas has remained decidedly urban. Despite Katz's important observation in his 1976 commentary that capitalism as a system of wage labour preceded urban industrialisation, both Marxists and their critics have tended to equate capitalism with industrial capitalism, preserving the pre-industrial–industrial and the rural–urban dichotomies.[30] This equation has muddied the debate, as outside of England the establishment of mass public school systems has tended to pre-date the rise of large-scale factory production. In consequence, we still know little about the rise of capitalism and its link to schooling because there has been little intensive investigation of the social and institutional forms associated with the growth of commercial capitalism, the transition from handicraft to other types of manufacturing prior to industrialisation and, significantly, capitalist penetration of agriculture.[31] We believe that our understanding of the rise of mass schooling in both rural and urban areas would be deepened if historians of education moved toward a much more comprehensive theory of capitalist development, the role(s) of the state in these developments and the implications for the ordering of social relationships, a theory which, if correctly conceptualised, transcends the rural–urban dichotomy.

Similarly, as we have indicated in earlier sections of this survey, much recent theory regarding the primacy of patriarchal relations and the sexual division of labour has important implications for the writing of the history of education which subsumes urban–rural differences. While there has been an upsurge of feminist research in recent years which has focused on such issues as the 'feminisation' of teaching, equality of access and the sexual division of labour in the bureaucracy, most historians working in the field have been slow to adopt an analysis which fully incorporates a patriarchal ordering of social relations into the argument. Partly, this omission derives from the preoccupations with the debate over schooling and capitalism and the role of social class. Partly, it stems from a tendency towards functional analyses of the family, school and work complex in which little consideration is given to the internal relations in the family. Partly, it reflects the fact that much feminist research has been Marxist–feminist in its orientation and has either concentrated on those aspects of patriarchal relations which are functional for capitalism or subordinated gender to class. Partly, it stems from the fact that most professional historians of education are men. It seems to us that the rapid development of feminist theory and historical writing, including the increasing questioning of the compatibility of Marxism and feminism, deserves the most serious attention of all historians of education.[32] If we accord the power relations between the sexes the centrality the theory demands then the analyses of rural–urban, bourgeois–working class and black–white relations need to be dramatically reconstructed.

We conclude with the claim that the work of reconstruction in these areas in Australia in recent years is equally applicable in other societies. It received particular help during the 1980s with the publication of a highly influential book from a group of historically trained sociologists, *Making the Difference*. This book about class, gender and schooling in Australia is based on a complex understanding of the processes of class and gender formation. The authors state that

Both class and gender are, in their different ways, structures of power. They involve control by some people over others, and the ability of some groups to organize social life to their own advantage. As power is exercised and contested, social relations are organized, and come to be in some degree a system. So an important corollary about class and gender is that they are systematic rather than random. But ... this does not mean being systematic in a mechanical sense, like an air-conditioning system. Both class and gender are *historical* systems, riddled with tension and contradiction, and always subject to change. Indeed it may be better to think of them as *structuring processes* rather than 'systems', that is, ways in which social life is constantly being organized (and ruptured and disorganized) through time.[33]

We believe that this conceptualisation of class and gender, and race and ethnicity,[34] as structuring processes is exceptionally important and, as they are being taken up here by historians of education, will enable us to move beyond the rather crude categories of analysis that have usually been adopted. It requires us to become far more theoretically sophisticated in our approach and to pursue close-grained empirical analyses of the relationships between these structuring processes and social institutions like the family and the school.[35] It also means that we abandon the rural–urban distinction as an overarching organising principle. The interactions of these structuring processes can be observed at work in the shaping of social relations in both rural and urban sites. While these sites may provide the context, they cannot guarantee the explanation.

NOTES

1 D. A. Reeder (ed.), *Urban Education in the Nineteenth Century* (London: Taylor and Francis, 1977); David B. Tyack, *The One Best System: A History of American Urban Education* (Cambridge, MA: Harvard University Press, 1974).
2 See, for example, the special issue of *Australian Historical Studies*, Vol. 23 (1988), 'Making the bicentenary'; and Verity Burgmann and Jenny Lee (eds.), *A People's History of Australia since 1788*, 4 vols. (Melbourne: McPhee Gribble/ Penguin, 1989). The major historical contribution is the ten-volume series *Australians: A Historical Library* under the general editorship of A. D. Gilbert, K. S. Inglis, F. Crowley and P. Spearritt (Broadway, NSW: Fairfax, Syme and Weldon, 1987–8).
3 For example, James Walter (ed.), *Australian Studies: A Survey* (Melbourne: Oxford University Press, 1989).
4 For example, A. G. Austin, *Australian Education 1788–1900: Church, State and Public Education in Colonial Australia* (Melbourne: Pitman, 1961).
5 Helen Bannister, 'The centralization problematic', *Australian Journal of Education*, Vol. 24 (1980), 246–64.
6 For Australian studies with an urban focus, see Richard Teese, 'Gender and class in the transformation of the public high school in Melbourne, 1946–85', *History of Education Quarterly*, Vol. 29 (1989), 237–59; Kerry Wimshurst, 'Child-saving and urban school reform in South Australia at the turn of the century', *Melbourne Studies in Education* (1983), 203–21; and Robert Van Krieken, 'Towards "good and useful men and women": the state and childhood in Sydney, 1840–1890', *Australian Historical Studies*, Vol. 23 (1989), 405–25.
7 An example of this long tradition is C. Turney (ed.) *Pioneers in Australian Education*, Vols. I–III (Sydney: Sydney University Press, 1969, 1972, 1982). An early historical survey that did question the equality rhetoric was B. K. Hyams and B. Bessant, *Schools for the People?* (Melbourne: Longman, 1972).
8 To take one example, Andrew Spaull has been prolific in the history of teacher unionism and industrial matters, see for example, B. Bessant and A. Spaull, *Teachers in Conflict* (Melbourne: Melbourne University Press, 1972); A. Spaull (ed.), *Australian Teachers: From Colonial School-Masters to Militant Professionals* (Melbourne: Macmillan, 1977); A. Spaull, 'The state and the formation and growth of Australian teachers' unions, 1915–1925', *History of Education Review*, Vol. 15 (1986), 34–48; A. Spaull, 'The establishment of a national teachers' union in Australia, 1921–1937', *History of Education Review*, Vol. 18 (1989), 26–42.
9 R. J. W. Selleck and M. Sullivan (eds.), *Not So Eminent Victorians* (Melbourne: Melbourne University Press, 1984).
10 Pavla Cook, Ian Davey and Malcolm Vick, 'Capitalism and working class schooling in late nineteenth century South Australia', *Australian and New Zealand History of Education Society Journal*, Vol. 8 (1979), 36–48.
11 Pavla Miller, *Long Division: State Schooling in South Australian Society* (Adelaide: Wakefield Press, 1986). Miller's book is a major contribution from the 'Adelaide School' of educational historians who collaborated on a number of projects in the 1980s working largely within Marxist and Marxist–feminist paradigms.
12 Pavla Miller and Ian Davey, 'Family formation, schooling and the patriarchal state', in R. J. W. Selleck and M. Theobald (eds.), *The Family, School and State in Australian History* (Sydney: Allen and Unwin, 1990), 1–24.

13 See, for example, Marjorie Theobald, 'Discourse of danger: gender and the history of elementary schooling in Australia, 1850–1880', *Historical Studies in Education*, Vol. 1 (1989), 29–52.
14 Much work has appeared during the 1980s on the history of women's education. See, for example, Paige Porter, 'The state, the family, and education: ideology, reproduction and resistance in Western Australia, 1900–1929', *Australian Journal of Education*, Vol. 27 (1983), 121–36; Alison Mackinnon, *One Foot on the Ladder: Origins and Outcomes of Girl's Secondary Schooling in South Australia* (Brisbane: University of Queensland Press, 1984); Noeline Kyle, *Her Natural Destiny: The Education of Women in New South Wales* (Kensington: New South Wales University Press, 1986); and Helen Jones, *Nothing Seemed Impossible: Women's Education and Social Change in South Australia, 1875–1915* (Brisbane: University of Queensland Press, 1985). Also, the special issue on women's education, *History of Education Review*, Vol. 13 (1984).
15 For a survey of the historiography of childhood and youth, see P. Hetherington, 'Childhood and youth in Australia', *Journal of Australian Studies*, No. 18 (1986), 3–18; and the special issue on childhood, *History of Education Review*, Vol. 15 (1986). For changing definitions of youth, including gender-bound conceptions of deviant youth, see Lesley Johnson, 'The teenage girl: the social definition of growing up for young Australian women, 1950–1965', *History of Education Review*, Vol. 18 (1989), 1–12; and Kerry Wimshurst, 'Control and resistance: reformatory school girls in late nineteenth century South Australia', *Journal of Social History*, Vol. 18 (1984), 273–87.
16 See, for example, Ian Davey, 'Growing up in a working-class community: school and work in Hindmarsh', in P. Grimshaw, C. McConville and E. McEwen (eds.), *Families in Colonial Australia* (Sydney: George Allen and Unwin, 1985), 163–71; and Kerry Wimshurst, 'Child labour and school attendance in South Australia, 1890–1915', *Historical Studies*, Vol. 19 (1981), 388–411. In addition, see n. 6.
17 Weston Bate, *Lucky City: The First Generation at Ballarat, 1851–1901* (Melbourne: Melbourne University Press, 1978); Graeme Davison, *The Rise and Fall of Marvellous Melbourne* (Melbourne: Melbourne University Press, 1978).
18 A good short account of early urbanisation is Sean Glynn, *Urbanisation in Australian History, 1788–1900* (Sydney: Nelson, 1970). For historiographical developments to 1980, see Max Neutze, 'Australian cities (1938–1988)', *Australia 1939–1988: A Bicentenial History Bulletin*, (1981), 19–26. For the relationship between the city and the bush, see Graeme Davison, 'Sydney and the bush: an urban context for the Australian legend', *Historical Studies*, Vol. 18 (1978), 191–209.
19 Examples of major urban histories include C. T. Stannage, *The People of Perth: A Social History of Western Australia's Capital City* (Perth: Perth City Council, 1979); Janet McCalman, *Struggletown: Public and Private Life in Richmond* (Melbourne: Melbourne University Press, 1984); and Shirley Fitzgerald, *Rising Damp, Sydney 1870–90* (Melbourne: Oxford University Press, 1987).
20 Max Kelly (ed.), *Nineteenth Century Sydney: Essays in Urban History* (Sydney: Sydney University Press, 1978).
21 Jill Roe (ed.), *Twentieth Century Sydney: Studies in Urban and Social History* (Sydney: Hale and Iremonger, 1980).
22 Graeme Davison, 'The city-bred child and urban reform in Melbourne, 1900–1940', in P. Williams (ed.), *Social Process and the City* (Sydney: George Allen and Unwin, 1983), 143–74; and G. Davison, D. Dunstan and C. McConville (eds.),

The Outcasts of Melbourne: Essays in Social History (Sydney: Allen and Unwin, 1985).

23 H. J. Dyos (ed.), *Urban History Yearbook* (Leicester: Leicester Univesity Press, 1977), 3.

24 See, for example, Judith Allen, 'Octavius Beale re-considered: infanticide, baby-farming and abortion in NSW, 1880–1939', 111–29; and Mark Finnane, 'Sexuality and social order: the state versus Chidley', 192–219, in Sydney Labor History Group (ed.), *What Rough Beast? The State and Social Order in Australian History* (Sydney: George Allen and Unwin, 1982).

25 Kerreen Reiger, *The Disenchantment of the Home: Modernizing the Australian Family 1880–1940* (Melbourne: Oxford Univesity Press, 1985).

26 Marilyn Lake, *The Limits of Hope: Soldier Settlement in Victoria, 1915–38* (Melbourne: Oxford University Press, 1987). See also M. Lake, 'The politics of respectability: identifying the masculinist context', *Historical Studies*, Vol. 22 (1986), 116–31.

27 Maris Vinovskis, 'Quantification and the analysis of American ante-bellum education', *Journal of Interdisciplinary History*, Vol. 13 (1983), 761–86.

28 Carl F. Kaestle and Maris A. Vinovskis, *Education and Social Change in Nineteenth-Century Massachusetts* (Cambridge: Cambridge University Press, 1980).

29 Pertinent examples are Samuel Bowles and Herbert Gintis, *Schooling in Capitalist America: Educational Reform and the Contradictions of Economic Life* (New York: Basic Books, 1976); and Richard Johnson, 'Notes on the schooling of the English working class, 1780–1850', in R. Dale *et al.* (eds.), *Schooling and Capitalism: A Sociological Reader* (London: Routledge and Kegan Paul and the Open University Press, 1976), 44–54.

30 Michael Katz, 'The origins of public education: a reassessment', *History of Education Quarterly*, Vol. 16 (1976), 381–407.

31 For a comparative review of some recent work on the development of mass schooling in pre-industrial societies, see Ian Davey, 'Rethinking the origins of British colonial school systems', *Historical Studies in Education*, Vol. 1, (1989), 149–59.

32 In the Australian context see, for example, Judith Allen, 'Marxism and the man question', 91–111, and Mia Campioni and Elizabeth Gross, 'Love's Labours lost', 113–41 in Judith Allen and Paul Patton (eds.), *Beyond Marxism? Interventions After Marx* (Sydney: Intervention Publications, 1983).

33 R. W. Connell, D. J. Ashenden, S. Kessler and G. W. Dowsett, *Making the Difference: Schools, Families and Social Division* (Sydney: George Allen and Unwin, 1982), 180 (original emphasis).

34 Race and ethnicity have not been areas of major research activity in the history of Australian education. The *History of Education Review*, for example, in the ten years 1979–89 carried one article on aboriginal education, although the wider history of black–white race relations does have a fairly extensive scholarship. Accounts of the historical experiences of some ethnic groups have appeared, see, for example, C. McConville, *Croppies, Celts and Catholics: The Irish in Australia* (Caulfield, Victoria: Edward Arnold, 1987).

35 For an American example, using this approach in class analyses, see David Hogan, *Class and Reform: School and Society in Chicago, 1880–1930* (Philadelphia, PA; University of Pennsylvania Press, 1985).

4 Out of the shadows: retrieving the history of urban education and urban childhood in Canada

Neil Sutherland and Jean Barman

The lives of urban children in Canada have differed greatly across time and space.[1] François-Xavier Garneau was born on 15 June 1809 in the city of Quebec, the oldest of four children of François-Xavier Garneau and Gertrude Amiot-Villeneuve.[2] His father, with neither wealth nor profession, met the needs of his growing family by being in turn a saddler, a carter, the captain of a merchant schooner and finally an innkeeper. Young Garneau, whose lively mind apparently attracted attention quite early, was put in the local school, run by an aged teacher known as 'the Good Parent'. Tradition has it that he was a serious and brilliant pupil.

By the time Garneau was twelve, he had absorbed all the knowledge that his teacher could offer and entered another school which had opened in the basement of a nearby chapel. Garneau spent two years there in what was called in French a 'mutual' school. Teaching was conducted according to the Lancasterian method, the most advanced pupils being used as instructors. When he left that school, Garneau wanted to enter the local seminary, the only institution where boys could get a secondary education. However, his parents lacked the necessary means, and the seminary was reluctant to assist young people who felt no attraction to holy orders.

Garneau therefore had to abandon his hope of studying the humanities, and instead took a job in the office of the clerk of court of the King's Bench, Joseph-François Perrault, who was also an educator of note. Garneau stayed there for two years, during which time Perrault gave him lessons in English, Latin and history. In 1825, Garneau chose the profession of notary, and began indentures for his legal training. Garneau devoted himself to his work but also used his leisure time to delve into his master's library which contained a good collection of English, Latin and French classical works. He continued to teach himself Latin, which he had begun to study under Perrault, and eventually was able to read Horace by sight. Garneau also learned Italian on his own and improved his English by reading Byron, Milton and Shakespeare.

Garneau's contemporary, Joseph Montferrand, had a very different childhood.[3] The son of a voyageur, young Montferrand was born on 25

October 1802 in Montreal's *faubourg* Saint-Laurent. In this working-class district with 'some ten boxing halls and many taverns', people made a fetish of physical skill and strength. Joseph's younger sister Helene is reputed to have taught him the shorter catechism, which seems to have been the beginning and end of his bookish education. Early in life, he picked up the art of foot fighting and boxing. At age sixteen, Montferrand was fully grown at six feet four inches and had a reputation as a *boule* (from the English 'bully'). By trade a carter, his thrashing of three hooligans who were terrorising the area made him the cock of the walk in the *faubourg* Saint-Laurent. At about the same time, Montferrand challenged an English boxer who had declared himself champion and knocked him out with one punch. People began to say that Jos Montferrand, as he was known, 'struck like the kick of a horse,' and that he 'used his leg like a whip'. These events initiated a career that included periods of time spent as a voyageur and a logger, and increased his fame as a strong man.

A half-century later, in the autumn of 1897, Mackenzie King, a graduate student interested in social problems, investigated the 'sweating system' in Toronto.[4] In King's brief account of a visit to a one-room home workshop we get a rare and all-too-limited glimpse into the childhood of some of the respectable poor. King found a sick woman 'who could hardly speak with a consumptive cough' and her three daughters. For the past eight years, the 'thin and sickly' sixteen-year-old had worked out at a wholesale house but now assisted her mother with the sewing that she did on a piece-work basis for a contractor. Her nine-year-old sister also helped with the family economy, working in the same room on her own sewing machine. The third daughter sometimes worked out making buttonholes in a nearby shop. The mother told King she regretted that, despite her being a skilled worker in the garment trades, she had been unable to save enough so that any of the girls could attend school.

Two decades later, in 1915 Sing Lim was born in Vancouver's Chinatown.[5] He had four older brothers and one older sister. His father, Low Lim, worked as a cobbler and his mother, Chow Shee, took in sewing from local tailor shops. The family lived on the fifth floor of a large building in an apartment consisting of a small parlour, two bedrooms, a kitchen and a washroom. They used 'every inch of space, even the fire escapes outside' to hang fish and greens to dry. Sing Lim first attended Central School and, later, also Chinese school in the evenings. He helped supplement the family fuel supply by collecting spilled coal along the railroad tracks and discarded packing crates in back alleys. When Sing Lim was nine years old, he began to spend his summers working full time on the farm of a friend of his father. Yet he continued in school and even managed to go on from Central School to the Vancouver Technical School and then to the Vancouver School of Art.

Implicit in these four stories are the central characteristics of the education of children in urban Canada until quite recently. They learned, in good part by doing, the skills and practices that would form the basis of their life's work. They also acquired enough of their cultural heritage, a set of beliefs, a code of acceptable conduct and, perhaps, the ability to read and write, to enable them to function within their society. Usually, urban parents both controlled and organised the education of their youngsters, and much of it took place within the family. From the time of the earliest European settlers in New France the family took priority over nearly all other dimensions of life. During the nineteenth century, the social and vocational requirements of an increasingly complex society meant that children had to spend more time at their formal education. The state, by expanding its institutional support, mostly although not entirely in the form of schools, assumed greater responsibility both for the transmission of culture and for the acquisition of occupational skills. Yet the family retained its role as educational strategist, by making, or failing to make, the necessary choices enabling their youngsters to find the occupation most agreeable to them. This essay lays out the principal sources telling the story of children's lives in urban Canada over the past 400 years.[6]

I

Canadians have tended in ever greater proportions to live in towns and cities. As elsewhere across the industrialising world, Canadian rates of urbanisation began to grow rapidly during the second half of the nineteenth century. The first census after Confederation, that of 1871, showed that one fifth of the population lived in incorporated centres with 1,000 or more people. By 1911, over 40 per cent of Canadians lived in such places, half of them in towns or cities of 20,000 or more people. Half a century later, one out of every two Canadians lived in cities, almost 70 per cent of them in urban centres of 1,000 or more. As the Canadian census monograph on the topic noted, 'by 1961 Canada was firmly among the top one fifth of the world's most highly urbanized countries'.[7] Only in the last years has urbanisation begun to moderate: between 1971 and 1981 the proportion of Canadians living in urban areas of 1,000 or more remained constant at just over three-quarters.

Despite high rates of urbanisation, Canadian scholars long focused their attention not on their country's urban character but rather on the role of geography in shaping the past. Thirty years after his visit to the Toronto tenement, Prime Minister Mackenzie King told the House of Commons that 'If some countries have too much history, we [Canadians] have too much geography.' In 1930, the economic historian Harold Innis put forward what came to be called the 'Laurentian thesis', the notion that Canada had an intrinsic geographical coherence: the nation had been constructed not in defiance of North American geography but because of it.[8] A system of east-west waterways that extended from the St Lawrence estuary, via the Great Lakes, Canadian Shield, the prairies and through the mountains to the Pacific Ocean led to the creation of staple-based national economies.

While studies of the staples trade by Innis and others encompassed urban relationships, it was only in 1954 that J. M. S. Careless began work that emphasised the central role played by cities in the creation of a single national entity. In its focus on the influence of urban areas over their hinterlands, Careless' 'metropolitan thesis' was the obverse of explanations based on frontier expansionism. The city in an 'almost feudal chain of vassalage' supplied capital, markets, marketing facilities, communication, transportation and culture to the frontier. Canada's very small number of dominant cities were, in turn, vassals of such external metropolitan centres as London, New York and San Francisco. As explained by Careless: 'Winnipeg is Montreal's subsidiary but it is the metropolis of a large area of prairie West. The Toronto metropolis is a subsidiary of both New York and Montreal, while Canada's main metropolitan centre, Montreal, has traditionally been bound to London.'[9] The metropolitan thesis, while eventually challenged and then superseded by such concepts as regionalism, turned the attention of Canadian historians to systematic study of their urban heritage.

Historians of education were at first little affected by the metropolitan thesis, continuing through the 1960s to describe the past in mainly descriptive and celebratory terms. Although written outside the mainstream of Canadian history, the work of C. E. Phillips, F. Henry Johnson, F. W. Rowe, K. C. N. MacNaughton and John W. Chalmers did implicitly reveal the central role played by cities in the development of schooling.[10] Their writings made clear that, from the mid-nineteenth century onward, English Canadians in urban centres worked to create systems of education not only for themselves but also for those in their hinterlands. Like the reformers these historians described, they themselves took the urban school system, with its separate, age-graded classrooms and its administrative hierarchy, to be the norm. Again following the practice of their subjects, they described and evaluated rural schooling against urban models.

In the 1970s, several historians of education examined certain chains of metropolitan influence at work in both education and child care. F. Henry Johnson argued that the centralising educational tendencies of Ontario's first Superintendent of Education, Egerton Ryerson, were carried west to British Columbia.[11] Robert Stamp revealed the influence of the urban Ontario model of the late nineteenth century on urban Alberta.[12] Neil

Sutherland explained the central role that Canadian cities, and especially Toronto, played in devising and introducing new notions designed to improve the health, education and welfare of Canadian children.[13] He argued that urban dwellers perceived problems in their own environments and devised, or copied from other cities, programmes that were supposed to deal with these conditions. Since, constitutionally, Canadian provincial governments are paramount in the fields of health, education and social welfare, urban reformers naturally pressed their provincial governments to assume responsibility for implementing universally their new programmes for children. Thus new ideas entered each region through its cities and towns. By the time they moved into the countryside, they had taken on a distinctly urban form which may not have been altogether appropriate to a rural environment.

Canadian historical scholarship underwent a series of major changes during the 1960s and early 1970s. New notions in the social sciences emanating from Britain, France and especially the United States began to exert their influence. Many fledgling Canadian academics took their graduate training in other countries. Higher education began to expand in Canada itself during the 1960s, attracting American and other foreign scholars to its universities.

It was within this context, fortified by the continuing appeal of the metropolitan thesis, that historians of Canada joined in a growing worldwide interest in urban history.[14] Much of their focus turned on 'the city as a physical entity', or 'as an artifact'.[15] Thus, a major research and publishing project centred on the production of 'urban biographies' of the principal Canadian cities, emphasising such common themes as the physical landscape, population growth, the economy, civic politics and, only secondarily, social infrastructure.[16]

Most institutional histories of urban education in Canada, some earlier in time in their inception, can be roughly placed into his 'biographical' framework. Studies, for the most part methodologically unsophisticated and often commemorative, chronicled schools in Ottawa, Toronto, Guelph, Calgary, Vancouver and elsewhere.[17] In addition, many local histories, whether of major cities or of small communities, have included a section on schooling variously based on oral recollections, local records and the official reports of provincial Departments of Education. Several Canadian provinces have publicly supported Catholic school systems, and these too have been profiled for major cities.[18] Some studies of individual schools, both public and private, appeared.[19] Under the auspices of Parks Canada, Dana Johnson compiled illustrated histories of school architecture which document the growth of a distinctive urban style.[20] Numerous graduate theses, most often at the master's level, detailed developments in a wide variety of Canadian cities.[21]

II

In another manifestation of the transformation of historical studies in Canada in the 1960s and early 1970s, historians turned to the systematic study of many aspects of social history, including the social history of education, which very rapidly became one of the most extensively investigated aspects of the Canadian past. Indeed, historians of education played an important role in shifting the historical mainstream in Canada away from studies of economic, political and constitutional themes toward analysis of the social dimensions of the past.

Easily the most controversial dimension of the new social history of Canadian education was the investigation of the relationships between urbanisation and the development of structures of schooling in the nineteenth century, especially in Ontario. In the late 1960s, the Harvard-trained academic Michael Katz came to the Ontario Institute for Studies in Education, the University of Toronto's graduate school of education. Katz soon thereafter began the Canadian Social History Project. Much of the project's work was undertaken within an intellectual context derived from sociology, including the concept of 'social control'. Historians who employed the social control hypothesis in their study of Canadian education – sometimes described as radical revisionists – found a fourfold explanation for the creation, in nineteenth-century Ontario, of educational and other social structures. In their view, these changes were a direct consequence of the growth of cities, the development of industries, a perceived need to provide institutional means to counter the danger of social disruption and the emergence of new forms of the family out of a social and economic environment in a state of flux.

Two of Katz's students, Susan Houston and Alison Prentice, put forward most forcefully the radical revisionist argument. In an article published in 1972 in the country's major historical journal, the *Canadian Historical Review,* Houston asserted that, 'while by 1851, roughly 15 percent of the [Ontario] population lived in incorporated places, the model of society provided by larger commercial centres such as Toronto and Kingston clearly exercised a commanding influence'.[22] 'This "urban outlook" provided sufficient ground for a consensus favouring common school promotion to secure bipartisan support for school legislation.' This legislation, in turn, bore 'witness to the pervasive influence of attitudes susceptible to the promises of an educational solution to social problems'. The bulk of this seminal essay then centred on the process through which such legislation was achieved.

In *The School Promoters,* published five years later, Prentice took up Houston's concept of an urban consensus.[23] Between about 1820 and 1850, large-scale immigration led to enormous growth in Ontario. The concentration of working-class families in urban areas, most notably Toronto, generated fears of social disorder. Torontonians and other urban dwellers increasingly perceived traditional patterns of child care and education by family and church as inadequate. A relatively small group of urban-based middle-class 'school promoters' became convinced of the necessity for a system of compulsory common schooling through which 'the poor would be elevated by means of the discipline considered essential for urban industrial living'. Put another way, an important function of education reform was 'one of providing a safe and disciplined lower class, the necessary labourers over whom those who had bettered themselves could exercise their newly won power'.

Katz's own major quantitative research project focused on nineteenth-century Hamilton. He used that mid-sized Ontario city, which in the thirty years after 1850 changed from a small prosperous commercial centre into an industrial one, as a laboratory to explore the relationship between urbanisation, industrialisation, family structure and schooling that had been propounded by Houston and Prentice. Both on his own, and in conjunction with others, Katz authored two monographs and several articles on Hamilton with important educational dimensions.[24] This work, and that of his graduate students Ian E. Davey and Harvey J. Graff, argued that the mid-nineteenth-century extension of schooling maintained and even furthered existing social and economic inequalities in Hamilton.[25] Katz, Davey and another graduate student, Haley Bamman, related attendance patterns in Hamilton and Toronto to larger socio-economic changes in the two cities.[26] During these same years two other scholars, Frank Denton and Peter George, similarly analysed attendance in Hamilton and came up with conflicting results.[27]

Prentice and Houston continued to pursue similar themes. In an essay on compulsory attendance in Toronto schools, Houston concluded that it was 'ineffective as a solution to the problems posed by a class of urban poor'.[28] Using evidence from both Toronto and Halifax, Prentice argued that graded school systems and professional hierarchies led to the feminisation of teaching occurring most rapidly in urban areas.[29] In a triad of essays with the late Marta Danylewycz, Prentice compared the female teaching forces in Ontario and Quebec during the years 1851–81.[30] In the cases of Toronto and Montreal, so they argued, 'growing school systems offered radically different opportunities to the men and women who staffed the schools', not surprisingly so since bureaucratic structures were developed 'chiefly with male administrators in mind'.[31]

Thus the radical revisionist thrust, whether centred on general or specific issues, made a singular point: the development of schooling in nineteenth-century Ontario, and by implication or comparison also in other parts of the country, had its impetus in urban priorities. As well as maintaining or even extending social, economic and gender inequalities, the changes imposed urban models on metropolis and hinterland alike.

III

During the 1980s, Canadian historians of education offered alternative explanations for the rise of common schooling which vigorously challenged the social control hypothesis so dominant in the previous decade. Even Houston and Prentice, in their fine survey of the history of education in Ontario to 1871, provided a more complex, multi-faceted explanation for the creation of a state system of education in that province.[32] Especially prolific was Robert Gidney, who in a series of well-sculpted studies with the late Douglas Lawr and then with W. P. J. Millar demonstrated that trustees and school users in rural and small-town Ontario were as concerned as were their urban counterparts with the creation of efficient structures and in fact frequently shaped policy to their distinctive needs.[33] Chad Gaffield pointed out that urban and rural priorities did not always coincide and that, moreover, the former did not necessarily override the latter.[34] In contrast, J. Donald Wilson demonstrated the great extent to which structures of rural schooling, in comparison to urban counterparts, remained simplistic and even primitive well into the twentieth century.[35] Thomas Fleming provided part of the explanation in two essays, which used as did Wilson the British Columbia experience and examined the rise of administrative frameworks that were largely based in urban priorities if not also urban assumptions.[36] Somewhat earlier, in essays comparing urban Ontario, Quebec and Alberta, Robert Stamp stressed the complexities of urban schooling, as did Neil Sutherland in his portrait of the urban school system in Saint John, New Brunswick, in the 1890s.[37] Patrick Harrigan contributed a useful comparison of rural and urban enrolment patterns across Canada during the first half of the twentieth century.[38]

Other historians argued persuasively for the high priority given to gender socialisation in the establishment of schools, especially in the case of Catholic female religious orders in urban Quebec. Nadia Fahmy-Eid focused on the Ursulines, A. J. B. Johnston on the Sisters of the Congregation of Notre Dame.[39] Michel Verrette explored literacy rates in Quebec City.[40] The continued role played by single-sex church schooling facilitated similar analyses of nineteenth- and twentieth-century girls' schools in Montreal and elsewhere by Fahmy-Eid, Micheline Dumont and others.[41] Writing more generally, Veronica Strong-Boag emphasised the extent to which girls growing up in inter-war Canada were caught in a web of traditional gender-based assumptions concerning first their schooling and then their destined roles in the larger society.[42] Nancy S. Jackson and Jane S. Gaskell explored the role of commercial education in Ontario and British Columbia during the turn of the century.[43]

The importance of working people in shaping educational structures in urban Canada also generated considerable interest. From a Marxist perspective, Bryan Palmer questioned the whole theoretical basis of the radical revisionist approach. He accused Katz in particular of ignoring the 'working-class record' of resistance to imposition. History 'must pay attention to the development of events if analysis is to mean anything'.[44] Bill Maciejko and Jean Barman took up the challenge to somewhat different ends. Maciejko interpreted Winnipeg workers' educational priorities, 1914–21, largely within a resistance framework.[45] In a pair of essays Barman argued that class interests were not as sharply divided as theory would sometimes suggest that they were.[46] Combining voting patterns for school trustees with demographic and other data, she concluded that in Vancouver in the 1920s socio-economic status influenced preferences at the polls. Because many working families genuinely believed that better conditions of schooling were in their own best interests, they combined with middle-class voters, and against the business establishment, to elect trustees committed to school improvement.

In a framework structured in part by Marxist notions of class and in part by Foucaultian ones on power, Bruce Curtis challenged the very core of Katz's and Prentice's argument: their attribution of educational reform in nineteenth-century Ontario to 'an attempt to control urban poverty and crime, an attempt to repress the menace of class struggle on the part of the working class, or both'. 'The peculiarity resides in the fact that the Upper Canadian [educational] system, as organized in the 1840s, was a specifically industrial or capitalist system, while capitalist industrialization in Upper Canada was only slightly developed.' The model was derived from other countries' responses 'to common problems faced by liberal reformers in all capitalist societies in the middle of the nineteenth century'. It was adopted in Upper Canada, according to Curtis, not so that one group in the society could exercise control over another but rather as 'an important mechanism for state building', as 'politically organized subjection'. Superintendent of Education Egerton Ryerson deliberately 'set out to transform education into a state-directed political socialization'.[47] Although Curtis did not view his interpretation as embodying a social control approach, some critics were quick to point up similarities with the very generation of scholars that he sought to replace.[48] 'Bourgeois hegemony' was the common goal. Clearly, discussion of the origins and character of urban schooling is far from over in Canada.

IV

A complementary thrust of recent Canadian scholarship in the history of urban education has been its move out of the classroom. As early as 1969, Sutherland suggested in an essay entitled 'The urban child' that 'what we really need to know for any particular time is just how the young were socialized'.[49] Acceptance by Canadian historians of a broader definition of education was encouraged by the publication in 1976 of his *Children in English–Canadian Society: Shaping the Twentieth-Century Consensus*, one of the few monographs published in North America focusing on children themselves as opposed to the institutions bounding their lives. There, Sutherland argued that between the 1880s and 1920s Anglophone Canadians created a new set of social priorities for their children. These policies affected youngsters not only in school but in their families and in other institutions concerned with their health, education and welfare. As was the case in school reform, urban Canadians devised policies not only for themselves but also for their rural hinterlands.

This new direction, described by Wilson as the study of 'family strategies', produced a wide variety of richly textured scholarship, much of it set in an urban environment.[50] The nature of childhood and family life amongst what might be described as 'ordinary' Canadians received particular attention. Judith Fingard looked at the education of the poor in colonial Halifax.[51] One of Davey's several essays on mid-nineteenth-century Hamilton emphasised the role of the family economy in determining school attendance.[52] Terrence Morrison examined the efforts made by female reformers to improve the conditions of childhood in urban Ontario during the late nineteenth century.[53] In a path-breaking dissertation, the late John Bullen analysed the extent to which work structured the lives of working-class children in late nineteenth-century Ontario, contending that, as the 'poorest', most powerless and least secure members of industrial society, children of the working class most visibly bore the scars inflicted by a social system designed to serve middle- and upper-class interests.[54] Lorna F. Hurl examined attempts to restrict child factory labour in late nineteenth-century Ontario.[55] Jane Synge carried a similar focus forward in time and demonstrated that family priorities still governed the schooling of working-class children in early twentieth-century Hamilton.[56]

Considerable attention was accorded French Canada. Peter Moogk emphasised the dominance of non-institutional education in New France, with schools being concentrated in the towns.[57] The lives of the working poor and their children in Montreal were graphically portrayed by Bettina Bradbury for the years 1860–85 and Terry Copp for the time period 1897–1929.[58] Micheline Dumont-Johnson examined the day care provided after 1860 to the poor in Montreal and elsewhere by the Grey Nuns.[59] Therese Hamel attributed the very low school attendance of Quebec children during the first half of this century to the continued importance of child labour both in factories and on farms.[60]

Other research focused on western Canada. Rebecca Coulter examined working-class youth in Edmonton during the 1920s and Norah Lewis the health care of urban children in British Columbia during the first four decades of the twentieth century.[61] As part of a major study analysing the impact on Canadian children of 'the twentieth-century consensus', Sutherland graphically portrayed school life, the culture of childhood and the paid and unpaid labour of children in Vancouver between the 1920s and 1960s.[62]

The harsh living conditions of working men and women in Canadian cities meant that their children's education often occurred outside the family circle. Paul Couett and Marianna O'Gallagher examined the care of orphans in Halifax in the mid-eighteenth century and in Quebec City a century later.[63] Mary Mulcahy described schools of industry in St John's.[64] Andrew Jones and Leonard Rutman wrote uncritically of the central role played by J.J. Kelso in the creation of a large network of mostly urban children's aid societies in Ontario in the late nineteenth and early twentieth centuries.[65] Henry Klassen described the origins of the Children's Aid Society of Calgary.[66] David Macleod examined the work of the YMCA in assisting urban youth, Kari Dehli that of public health nurses in the schools of early twentieth-century Toronto.[67] Theresa Richardson analysed the role of the mental hygiene movement in setting social policy.[68]

Of particular interest was the work of Patricia T. Rooke and R.L. Schnell, who closely documented for English Canada how attitudes toward the neglected and orphaned changed sharply over time, with a reliance on institutions gradually giving way to programmes of social assistance designed to keep children within a family setting.[69] Rooke and Schnell developed out of the example of these children a thesis regarding the role of childhood in Western society as a whole. They argued that the 'discovery' of childhood gave rise to what they called an ideology of childhood that was articulated through the four criteria of dependence, protection, segregation and delayed responsibility. In an effort to protect children from physical and moral dangers and to segregate them from the pernicious aspects of adult life, those in the middle class in particular extended youthful dependency and thus delayed youngsters from assuming full responsibility for their lives.

The delinquent and the 'pre-delinquent' attracted scholarly attention. Houston argued that the urban consensus of mid-nineteenth-century Ontario was centred in middle-class anxiety regarding the apparently deviant life-style of working-class children.[70] Vagrancy easily became equated with delinquency, and its remedy was sought in remedial care in industrial schools. Morrison and Paul W. Bennett discussed the role of industrial schools in urban Ontario, Indiana Matters their nature in urban British Columbia.[71]

As has occurred all over the world, most radical and ethnic minorities in Canadian cities have faced special problems. While the rapid growth of ethnic studies in Canada over the last two decades produced an extensive and wide-ranging examination of the experiences of different groups, little of it focused on childhood and schooling. Among the exceptions were John Abbott's examination of the role of ethnicity in the schools of Sault Ste. Marie, Ontario, in the early twentieth century.[72] Several scholars explored the educational strategies of Jews in Montreal and Toronto.[73] Elouessa Polyzoi, Murry Nicolson and Lillian Petroff examined those of Toronto's Greek, Irish and Macedonian communities.[74] Other studies described the role played by Italian and Slovak language schools in Toronto and Windsor.[75] Moving west, David Chuenyan Lai and Timothy J. Stanley looked at discrimination in Victoria's schools during the first decades of the twentieth century.[76] Among the most vivid insights into the childhood of ethnic minorities have been recollections and novels by such writers as John Marlyn, Laura Goodman Salverson and Mordecai Richler.[77]

V

Over the past two decades, the history of urban education has generated considerable interest in Canada. As educational historians moved into the historical mainstream during the 1970s, their 'revisionist' stance made the city the most appropriate laboratory for analysis. At the same time, interest in urban education remained relatively sparse, particularly when compared with the country's southern neighbour. Part of the reason was fairly straightforward. In the United States, much of the scholarly interest was generated by what was perceived as the unsatisfactory condition of much of urban schooling. Canadians have, on the other hand, remained reasonably satisfied with their school systems. Scholars have thereby lacked the practical impetus spurring on many of their American colleagues.

Thus, many issues central to the history of urban schooling and urban childhood remain unexamined in Canada. Even when these issues eventually receive the attention that they deserve, the city will probably not be the principal unit of analysis. As in other countries, Canadian historians have increasingly come to believe that such concepts as 'urban' and 'urbanisation' offer less explanatory bite than do 'gender', 'class' and 'ethnicity'. To change units of analysis does not, however, alter the historical reality that increasing proportions of Canadians have come to live in towns and cities. Urban children will still be the dominant metaphor as historians explore such topics as the varying strategies used by parents, both within the dominant society and as members of ethnic and radical minorities, to educate their daughters and sons; the roles played by voluntary associations and by congregations in socialising their young members; and the transition from school to work. More and more of the lives of urban children in Canada over the past four centuries will emerge from the shadows. The children who opened this essay will be joined by many others, and we will gain a much stronger sense as to how each of their lives has fitted into Canadian society as a whole.

NOTES

1 We have benefited from the insights of Robert McDonald, Peter Moogk and J. Donald Wilson. We are also grateful to the Social Sciences and Humanities Research Council of Canada for its support of the Canadian Childhood History Project, under whose auspices some of the ideas finding their way into this essay originated.
2 *Dictionary of Canadian Biography*, Vol. IX, 297–306.
3 *Dictionary of Canadian Biography*, Vol. IX, 561–4.
4 *Toronto Daily Mail and Empire*, 9 October 1897, 10.
5 Sing Lim, *West Coast Chinese Boy* (Montreal: Tundra Books, 1979).
6 Two new bibliographies provide virtually complete coverage to the literature on the history of Canadian education and of Canadian childhood: E. G. Finley, *Education in Canada: A Bibliography / L'Education au Canada: une bibliographie*, 2 vols. (Toronto and Oxford: Dundern Press in co-operation with the National Library of Canada and the Canadian Government Publishing Centre, Supply and Services Canada, 1989); and Neil Sutherland, Jean Barman and Linda Hale, *History of Canadian Childhood and Youth: A Bibliography* (Westport, CT: Greenwood Press, 1992).
7 Leroy O. Stone, *Urban Development in Canada* (Ottawa: Dominion Bureau of Statistics, 1967), 17.
8 See Harold Innis' classic studies, *The Fur Trade in Canada: An Introduction to Canadian Economic History* (New Haven, CT: Yale University Press, 1930), and *The Cod Fisheries: The History of an International Economy* (New Haven, CT: Yale University Press, 1940). For a detailed examination of historiography, see Carl Berger, *The Writing of Canadian History: Aspects of English–Canadian Historical Writing since 1900* (2nd edn, Toronto: University of Toronto Press, 1986).
9 J. M. S. Careless, 'Frontierism and metropolitanism in Canadian history', *Canadian Historical Review*, Vol. 35 (1954), 1–21; and J. M. S. Careless, *Frontier and Metropolis: Regions, Cities, and Identities in Canada before 1914* (Toronto: University of Toronto Press, 1989).
10 C. E. Phillips, *The Development of Education in Canada* (Toronto: Gage, 1957); F. Henry Johnson, *A Brief History of Canadian Education* (Toronto: McGraw-Hill, 1968), and *A History of Public Education in British Columbia* (Vancouver: University of British Columbia, 1964), F. W. Rowe, *The History of Education in*

Newfoundland (Toronto: Ryerson, 1952), and *The Development of Education in Newfoundland* (Toronto: Ryerson, 1964); K. C. N. MacNaughton, *The Development of the Theory and Practice of Education in New Brunswick 1784–1900* (Fredericton: University of New Brunswick, 1947); and John W. Chalmers, *Schools of the Foothills Province* [Alberta] (Toronto: University of Toronto Press, 1967).

11 F. Henry Johnson, 'The Ryerson influence on the public school system of British Columbia', *BC Studies*, Vol. 10 (Summer 1971), 26–34. Johnson's argument was extended and to some extent challenged in Jean Barman, 'Transfer, imposition or consensus? The emergence of educational structures in nineteenth-century British Columbia', in Nancy M. Sheehan, J. Donald Wilson and David C. Jones (eds.), *Schools in the West: Essays in Canadian Educational History* (Calgary: Detselig, 1986), 261–4.

12 Robert Stamp, 'The response to urban growth: the bureaucratization of public education in Calgary, 1884–1914', in A. W. Rasporich and H. C. Klassen (eds.), *Frontier Calgary* (Calgary: University of Calgary Press, 1975), 153–68.

13 Neil Sutherland, *Children in English–Canadian Society: Shaping the Twentieth-Century Consensus* (Toronto: University of Toronto Press, 1976).

14 See Gordon Stelter, 'Urban history', in J. L. Granatstein and P. Stevens (eds.), *A Reader's Guide to Canadian History* (Toronto: University of Toronto Press, 1982), 96–113; and Donald F. Davis, 'The "metropolitan thesis" and the writing of Canadian urban history', *Urban History Review*, Vol. 14 (1985), 95–113.

15 See Bruce M. Stave, 'A conversation with Gilbert A. Stelter: urban history in Canada', *Journal of Urban History*, Vol. 6 (1980), esp. 187–91 and 199, and his 'Urban history in Canada: a conversation with Alan F. J. Artibise', *Urban History*, Vol. 3 (1980), esp. 119–22 and 142–3.

16 For example, Patricia E. Roy, *Vancouver: An Illustrated History*, History of Canadian Cities Series (Toronto: James Lorimer and National Museum of Man, 1980).

17 H. R. Cummings and W. T. MacSkimming, *The City of Ottawa Public Schools: A Brief History* (Ottawa: Board of Education, 1971); Honora M. Cochrane (ed.), *Centennial Story: The Board of Education for the City of Toronto, 1850–1950* (Toronto: Nelson, 1950); Greta Shutt, *The High Schools of Guelph* (Toronto: University of Toronto Press, 1961); Robert M. Stamp, *School Days: A Century of Memories* (Calgary: Board of Education, 1975); and Chuck Gosbee and Leslie Dyson (eds.), *'Glancing Back': Reflections and Anecdotes on Vancouver Public Schools* (Vancouver: Vancouver School Board, 1988).

18 For example, Lucien Brault, *Un siècle d'administration scholaire: la Commission des écoles catholiques de Hull, 1866–1966* (Hull: La Commission des Écoles Catholiques de Hull, 1966); Louis J. Flynn, *At School in Kingston, 1850–1973* (Kingston: Roman Catholic Separate School Board, 1973); and Michael J. Donovan, 'The establishment of Roman Catholic separate schools in Port Arthur in the 1880s', Thunder Bay Historical Society, *Papers and Records*, Vol. 3 (1975), 9–15.

19 Indicative of such studies' diversity were Robert J. Bolton, *History of the Central Public School, Peterborough, 1860–1960* (Peterborough: n.p., 1960); Richard B. Howard, *Upper Canada College 1829–1979* (Toronto: Macmillan, 1979), G. M. Theal, 'Schooldays, schooldays ... Cocagne Academy in the 1840s', *Acadiensis*,

Vol. 6 (1976), 132–7; Peter L. Smith, *Come Give a Cheer! One Hundred Years of Victoria High School, 1876–1976* (Victoria: Victoria High School Centennial Celebrations Committee, 1976); and the pupil-produced *Lucky to Live in Cedar Cottage: Memories of Lord Selkirk School and Cedar Cottage Neighbourhood, 1911–1963*, ed. Seymour Levitan and Carol Miller (Vancouver: Vancouver School Board, 1986).

20 For instance, Dana Johnson, 'Going to school in Ontario: the urban primary school 1850–1930', Parks Canada, *Research Bulletin*, Vol. 213 (1984).

21 Exemplary were P.W. Fleming, 'The development of secondary education in Saint John, New Brunswick, Canada, from 1805' (MA thesis, University of Leeds, 1977); W.C. Nesbitt, 'The development of the Saint John System to 1871' (MEd thesis, University of New Brunswick, 1970); M.W. Williams, 'Early history of education in the district of Bathurst' (MA thesis, University of Ottawa, 1951); H. Dukham, 'The development of the junior high school and the senior high school in metropolitan Toronto' (MEd thesis, University of Toronto, 1959); Donald A. Lapp, 'The schools of Kingston: their first one hundred and fifty years' (MA thesis, Queen's University (Kingston), 1937); John J.D. Londerville, 'The schools of Peterborough: their first hundred years' (MA thesis, Queen's University (Kingston), 1942); F. Vernon, 'Some aspects of the development of public education in the city of St. Catharines' (MEd thesis, University of Toronto, 1960); G.S. Belton, 'A history of the origin and growth of schools in the city of St. Boniface' (MEd thesis, University of Manitoba, 1959); Carl Bjarnason, 'The Brandon school system: a historical survey' (MEd thesis, University of Manitoba, 1962); W.H. Lucow, 'The origin and growth of the public school system in Winnipeg' (MEd thesis, University of Manitoba, 1959); Kaspar C. Morgenroth, 'The development ... of the Saskatoon school system, 1884–1947' (MEd thesis, University of Saskatchewan, 1949); Robert G. Neely, 'The growth and development of the Regina educational system from its beginnings to 1944' (MEd thesis, University of Saskatchewan, 1946); L.A. Daniels, 'the history of education in Calgary' (MA thesis, University of Washington, 1954); J.R. Houghton, 'The Calgary public school system, 1939–1969' (MEd thesis, University of Calgary, 1971); Phyllis Weston, 'The history of education in Calgary' (MA thesis, University of Alberta, 1951); and Elsie Watts, 'Attitudes of parents toward the development of public schooling in Victoria, BC, during the colonial period' (MA thesis, Simon Fraser University (Barnaby), 1988).

22 Susan Houston, 'Politics, schools and social change in Upper Canada', *Canadian Historical Review*, Vol. 53 (1972), 249–71, esp. 250, 252 and 271. See also Peter N. Ross, 'The free school controversy in Toronto, 1848–1852', *History of Education Quarterly*, Vol. 12 (1972), 358–80. Essays from this special issue were reprinted along with several others as M.B. Katz and P.H. Mattingly (eds.), *Education and Social Change: Themes from Ontario's Past* (New York: New York University Press, 1975). The same notion was expressed two years earlier by J.D. Wilson, in 'The Ryerson years in Canada West', in J.D. Wilson, R.M. Stamp and L.-P. Audet (eds.), *Canadian Education: A History* (Scarborough: Prentice-Hall, 1970), 214–40, esp. 224.

23 Alison Prentice, *The School Promoters: Education and Social Class in Mid-Nineteenth Century Upper Canada* (Toronto: McClelland and Stewart, 1977), esp. 45–6, 115 and 181–2.

24 Michael B. Katz, *The People of Hamilton, Canada West: Family and Class in a Mid-Nineteenth-Century City* (Cambridge, MA: Harvard University Press, 1976); Michael B. Katz, Michael J. Doucet and Mark J. Stern, *The Social Organization of Early Industrial Capitalism* (Cambridge, MA: Harvard University Press, 1982); Michael B. Katz, 'The people of a Canadian city: 1851–52', *Canadian Historical Review*, Vol. 53 (1972), 402–26; Michael B. Katz, 'Who went to school?', *History of Education Quarterly*, Vol. 12 (1972), 432–54; Michael B. Katz and Ian E. Davey, 'Youth and early industrialization in a Canadian city', in John Demos and A. S. Boocock (eds.), *Turning Points: Historical and Sociological Essays on the Family* (Chicago, IL: University of Chicago Press, 1978), 81–119; and Michael B. Katz and Ian E. Davey, 'School attendance and early industrialization in a Canadian city: a multivariate analysis', *History of Education Quarterly*, Vol. 18 (1978), 271–94.

25 Ian E. Davey, 'School reform and school attendance: the Hamilton central school, 1853–1861', in Katz and Mattingly (eds.), *Education and Social Change*, 294–314; Ian E. Davey, 'Trends in female school attendance patterns', *Social History*, Vol. 8 (1975), 238–54; Ian E. Davey, 'The rhythm of work and the rhythm of school', in Neil McDonald and Alf Chaiton (eds.), *Egerton Ryerson and his Times* (Toronto: Macmillan Canada, 1978), 221–53; Harvey J. Graff, *The Literacy Myth: Literacy and Social Structure in a Nineteenth Century City* (New York: Academic Press, 1979); Harvey J. Graff, 'Towards a meaning of literacy: literacy and social structure in Hamilton, Ontario', *History of Education Quarterly*, Vol. 12 (1972), 411–31; Harvey J. Graff, 'The reality behind the rhetoric: the social and economic meanings of literacy in the mid-nineteenth century', in McDonald and Chaiton (eds.), *Ryerson*, 187–220; and Harvey J. Graff, 'Respected and profitable labour: literacy, jobs and the working class in the nineteenth century', in G. S. Kealey and Peter Warrian (eds.), *Essays in Canadian Working Class History* (Toronto: McClelland and Stewart, 1976), 58–82.

26 Katz, 'Who went'; Katz and Davey, 'School attendance'; Davey, 'School reform'; Davey, 'Trends'; and Bamman, 'Patterns of school attendance in Toronto, 1844–1878: some spatial considerations', *History of Education Quarterly*, Vol. 12 (1972), 381–410.

27 Frank Denton and Peter George, 'Socio-economic influences in school attendance: a study of a Canadian county in 1871', *History of Education Quarterly*, Vol. 14 (1974), 223–34.

28 Susan Houston, 'Social reform and education: the issue of compulsory schooling, Toronto, 1851–71', in McDonald and Chaiton (eds.), *Ryerson*, 254–76.

29 Alison Prentice, 'The feminization of teaching in British North America and Canada, 1845–1876', *Social History*, Vol. 8 (1975), 5–20. On related themes were A. M. Kojder, 'The Saskatoon Women Teachers' Association: a demand for recognition', *Saskatchewan History*, Vol. 30 (1977), 56–62; and E. K. Walker, *The Story of the Women Teachers' Association of Toronto* (Toronto: Copp Clark, 1963).

30 Marta Danylewycz and Alison Prentice, 'Teachers, gender, and bureaucratizing school systems in nineteenth century Montreal and Toronto', *History of Education Quarterly*, Vol. 24 (1984), 75–100; Marta Danylewycz, Beth Light and Alison Prentice, 'The evolution of the sexual division of labour in teaching: a nineteenth-century Ontario and Quebec case study', *Histoire Sociale/Social*

History, Vol. 16 (1983), 81–109; and Marta Danylewycz and Alison Prentice, 'Teachers' work: changing patterns and preceptions in the emerging school systems of nineteenth and early twentieth century central Canada', *Labour / Le Travail*, Vol. 17 (1986), 59–80. Also see Marta Danylewycz, 'Sexes et classes sociales dans l'enseignement: le cas de Montreal à la fin du 19e siècle', in Nadia Fahmy-Eid and Micheline Dumont (eds.), *Maitresses de maison, maitresses d'école: femmes, famille et éducation dans l'histoire du Québec* (Montreal: Boreal Express, 1983), 93–118.

31 Danylewycz and Prentice, 'Teachers, gender', 78. A somewhat different perspective was advanced in Jean Barman, 'Birds of passage or early professionals? Teachers in late nineteenth-century British Columbia', *Historical Studies in Education*, Vol. 2 (1990), 17–36. Related were Cecilia Reynolds, 'Hegemony and hierarchy: becoming a teacher in Toronto, 1930–1980', *Historical Studies in Education*, Vol. 2 (1990), 95–118; and Susan Gelman, '"The 'feminization' of the high schools"? Women secondary school teachers in Toronto: 1871–1930', *Historical Studies in Education*, Vol. 2 (1990), 119–48.

32 Susan E. Houston and Alison Prentice, *Schooling and Scholars in Nineteenth-Century Ontario* (Toronto: University of Toronto Press, 1988).

33 Especially Robert Gidney and Douglas Lawr, 'Who ran the schools? Local influence on educational policy in nineteenth-century Ontario', *Ontario History*, Vol. 72 (1980), 131–43; Robert Gidney and Douglas Lawr, 'Bureaucracy vs. community? The origins of bureaucratic procedure in the Upper Canadian school system', *Journal of Social History*, Vol. 13 (1980), 438–57; Robert Gidney and W. P. J. Millar, 'From voluntarism to state schooling: the creation of the public school system in Ontario', *Canadian Historical Review*, Vol. 66 (1985), 443–73; and Robert Gidney and W. P. J. Millar, *Inventing Secondary Education: The Rise of the High School in Nineteenth-Century Ontario* (Montreal: McGill–Queen's University Press, 1990).

34 Chad Gaffield, 'Schooling, the economy, and rural society in nineteenth-century Ontario', in Joy Parr (ed.), *Childhood and Family in Canadian History* (Toronto: McClelland and Stewart, 1982), 69–83. Also see Chad Gaffield and David Levine, 'Dependency and adolescence on the Canadian frontier: Orillia, Ontario, in the mid-nineteenth century', *History of Education Quarterly*, Vol. 18 (1978), 35–47; and Chad Gaffield and Gérard Bouchard, 'Literacy, schooling, and family reproduction in rural Ontario and Quebec', *Historical Studies in Education*, Vol. 1 (1989), 201–18. In *Language, Schooling, and Cultural Conflict: The Origins of the French-Language Controversy in Ontario* (Kingston: McGill–Queen's University Press, 1987), Gaffield put his ideas respecting rural education into their broader social and economic framework.

35 J. Donald Wilson, 'The visions of ordinary participants: teachers' views of rural schooling in British Columbia in the 1920s', in Patricia E. Roy (ed.), *A History of British Columbia: Selected Readings* (Toronto: Copp Clark Pitman, 1989), 239–53; and J. Donald Wilson and Paul J. Stortz, '"May the Lord Have Mercy on You": the rural school problem in British Columbia in the 1920s', *BC Studies*, Vol. 79 (Autumn 1988), 24–58.

36 Thomas Fleming, '"Our boys in the field": school inspectors, superintendents, and the changing character of school leadership in British Columbia', in Sheehan, Wilson and Jones (eds.), *Schools in the West*, 285–303; and Thomas Fleming, 'In

37 Stamp, 'Response'; Robert Stamp, 'Urbanization and education in Ontario and Quebec, 1867–1914', *McGill Journal of Education*, Vol. 3 (1968), 127–35; and Neil Sutherland, 'Albert School, Saint John, N.B.: a case study of urban schooling in the 1890's', *Journal of Education*, Vol. 19 (1973), 63–73.

38 Patrick Harrigan, 'A comparison of rural and urban patterns of enrolment and attendance in Canada, 1900–1960', *Canadian History of Education Association Bulletin*, Vol. 5 (October 1988), 27–48.

39 Nadia Fahmy-Eid, 'L'Education des filles chez les Ursulines de Québec sous le Régime Français', in Fahmy-Eid and Dumont (eds.), *Maitresses*, 49–76; A. J. B. Johnston, 'Education and female literacy in eighteenth century Louisbourg: the work of the Soeurs de la Congrégation de Notre Dame', in J. D. Wilson (ed.), *An Imperfect Past: Education and Society in Canadian History* (Vancouver: Centre for the Study of Curriculum and Instruction, University of British Columbia, 1984), 48–66; and A. J. B. Johnston, 'Formal education at colonial Louisbourg', Parks Canada, *Research Bulletin*, Vol. 136 (1980).

40 Michel Verrette, 'L'Alphabétisation de la population de la ville de Québec de 1750 a 1849', *Revue d'histoire de l'Amérique français*, Vol. 39 (1985), 51–76.

41 Especially Micheline Dumont and Nadia Fahmy-Eid, *Les Couventines: l'education des filles au Québec dans les congrégations religieuses enseignantes, 1840–1860* (Montreal: Boréal, 1986); and the various essays in Fahmy-Eid and Dumont (eds.), *Maitresses*. Exemplary of theses were Ruby Heap, 'L'Eglise, l'état et l'enseignement primaire public catholique au Québec, 1897–1920 (PhD thesis, University of Montreal, 1987); Marie-Josée Delorme, 'Le Financement du Pensionnat Saint-Marie: une institution indépendante et sous-contrôle' (MA thesis, University of Sherbrooke, 1987); and Lucie Champagne, 'Le Financement des pensionnats de jeunes filles au Québec: le modèle des Soeurs de Sainte-Anne 1850–1950' (MA thesis, University of Sherbrooke, 1989). Related were Lucie Champagne and Micheline Dumont, 'Le Financement d'un séminaire diocésain: le Séminaire de Sherbrooke, 1915–1950. Comparison avec le financement des pensionnats de religieuses', *Historical Studies in Education*, Vol. 2 (1990), 339–97; Anne Gagnon, 'The Pensionnat Assomption: religious nationalism in a Franco-Albertan boarding school for girls, 1926–1960', *Historical Studies in Education*, Vol. 1 (1989), 95–117; and Anne Drummond, 'Gender, profession, and principals: the teachers of Quebec Protestant academies, 1875–1900', *Historical Studies in Education*, Vol. 2 (1990), 59–71.

42 Veronica Strong-Boag, 'Growing up female', Chapter 1 in *The New Day Recalled: Lives of Girls and Women in English Canada, 1919–1939* (Markham: Penguin, 1988).

43 Nancy S. Jackson and Jane S. Gaskell, 'White collar vocationalism: the rise of commercial education in Ontario and British Columbia, 1870–1920', *Curriculum Inquiry*, Vol. 17 (1987), 177–201.

44 Bryan Palmer, 'Emperor Katz's New Clothes; or with the Wizard in Oz', *Labour / Le Travail*, Vol. 13 (1984), 190–7, esp. 193–4. For another critique of Katz, see Geoffrey Partington, 'Two Marxisms and the history of education', *History of Education*, Vol. 13 (1984), 251–70.

45 Bill Maciejko, 'Public schools and the workers' struggle: Winnipeg, 1914–1921', in Sheehan, Wilson and Jones (eds.), *Schools in the West*, 213–37.

46 Jean Barman, 'Neighbourhood and community in interwar Vancouver: residential differentiation and civic voting behaviour', in Robert A. J. McDonald and Jean Barman (eds.), *Vancouver Past: Essays in Social History* (Vancouver: University of British Columbia Press, 1986), 97–141; and Jean Barman, '"Knowledge is essential for universal progress but fatal to class privilege": working people and the schools in Vancouver during the 1920s', *Labour / Le Travail*, Vol. 22 (1988), 9–66.

47 Bruce Curtis, 'Preconditions of the Canadian state: educational reform and the construction of a public in Upper Canada, 1837–1846', *Studies in Political Economy*, Vol. 10 (1983), 99–121, esp. 99, 102, 107 and 103; and Bruce Curtis, *Building the Educational State: Canada West, 1836–1871* (Ontario: Falmer Press and London, Ont. Althouse Press, 1988), esp. 106.

48 For instance, review of *Building the Educational State* by Douglas Owram in *History of Education Quarterly*, Vol. 29 (1989), 138–40.

49 Neil Sutherland, 'The urban child', *History of Education Quarterly*, Vol. 9 (1969), 305–11.

50 J. Donald Wilson, 'From social control to family strategies: some observations on recent trends in Canadian educational history', *History of Education Review*, Vol. 13 (1984), 1–13. Useful later assessments were Chad Gaffield, 'Back to school: towards a new agenda for the history of education', *Acadiensis*, Vol. 15 (1986), 169–90; and J. Donald Wilson, 'The new diversity in Canadian educational history', *Acadiensis*, Vol. 19 (1990), 148–70.

51 Judith Fingard, 'Attitudes toward the education of the poor in colonial Halifax', *Dalhousie Review*, Vol. 50 (1970–1), 510–16.

52 Davey, 'Rhythm'.

53 Terrence Morrison, '"Their proper sphere": feminism, the family and child centred social reform in Ontario, 1875–1900', *Ontario History*, Vol. 68 (March 1976), 45–64 and 68, and (June 1976), 66–74.

54 John Bullen, 'Children of the industrial age: children, work, and welfare in late nineteenth century Ontario' (PhD thesis, University of Ottawa, 1989); also John Bullen, "Hidden workers": Child labour and the household economy in late nineteenth-century urban Ontario', *Labour / Le Travail*, Vol. 18 (1986), 163–87; and John Bullen, 'Orphans, idiots, lunatics, and historians: recent approaches to the history of child welfare in Canada', *Histoire Sociale / Social History*, Vol. 18 (1985), 133–45. Somewhat earlier, Greg Kealey edited, albeit severely, with about 5 per cent of the evidence remaining, the Royal Commission on the Relations of Labour and Capital, which gave working-class children of the turn of the century a rare opportunity to talk about their lives. Greg Kealey (ed.), *Canada Investigates Industrialism* (Toronto: University of Toronto Press, 1973). Another reprinted contemporary account of the lives of poor children was C. S. Clark, *Of Toronto the Good: The Queen City of Canada as It Is* (Toronto: Coles, 1970; orig., Toronto Publishing Co., 1898).

55 Lorna F. Hurl, 'Overcoming the inevitable: restricting child factory labour in late nineteenth century Ontario', *Labour / Le Travail*, Vol. 21 (1988), 87–121.

56 Judith Synge, 'Growing up working class in Hamilton in the early twentieth century', in K. Ishwaran (ed.), *Childhood and Adolescence in Canada* (Toronto: McGraw-Hill Ryerson, 1979), 249–69.

57 Especially Peter Moogk, 'Manual education and economic life in new France', *Studies on Voltaire and the Eighteenth Century* (Geneva), Vol. 167 (1977), 125–68.

Related was Jean-Pierre and David Thierry-Rud, *Les Apprentis artisans a Québec, 1660–1815* (Montreal: Les Presses d'Université du Quebec, 1977).

58 Bettina Bradbury, 'The fragmented family: family strategies in the face of death, illness, and poverty, Montreal, 1860–1885', in Parr (ed.), *Childhood and Family*, 109–28; Bettina Bradbury, 'The family economy and work in an industrializing city: Montreal in the 1870s', Canadian Historical Association, *Historical Papers* (1979), 71–96; Terry Copp, *The Anatomy of Poverty: The Condition of the Working Class in Montreal, 1897–1929* (Toronto: McClelland and Stewart, 1974).

59 Micheline Dumont-Johnson, 'Des garderies au XIXe siècle: les salles d'asile des Soeurs Grise à Montreal', *Revue d'histoire de l'Amérique français*, Vol. 34 (1980), 27–55.

60 Therese Hamel, 'Obligation scolaire et travail des enfants au Québec, 1900–1950', *Revue d'histoire de l'Amérique français*, Vol. 38 (1984), 39–58; and Therese Hamel, 'L'Obligation scolaire au Québec: lieu et enjeu de la lutte des classes' (PhD thesis, Université de Paris V, Rue Descartes, 1981).

61 Rebecca Coulter, 'The working young of Edmonton, 1921–1931', in Parr (ed.), *Childhood and Family*, 143–59; and Norah Lewis, 'Physical perfection for spiritual welfare: health care for the urban child, 1900–1939', in P. T. Rooke and R. L. Schnell (eds.), *Studies in Childhood History: A Canadian Perspective* (Calgary: Detselig, 1982), 135–66. Related were Norah Lewis, 'Creating the little machine: child rearing in British Columbia', *BC Studies*, Vol. 56 (Winter 1982/3), 44–60; and Neil Sutherland, 'Social policy, "deviant" children, and the public health apparatus in British Columbia between the wars', *Journal of Educational Thought*, Vol. 14 (1980), 80–91.

62 Neil Sutherland, 'The triumph of "formalism": elementary schooling in Vancouver from the 1920s to the 1960s', in McDonald and Barman (eds.), *Vancouver Past*, 175–210; Neil Sutherland, '"Everyone seemed happy in those days": the culture of childhood in Vancouver between the 1920s and the 1960s', *History of Education Review*, Vol. 15 (1986), 37–51; Neil Sutherland, '"We always had things to do": the paid and unpaid work of Anglophone children between the 1920s and the 1960s', *Labour / Le Travail*, Vol. 25 (Spring 1990), 105–41 and Neil Sutherland, *Growing up in Modern Canada: The Children's Perspective* (Toronto: University of Toronto Press, forthcoming).

63 Paul Couett, 'The Halifax orphan home, 1752–1787', *Nova Scotia Historical Quarterly*, Vol. 6 (1976), 281–91; and Marianna O'Gallagher, 'Care of the orphaned and the aged by the Irish community of Quebec City, 1847, and the years following', Canadian Catholic Historical Association, *Study Sessions*, Vol. 43 (1976), 39–56.

64 Mary Mulcahy, 'The St. John's schools of industry', *Newfoundland Quarterly*, Vol. 78 (1983), 17–22.

65 Andrew Jones and Leonard Rutman, *In the Children's Aid: J. J. Kelso and Child Welfare in Ontario* (Toronto: University of Toronto Press, 1980).

66 Henry Klassen, 'In search of neglected and delinquent children: the Calgary Children's Aid Society, 1909–1920', in A. F. J. Artibise (ed.), *Town and City: Aspects of Western Canadian Urban Development* (Regina: University of Regina, 1981), 375–91.

67 David Macleod, 'A live vaccine: the YMCA and male adolescence in the United

States and Canada, 1870–1920', *Histoire Sociale / Social History*, Vol. 11 (1978), 5–25; and Kari Dehli, '"Health scouts' for the state? School and public health nurses in early twentieth-century Toronto', *Historical Studies in Education*, Vol. 2 (1990), 247–64.
68 Theresa Richardson, *The Century of the Child: The Mental Hygiene Movement and Social Policy in the United States and Canada* (Albany: State University of New York Press, 1989).
69 Patricia T. Rooke and R. L. Schnell, *Discarding the Asylum: From Child Rescue to the Welfare State in English–Canada (1800–1950)* (Latham: University Press of America, 1983).
70 Susan Houston, 'Victorian origins of juvenile delinquency: a Canadian experience', *History of Education Quarterly*, Vol. 12 (1972), 254–80; and Susan Houston, 'The "waifs and strays" of a late Victorian city: juvenile delinquents in Toronto', in Parr (ed.), *Childhood and Family*, 129–42. Related was Rebecca Coulter, '"Not to punish but to reform": juvenile delinquency and Children's Protection Act in Alberta, 1909–1929', in Rooke and Schnell (eds.), *Studies*, 167–84.
71 Terrence Morrison, 'Reform as social tracking: the case of industrial education in Ontario, 1870–1900', *Journal of Educational Thought*, Vol. 8 (1974), 87–110; Paul W. Bennett, 'Taming the "bad boys" of the "dangerous class": child rescue and restraint at the Victoria Industrial School, 1887–1935', *Histoire Sociale / Social History*, Vol. 21 (1988), 71–96; Diane [Indiana] Matters, 'The Boys' Industrial School: education for juvenile offenders', in J. D. Wilson and D. C. Jones (eds.), *Schooling and Society in 20th Century British Columbia* (Calgary: Detselig, 1980), 63–70; and Diane [Indiana] Matters, 'Sinners or sinned against? Historical aspects of female juvenile delinquency in British Columbia', in Barbara Latham and Roberta J. Pazdro (eds.), *Not Just Pin Money: Selected Essays on the History of Women's Work in British Columbia* (Victoria: Camosun College, 1984), 265–77.
72 John Abbott, 'Ethnicity as a dynamic factor in the education of an industrializing town: the case of Sault Ste. Marie, 1895–1914', *Ontario History*, Vol. 79 (1987), 327–52.
73 William Shaffir, 'The organization of secular education in a Chassidic Jewish community', *Canadian Ethnic Studies*, Vol. 8 (1976), 38–51; Luigi Pennacchio, 'The defense of identity: Ida Siegel and the Jews of Toronto versus the assimilation attempts of the public school and its allies, 1900–1920', *Canadian Jewish Historical Society Journal*, Vol. 9 (1985), 41–60; Harvey A. Raben, 'Bringing order to chaos: the centralization of Jewish education in Toronto', *Canadian Jewish Historical Society Journal*, Vol. 10 (1988), 34–46; and Samuel Shammal, 'The Jews and the public education system: the students' strike over the "flag fight" in Toronto after the first world war', *Canadian Jewish Historical Society Journal*, Vol. 10 (1988), 46–53.
74 Elouessa Polyzoi, 'The Greek community school and cultural survival in pre-war Toronto', *Urban History Review*, Vol. 2 (1978), 74–95; Murry Nicolson, 'Irish Catholic education in Victorian Toronto: an ethnic response to urban conformity', *Histoire Sociale / Social History*, Vol. 17 (1984), 287–306; and Lillian Petroff, 'An all-important business: educating Macedonian youth in Toronto before world war II', *Polyphony*, Vol. 11 (1989), 24–8.

75 Luigi G. Pennacchio, 'Italian heritage language classes in pre-second world war Toronto', *Polyphony*, Vol. 11 (1989), 36–45; and Ladislav Bagin, 'Slovak language schools in Windsor, Ontario ', *Polyphony*, Vol. 11 (1989), 72–5. Related was Susan M. Papp, 'Hungarian language education in Ontario', *Polyphony*, Vol. 11 (1989), 75–80.

76 David Chuenyan Lai, 'The issue of discrimination in education in Victoria, 1901–1923', *Canadian Ethnic Studies*, Vol. 19 (1987), 47–67; and Timothy J. Stanley, 'White supremacy, Chinese schooling, and school segregation in Victoria: the case of the Chinese students' strike, 1922–23', *Historical Studies in Education*, Vol. 2 (1990), 287–305.

77 John Marlyn, *Under the Ribs of Death* (Toronto: McClelland and Stewart, 1971); Laura Goodman Salverson, *Confessions of an Immigrant's Daughter* (London: Faber and Faber, 1930; and Toronto: University of Toronto Press, 1981); and Mordecai Richler, *The Apprenticeship of Duddy Kravitz* (Toronto: McClelland and Stewart, 1969).

Part 2

Approaches to the social history of education: ecology, choice and culture

5 Social stratification and nineteenth-century English urban education

William E. Marsden

Introduction

One appraisal of educational provision in nineteenth-century England would have us believe that schooling faithfully reflected a social polarisation between upper classes and lower classes, marked by the provision of an extended private education for the elite, as distinct from the shortlife elementary schooling that was deemed sufficient for the lower orders. A revisionist explanation adds a value judgement but does not refine the dimensions. There are oppressors and oppressed, social controllers and controlled, reproduced in school systems which concentrated on the improvement of the mind for the one group, and on the dampening of the baser instincts of the other.[1]

There is plenty of evidence from the time which can be drawn upon to sustain this stereotype. As late as the Newcastle Commission, for example, elementary provision was still characterised as the 'education of the poor'. But as Hurt has observed, Robert Lowe (and others of his ilk) had little regard for the 'finer nuances' of the class system,[2] in a condition of dramatic social change, wrought by a rapidly expanding economy and an increasingly differentiated occupational structure. By the 1850s and 1860s, there was but an incipient recognition of the gradations which had developed *within* the middle classes (lumped with the upper classes in dichotomised explanations) and *within* the working classes.

Interaction between education and nineteenth-century society was truly ecological in respect of the capacity of individual participants in schooling to adapt to changing social niches. Ecological adjustment, however, appears a neglected concept in comparison with, say, social control, or socialisation, in attempts to interpret the impact of nineteenth-century educational provision.[3] This is not to say that at the aggregate level control mechanisms were not established. But at the same time, the individual family retained considerable room for manoeuvre in making decisions about schooling.

Much of the misunderstanding which has permeated academic debates about social class and school provision has resulted from the failure to take

111

account of the disjunction between official intent and not so much the aggregate response as the tangible individual family and group adjustments at the grass-roots. Even after compulsion began to 'bite', parents enjoyed considerable latitude in the choice of schools.[4]

More significant, perhaps, was the competition for the custom of the *regular* attenders, characteristically the children of the respectable groups which formed the 'middle orders' in Victorian society. Failure to appreciate the influence of this burgeoning and overwhelmingly urban cohort diminishes the credibility of explanations which stretch too far in time the centrality of the *industrial revolution*, imposition of schooling model, and omit to shift priority to the educational impact of the post-industrial *tertiary revolution* of the late nineteenth century, and the changing social values this embodied.

Both publicly provided and privately sponsored systems evolved a wide range of responses to the needs of increasingly differentiated social groups. Graduation of provision, a defensive, 'enclosure' principle, was applied at all social levels. Those regarded as needing the firmest enclosure were at the top and bottom ends of the social scale, the 'elite' and the incipiently criminal 'residuum', both, in their different ways, requiring the oversight of boarding accommodation. But at all levels, whether in boarding or in day schools, parents responded to the threat posed by the urban social mix by quarantining their children from contamination by those of alien groups. The graduation principle was a characteristically urban response. The complexity of the graduation of schools reflected faithfully intricate perceptions of social status by urban people, which might be based on wealth, or on something less tangible. Graduation of fees became an underlying mechanism of a responsive educational differentiation.

The most underexplored arena of conflict was not, however, between rich and poor, the controllers and controlled, but among the middling groups of society. These, Brereton portrayed as including 'the great mass of the nation', in which moderate means did not preclude the attainment of 'moral and intellectual excellence'. There was the prospect of widening of 'the margin between the higher classes and the lower as practically to make any line imperceptible'.[5] The social situation of the late nineteenth century was fluid. With an expanding lower middle class, a considerable prospect of social mobility, albeit qualitatively limited, was necessary, acceptable and made available. While there was little chance of the sons of labourers becoming cabinet ministers, there was plenty of opportunity for the son of a mechanic to become a clerk or, more tellingly, for the son of a clerk to drop a rung in the occupational status ladder to the level of the mechanic. Clerkly and mechanical occupations were mingled in many families, fuelling domestic tensions. Active trade unionists, urging working-class solidarity in the

Table 5.1. *Schools and social categories in the late nineteenth century*

Social category	Publicly provided schools	Privately sponsored schools	Boarding/day
Upper class		The 'great' public schools	
----------	----------	Other public boarding schools	Boarding
Upper middle class		Preparatory schools	

		1st grade secondary schools	
Lower middle class		2nd grade secondary schools Private schools ('commercial' type)	
----------	Higher grade and other high-fee (6d per week and over) board and voluntary elementary schools	----------	
Upper working class		3rd grade secondary schools	Day
	Middle-fee (3d–6d) board and voluntary elementary schools	Some urban private adventure, small-scale establishments	
Lower working class	Low-fee (2d and 1d) board schools ('Schools of special difficulty' in London) Many Catholic urban schools	Ragged schools 'Dame-type' child-minding establishments	

	Day industrial schools		
	Truant schools Industrial schools Reformatory schools		Boarding

---------- High degree of permeability
────────── Relatively impermeable

aggregate, were torn at the individual level into encouraging their children to seek more secure jobs.

Some awareness of the detail of educational divisions can be garnered from Table 5.1, illustrating the complexities which had evolved by the second half of the century. Certain aspects require emphasis. One is that the most clear-cut discontinuities were not at the conventionally attributed breaks between upper, middle and working classes. By this time the upper middle classes had gained entry to the corridors of power by achieving rights of passage into the major public schools and by colonising a first grade of day grammar schools and the equivalent classical divisions of proprietary schools. A sharper break appeared between the upper middle classes and, growing in influence, the lower middle classes, whose aspirations were hindered by their sheer weight of numbers and the desire of the upper middle classes, in conjunction with the upper classes, to keep narrow the ladder of opportunity to higher positions in the state.

The division between the lower middle and upper working classes was, as already noted, highly permeable (Table 5.1). As a result, a considerable overlap in the intakes of, for example, higher elementary and third grade secondary schools occurred.[6] The respectable working class was divided from the labouring poor by another sharp break. The true 'labouring poor' ranged from the 'poor but honest', dependent on the chances of the labour market for comfortable survival, to those Booth described as 'loafers and semi-criminals'.

Thus embodied in this discussion is not a class conflict explanation, but rather a pragmatic, adaptive ecological framework, which sheds light on an influence that was characteristically English, a compulsive, individualistic quest to achieve or preserve status, as distinct from the aggregate class consciousnesses that are presumed to have been so important as determinants. In the march of history, the ecological forces made possible finely shaded and gradual, though certainly not equitable, adjustments. Among the most striking aspects of this adaptation was the territorial segregation of the different urban social groups. The fineness of the tuning was something only required and that could only be provided in the larger towns and cities.

The development of the graduation principle in English education

While the graduation principle in education reached its peak in the late nineteenth century, its roots stretched back for more than a century. Consonant with eighteenth-century concepts of the pre-ordained ranking of society, Nelson offered advice about the appropriate type of education for each of his five social groups. 'There ought to be made a considerable Difference between the Children of inferior People, and those of Rank, with regard to their Tuition.'[7]

For the nobility and gentry, a learned education was essential. This, suitably modified, was also appropriate for the genteel trades, as the commercial aspirations of the nation demanded contact between men of trade and the gentry. While applauding the social aspirations of the respectable trading classes, Nelson was much less sympathetic towards the 'ostentatious education' sought by some common tradesmen, for whom a learned education was 'needless and improper' and 'even hurtful'. Their curriculum should include the three R's, drawing and knowledge of maps, but exclude the classics and foreign languages. The lower orders were seen as having 'but a small Share either of time or Abilities for Instruction'. Nelson distinguished, however, the agricultural peasantry, who were particularly in this situation, from their peers in London, who possessed the same ignorance but not the same degree of innocence. For these, he advocated some basic education to qualify for useful employment, at the same time holding out little hope that it would reform character.[8]

The classification of Mrs Sarah Trimmer, on the other hand, related specifically to education for the lower orders. She regarded it as proper to offer an educational opportunity to all the poor, 'to rescue the lower kinds of people from that deplorable state of ignorance, in which the greatest part of them are suffered to remain', but it would not be appropriate

> to train them *all* in a way which will most probably raise their ideas above the very lowest occupations in life, and disqualify them for those servile offices, which must be filled by some members of the community, and in which they may be equally happy with the highest, if they will do their duty.[9]

It was right, she felt, that schooling should reflect the finer gradations of society, and such gradations existed even among the poorer ranks.[10] In the charity schools, however, the different grades of the poor were mixed together. Mrs Trimmer's strategy was to integrate the charity schools, schools of industry and Sunday schools into a graded system of popular provision. The *charity schools* would offer a more comprehensive tuition for the *first degree* of the lower orders, who might be trained as charity school teachers, as traders' apprentices, or as higher grade domestic servants. The day *schools of industry*, by mixing labour and learning, would be 'particularly eligible' for children who would later be employed in manufacturing industry or 'other inferior offices of life, as well as for training those who are usually called *common servants*'. The *Sunday schools* would provide religious instruction for poor children whose labour could not be spared during the week, and would also 'serve as probationary schools to try the capacities of children previous to their admission into *Charity schools*'. The charity schools would thus provide the most 'liberal instruction' that could be envisaged, for a relatively limited number of scholars from the 'superior stations of humble life'[11] in which they would be protected from contact with 'the offspring of thieves and vagabonds'.[12]

Comparable thinking persisted in influential statements even into the 1850s and 1860s. Thus in a sermon at Salisbury, James Fraser, a major contributor to the Newcastle Commission on popular education, insisted that the American 'common school' system, open to all classes, was only possible in a young society where wealth had not yet set up class barriers,[13] and Matthew Arnold promulgated the idea of class-related school provision (1863–4).[14]

The complexity of class and status differentiation by the 1860s was heightened by the increasing concentration of population in large towns and cities, and the consequential residential segregation. The variety of social and economic circumstance that characterised urban society offered the opportunity for a sophisticated gradation of schools, as an article in the *Education Reporter* indicated:

> This completeness of classification is one of the greatest makeweights afforded to a town school. The larger the town, the more complete should be the graduation of its school children for purposes of instruction, and in the largest towns the *schools themselves* should be grouped into classes. Not, however, that they may become 'class schools'. We have already had too much of that sort of thing. 'Distinctions' there should be, but not 'social' ones. Let the scholars distinguish *themselves* – not their 'order'. There will be plenty of time for the cultivation and development of caste after school life is over. We want 'schools classed' – not 'class schools'.[15]

Opinion in the 1860s was thus veering towards a meritocratic view: that the aspirations of different social groups and the needs of state justified an educational system that at all levels could develop relevant skills and promote a degree of occupational mobility.

Mass urban provision threatened, as Sarah Trimmer had anticipated, the promiscuous mixing of the lower orders of society. The Newcastle Commissioners accepted that the most intractable problem was that posed by pauper and vagrant/criminal children, to be distinguished from the 'independent poor'. These disruptive children were characteristically accommodated in the lowest class of school provided, the 'ragged school', the epithet 'ragged' having been prefixed, according to Watson, to ward off self-respecting parents.[16] Mary Carpenter had been even more uncompromising in her definition of 'ragged schools' as designed for the 'scum of the populace'. At the same time, she rated these 'vermin' as people with 'mental and bodily powers often of the first order', and also as possessing 'mortal souls' in need of rescue by the school.[17]

In taking urchin children off the streets, the educational reformers faced fearful problems, not least cosmetic ones. Montague recounts the tribulations of the early voluntary women teachers in ragged girls' classes, the habits of whose occupants must have been 'abhorrent to delicately nurtured ladies' and whose physical appearance and smell was also offensive, in a period of 'bad and incomplete water supply' and 'a tax on soap'.[18]

Another major social reformer, William Booth, painted a lugubrious picture of the consequences of introducing destitute children into the public elementary system:

> The rakings of the human cesspool are brought into the school-room and mixed up with your children. Your little ones, who never heard a foul word and who are not only innocent, but ignorant, of the horrors of vice and sin, sit for hours side by side

with little ones whose parents are habitually drunk, and play with others whose ideas of merriment are gained from familiar spectacle of the nightly debauch by which their mothers earn the daily bread.[19]

Compulsion meant sweeping more and more unkempt children into the schools, in which circumstances respectable parents were held to have the right to demand 'separate development'. The *Edinburgh Review* pointed to the need for a 'conscience clause against the contagion of infectious disease or the worse contagion of bad example'.[20] The *School Board Chronicle* contended that the schools were not the arena in which to indoctrinate 'the rising generation of the working and labouring classes with the dogma of equality'. If 'unqualified mixture of grades' caused the more well-to-do 'repugnance, indignation and rebellion', then 'some special arrangement must be made for the uncivilised'.[21]

While official opinion was slow to acquire an appreciation of the subtleties of the class structure, those working at the grass-roots had for some time been aware of distinctive and differentiated responses among working-class consumers towards education, many of them not at all negative. Thus HMI Norris, in his 1851 report on Cheshire, Staffordshire and Shropshire, attached the stereotyping of working-class attitudes to education, and urged a more sensitive reaction:

If education really be instruction in a certain curricule of book learning, it is plainly absurd to expect an illiterate set of parents to appreciate it. But is this *their* definition of education? I do not say that their's is more likely to be right than our's; the presumption is quite the other way; yet it is very possible, nay highly probable, that there may be some portion of truth in their notion, and some admixture of error in our own; enough at least to make it well worthwhile to consider attentively what their definition is.[22]

The Newcastle Commissioners were to find this type of appeal to working-class opinion useful in that, like the lower-middle-class opinion previously cited, it tended to support an instrumental view of education consistent with the terms of reference of the Commission itself, which were to see what measures, if any, were required for the provision of 'sound and cheap elementary instruction to all classes of the people'.[23]

By the 1850s, the well-to-do working, joined by the lower middle, classes were seeking educational provision at modest cost which provided useful knowledge and avoided mixing with children of the low poor. This could be achieved through private adventure schools, which some parents chose. But their uninspected nature and variability in quality discouraged their widespread use. A gap existed which was quickly plugged by voluntary school managers, particularly in the Wesleyan and 'British' school sectors, who from the 1850s sought to provide a more exclusive elementary tuition. Thus in his report to the Newcastle Commission, Ralph Lingen noted that the children attending these schools consisted 'to a very great extent, of that class which is either the top of the working class or the bottom of the shopkeeping class; and, with regard to these persons, the contribution which they make to the schools is very much represented by a graduated set of fees'.[24]

Matthew Arnold had in fact already drawn attention to this phenomenon: noting that the Wesleyans were charging the majority of pupils in their elementary schools 3d or 4d, and some up to 8d per week, thus excluding children of the poor and specifically seeking to attract the offspring of aspiring families.[25] Arnold attached no blame to the Wesleyans for such opportunism (having been given as assurance from the Wesleyan Training Institution that there was no deliberate policy in this respect), arguing that they were responding to a legitimate demand. He also felt it only to be expected that a management committee able to fill a school with children paying 4d or 6d a week would not refuse to admit them in order to find room for those able to pay only half that, thus encouraging the trend for less profitable, irregularly attending children to be 'gradually eliminated to make room for a more desirable body of scholars'.[26]

The fact that separate inspectors had been recruited to oversee British, Wesleyan and other non-Anglican and Catholic denominational schools brought this important development into the open. In his report on the eastern counties for 1858, Alderson noted that in the larger towns the nonconformist schools he visited contained most children from the small tradesman, artisan and public service groups (policemen, railway clerks, porters, etc.) and charged higher fees. The advantages of this system, he suggested, related to finance, social prestige and civilising influences. The dangers lay in the possibility of teachers devoting more time to the more 'inviting' upper part of the school, where the children were more regular, more intelligent and better behaved.[27]

J. D. Morell, covering nonconformist schools in the Lakeland counties, noted in his evidence to the Newcastle Commission the practice of raising the fees to improve the school, attracting middle-class children and driving out the poor. Another policy was to graduate the fees within the school, allowing a wider social mix lower down, but not in the higher standards. Morell was well aware that graduation of fees was promoting social differentiation. If a school charged below 3d per week, the better class of children was withdrawn, as parents of lower-middle-class and upper-working-class children were prepared to pay up to 6d per week. When asked whether the effect of this process was to 'pauperise' relatively affluent parents, he agreed that there was ambiguity in the situation. The justification was that such parents were taking up places because of the quality of education being provided, and not to evade paying for schooling.[28]

Morell interpreted the problem as deriving from the varied circumstances of parents termed 'working class'. The working people of the manufacturing districts were often as affluent as members of the lower middle classes. The only alternative to excluding children of well-paid working men from elementary schools was the cheap boarding or private adventure day school, giving an inferior education, for the better schools of this type were enormously expensive.[29]

One of the Newcastle Commission witnesses, H. S. Skeats, was, by contrast, dismayed by the thought of the middle classes taking advantage of 'the superior system of the state-aided schools', forsaking private academies. If they had the right to do this, then 'let us all assert our moral and equitable claim to be supplied, at the public expense, with broughams and horses, fine houses and furniture, the best "Havannahs", and nothing inferior to hock at lunch and champagne at dinner'.[30]

The Rev. John Scott, Principal of the Wesleyan Training College, refuted the charge that Wesleyan parents were generally more well-to-do than those of Anglican elementary scholars, though he believed that in general they had better habits and were more industrious, and therefore better off than much of the working class. The fact that they paid fees meant that the pauperisation principle did not apply. In any case, many managers asked richer parents to pay a subscription in addition to the fees, kept the same for children of all groups.[31] The Rev. William Unwin, Principal of the Congregational Training College, Homerton, argued that the idea of bringing together the children of the more affluent workers and tradesmen with poorer children was a sound one, a healthier education being produced by the blending of children of different classes. The fact that the Congregational schools had to be self-supporting meant that they needed to charge fees of at least 3d and 4d. There were, however, a few instances of fees over 6d.[32]

It was clear that a new order of school had been established for the upper-working-class/lower-middle-class fringe population, that was very much 'in the nature of a proprietary school for the lower classes', largely self-supporting, and regulated in its clientele by a general scale of fees that was beyond the means of the poor.[33]

The debate intensified in the 1860s. Graduated fees were a new mechanism of selection. Far from driving children from schools, high fees, by elementary standards, increased attendance. But a system in which relatively well-to-do parents were being subsidised out of government grant, still perceived as primarily intended for the education of the poor, continued to excite disapproval. Fearon, in his 1869 report on Liverpool and Manchester, maintained that the intentions of the 1862 Code were being neglected: 'There is reason to fear that a certain number of children *not* of the poorer, but of the lower middle classes have been reckoned among the number of scholars on the roll and in actual attendance.'

Managers, not surprisingly, found it difficult to draw the line between the social groups. The more advantaged children earned grant more easily. The inspectors appealed to managers to do their duty, but were preoccupied with supervising annual examinations, and rarely went beyond exhortation.[34]

Horace Mann, architect of the 1851 Education Census was, like Skeats, appalled at a situation which would be regarded as pauperising those above the pauper class. He feared the possibility of this being taken to its logical conclusion, with subsidised education for all classes of the community.[35]

By the time of the 1870 Act, therefore, the social pressure for a 'higher level' elementary provision was inexorable. Through the nonconformists in particular an important principle in the extension of popular education had been implanted, one that had led to, and was increasingly to foster, a hierarchy of schools within the elementary sector.

Mass elementary education had been diffused relatively successfully over the country by 1870. But the impact had not been comprehensive in the towns and cities. As we have seen, the voluntary societies, and especially the nonconformists, were moving up-market, and failing to cater for the more deprived social groups. The intention of the 1870 Act was to fill these gaps. Among the many burning questions which followed were those regularly posed by voluntaryist interests, faithfully reflected in their journal, *The School Guardian*, in articles entitled: 'What is the proper use for board schools?',[36] or 'For what class of children are our board schools intended?'.[37]

The voluntaryists took the line that as subscriptions formed a major part of their income, it was appropriate that they should attract children whose parents could afford to pay reasonable fees. If elementary schools were to be subsidised by the rates, it should be the function of rate-supported board schools to concentrate on provision for the more needy who, as *The School Guardian* in 1876 innocently observed, 'do not feel comfortable among the more orderly and well-dressed children who are found in most of our Primary Schools'.[38]

HMI Sharpe in his 1873 report drew attention to the view that the prime function of board schools would be to replace ragged schools.[39] The situation did not evolve so straightforwardly, however. Well-to-do parents soon became aware of the qualitative advantages possessed by schools resourced by the rates. School boards such as London's were by the late 1870s erecting the most ambitious elementary schools yet envisaged.[40] The *School Board Chronicle*, organ of the school boards, foresaw in 1876 that while in the early stages the voluntary sector would be able to attract the more select children, the superior resources of the board schools would later reverse this trend, already operative by the mid-1870s, as Morell noted in his report on Greenwich and the City of London (1875):

The idea which at first prevailed when the new board schools were started was that they would be filled by scholars of a lower class, driven in by the operation of the compulsory clauses, and that the voluntary school would approach somewhat to the middle-class type adapted to the requirements of those who object to the indiscriminate mixture of their own children with those of rougher description. This idea, I find, has not by any means been realised. So far from that the tendency is rather the contrary, the board school, where circumstances favour it, showing a much more decided tendency to assume a middle-class form than the others.[41]

At the same time, the urban school boards could not evade their responsibility towards the poorer groups. But this was seen as one of a number of responsibilities, and by some as a necessary evil. In the early years of the London School Board, for example, there was considerable debate as to whether 'street arab' children should be educated promiscuously with the rest. One lady member proposed 'a sort of penal or purgatorial school – something distinctly unpleasant, or at least more unattractive to the unmanageable than the best board schools'.[42] The notion of 'best board schools' enraged the voluntary sector.

The School Guardian in 1876 contended that the consequences of this policy were that the poorest children were now worse off than in the days of the ragged schools. Institutions then charging 1d a week were now demanding 3d. The boards were turning away from the neglected, with 'ambitious aims', to educate the upper portion of the working class, showing their primary object was not 'the advancement of the education of the people, but the destruction of the schools which others have provided for that purpose'.[43]

By the 1880s, voluntaryist opinion on the London School Board was making itself more strongly felt, pressing the case of 'unfair competition', accusing the board of discouraging the admission of the poor, and preferring 'to see their schools filled with well dressed and well-to-do children'. In its riposte, the *School Board Chronicle* ridiculed the 'curious notion of the institution of a poverty-meter at the threshold of every Board School'.[44]

The survey of London elementary education by Charles Booth and his team at the end of the 1880s provided a more objective appraisal. While offering an uncomfortable level of competition at the upper end of the elementary spectrum, board schools were, at the same time, sharing with the Catholic sector the burden of providing for the disadvantaged. Booth's survey made clear the variety of provision offered by the London School Board, more wide-ranging than that of the Anglican, nonconformist or Catholic sectors. He divided the elementary schools of London into six

'Classes', ranging from 'schools of special difficulty' (his Class I), an 'Educational Priority Area'-type compensatory concept introduced by the London School Board, to the Class VI schools, highly regarded by respectable parents. The three upper classes of schools, though taking a minority of the overall scholar total, attracted to themselves big majorities of skilled artisan and lower-middle-class children. At the extremes, the Class I board schools, ninety-nine in number and accommodating 110,000 children, averaged 87.8 per cent in poverty. The Class VI, only eight in number but taking over 6,000 children, had only 6.6 per cent in poverty. Class VI voluntary schools housed 100 per cent of children in comfort, while the three top categories in this sector, with approaching 100,000 children, had over 80 per cent living in comfort.[45]

Crowning the elementary hierarchy came the higher grade schools, most firmly entrenched in manufacturing centres of northern England, where secondary provision was weak. These were roughly equivalent in social terms to third grade secondary schools (see Table 5.1), but educationally were probably superior. Two basic types emerged. One could be termed the Bradford pattern, a selective one, in which the schools were located peripherally in socially respectable areas, and attracted children of 'thoughtful and better-to-do working people, the children of clerks, managers, foremen and artizans, and some of what you would class as small tradesmen – the lower middle class'.[46] The second model was exemplified by Sheffield, intended for 'deserving and clever children', who were drawn from all over the city to a centrally placed school. It catered specifically for 'higher level' elementary education, with no standards provided for below the seventh.[47] The higher grade schools were generally meshed into a scholarship system which made possible entry into secondary education. They formed an important rung in the emerging but still narrow scholarship ladder, on which mostly upper-working- and lower-middle-class children fought for position. The higher grade schools rendered almost obsolete the concept of the third grade secondary school, but were too successful for their own good. They were invalidated by the Cockerton judgement of 1899, which decided the London School Board was acting illegally in spending public money on education beyond the elementary stage. As in other areas of English education, a combination of official failure to define the upper limit of elementary education clearly, and of local initiative taking advantage of this obscurity, had led to confusion.

The inevitability of such confusion reflected the ambiguities of the 1870 Act, which set as the upper limit of elementary provision a fee of 9d per week. This was a high limit, and was determined by administrative, as representing the average per capita cost maintenance of a child at a grant-aided school, rather than by social criteria.[48] The 9d fee provided plenty of scope for the board sector to replicate the existing voluntary strategy of grading elementary schools by varying school fees.

Although in parts of the board school sector, in East Lambeth, for example, low fees were charged, this was by no means the case for London as a whole. By fits and starts, the London School Board set out to cover the whole field, from the 'gutter child' to the aspirant to secondary school scholarships. By 1873, it had provided 28,000 places, of which 23,000 were paying fees of 1d or 2d, 3,670 of 3d, 990 of 4d and 870 of 6d.[49]

By contrast, about 60 per cent of children in voluntary schools paid 3d per week, and 18 per cent 4d to 9d. This meant that the average fee per child for 78 per cent of pupils in voluntary schools was 3½d, while for 75 per cent of children in board schools it was only 1½d. In addition, in the voluntary sector in particular, fees were graduated according to the different age phases in the school, infants paying the lowest fees.

Clearly, there was a social correlation here also, for the more well-to-do children tended to be those staying on into the higher standards. The headteacher of Newcastle Wesleyan School informed the Cross Commission that his fees were 2d in the infants, 4d in standards I and II, 5d in III, 6d in IV, 7d in V, 8d in VI and 9d in VII.[50] In more general terms, by 1891, 4.8 per cent of scholars were being schooled free, 15.6 per cent were paying 1d and less than 2d, 37.0 per cent 2d and less than 3d, 25.8 per cent 3d and less than 4d, 12.9 per cent 4d and less than 6d, 2.9 per cent 6d and less than 9d and 0.8 per cent 9d and over, giving an average of about 3d per child.[51]

A crucial correlation was, therefore, between fee level and residential area. The influence of social geography was pervasive. In Manchester, for example, HMI Oakeley identified four categories of elementary schools:

1 Those on the outskirts, where more well-to-do people had moved, and where fees of 6d to 9d per week could easily be paid.
2 Schools in poorer central areas 'whose great and well-deserved reputation prevented their natural extinction when the homes of their former scholars were replaced by warehouses', and to which 'a good class of scholars attend from considerable distances'.
3 Elementary schools 'of the second grade' in stable working-class areas, where fees averaged about 4d per week.
4 Schools attended by the very poor, where the maximum fee would be 2d or 3d per week.[52]

It was in the socially less desirable districts that voluntary schools tended to retain higher status, leaving the board sector to cater for the poorer children, as the following exchange between a school board visitor and a trade union secretary, T. E. Powell, from Southwark, and the Cross Commissioners, indicates:

52,898. You said that the voluntary school had higher fees; do you find many parents preferring them on that account? – Yes, some do prefer them, because they are higher fee'd; and some prefer them because the board school is rough. When the parents make an objection at all, it is 'Well, I do not care for your board schools; they are so rough; the children are so outrageous'; and, unfortunately, they say they are so dirty; consequently, we have no choice but to send them into this school here; it is a higher fee, but we will send them.[53]

With the tacit approval of the Education Department, however, school boards established high fee schools in better residential areas. When the London School Board resolved to raise fees at the prestigious Monmow Road Board School in Bermondsey in 1880 from 4d to 6d, for example, radical groups protested. Local divisional members of the board agreed with their reasoning, but the Education Department pointed out that its aim was to secure that fees be fixed 'so as to suit the particular class of children for which a particular school may have been erected', relying on local knowledge to decide on the level of fee suitable to a locality.[54] In another part of London, Notting Hill, local tradesmen petitioned the London School Board to fix fees at the Oxford Gardens Board School, opened in 1884, at 6d per week, to keep the school select. By 1891, it was one of two London board schools at which the maximum possible fee of 9d per week was charged.[55] Not so far away, in the desperate Notting Dale slum, under the self-same public body, the fee at St Clements Road Board School, designated a 'school of special difficulty', had long been 1d.[56]

Conclusion

So the English public educational system adapted itself to the complex status divisions of tertiary society. Historically, there had been a shift from a predominantly rural society, with its impermeable 'orders' or 'estates', in which any concept of an 'education for all' was contested; to (1) in the late eighteenth and early nineteenth centuries, an industrial society in which aggregate class feeling and vertical antagonism between groups (though never, in England, a revolutionary class consciousness) was generated, and in which the idea of a dual and polarised educational provision fitted; (2) in the late nineteenth century, an amazing growth of tertiary activities, to which came to be attached a more individualistic status consciousness and a meritocratic ideology. It is this development which has provided the main stimulus to this essay. It was this that was the most characteristically urban, for much early industrialisation had in fact been semi-rural. Many early industrial towns were mere congeries of industrial villages, without a typically 'urban' range of functions. It was tertiary urban society that predicated much more complex schooling arrangements, and overrode the rudimentary split between 'the education of the rich' and 'the education of the poor'.

It is thus contended that to date the social historiography of education has concentrated too much attention on aggregate 'labour history' and the influence of industrialisation, and carried over this paradigm largely unaltered into a later phase of socio-economic evolution. By the late nineteenth century, an urban revolution was virtually complete, achieving its 'most monstrous development' in Britain, with population aggregations on a scale 'new in the history of things, to which no former time can furnish any precedent or parallel'.[57] Anxieties plagued the more respectable groups of society as the burgeoning city slums were increasingly perceived as the breeding grounds of, on the one hand, a potentially revolutionary working-class consciousness and, on the other, of likely racial decay. Social interpretations of the principles of natural selection boded no good for urban populations.[58]

At the individual level, segregation of residence was seen as critical in the process of achieving familial security and maintaining social status, a sublimated form of a basic human need for survival at an acceptable level of well-being. Propinquity of urban districts of differentiated ranking provoked deep-rooted social tensions. To a stable residential area, a contiguous, in Park's terms, 'sub-social unit', communicated 'a pervasive sense of malaise as if in the presence of something not quite understood hence always a little to be feared'.[59] Fears became tangible realities when children from 'sub-social units' appeared in the classrooms. The 'enclosure' imperative, which had generated territorially bound, socially homogeneous communities, demanded parallelism in the schools. Such grass-root forces shaped the face of English education, and not least elementary education, in the late nineteenth century. Social stratification, territorial segregation and educational gradation comprised an interactive trinity, implicated in enabling the English school system to reproduce inequality. But this had been accomplished in large part through a sophisticated, adaptive and meritocratically based correspondence between urban educational provision and socio-economic status, subtly differentiated by relating it to market forces, parental choice and the need to produce a reasonable prospect of upward mobility for the decent, thrifty and therefore deserving. It was not accomplished through the undifferentiated, stereotyped and imperative historical macro-forces of the sort we have sometimes been led to understand were predominant.[60]

NOTES

1. S. Shapin and B. Barnes, 'Head and hand: rhetorical resources in British pedagogical writing, 1770-1850', *Oxford Review of Education*, Vol. 2 (1976), 231-54.
2. J. Hurt, *Elementary Schooling and the Working Classes 1860-1918* (London: Routledge and Kegan Paul, 1979), 22.
3. W. E. Marsden, 'Ecology and nineteenth-century urban education', *History of Education Quarterly*, Vol. 23 (1983), 29-53.
4. See, for example, Anonymous, 'Reaction at the London School Board', *The Nonconformist*, Vol. 7 (New Series, 4 February 1886), 104.
5. J. L. Brereton, *County Education: A Contribution of Experiments, Estimates and Suggestions* (London: Bickers and Son, 1874), 1-5.
6. W. E. Marsden, 'Schools for the urban lower middle class: third grade or higher grade?', in P. Searby (ed.), *Educating the Victorian Middle Class* (Leicester; History of Education Society, 1982), 45-56.
7. J. Nelson, *An Essay on the Government of Children* (London: R. & J. Dodsley, 1756), 33.
8. *Ibid.*, 320, 330, 338, 344, 365-7.
9. Mrs Trimmer, *The Oeconomy of Charity*, Vol. I (London: J. Johnson *et al.*, 1801), 22-3.
10. *Ibid.*, 24.
11. *Ibid.*, 27-9.
12. *Ibid.*, 24.
13. J. Fraser, *National Education* (London: Salisbury, 1868), 7.
14. See M. Arnold, 'A French Eton, or middle-class education and the state', in G. Sutherland (ed.), *Matthew Arnold on Education* (Harmondsworth: Penguin Education, 1973), 137.
15. *Educational Reporter*, Vol. 1 (1869), 1.
16. W. Watson, *Chapters on Ragged and Industrial Schools* (Edinburgh, 1872), 9.
17. A Worker (Mary Carpenter), *Ragged Schools: Their Principles and Modes of Operation* (London: Partridge and Oakey, 1850), 3.
18. C. J. Montague, *Sixty Years of Waifdom, or, the Ragged School Movement in English History* (London: C. Murray, 1904; Woburn Press Reprint, 1968), 114-15.
19. W. Booth, *In Darkest England, and the Way Out* (London: International Headquarters, 1890), 63-4.
20. Anonymous, 'Results of the Education Act', *Edinburgh Review*, Vol. 139 (1874), 231-2.
21. *School Board Chronicle* (9 November 1872), 397.
22. *Minutes of the Committee of Council on Education* (1851-2), 730.
23. For the most part, a sympathetic view towards parental opinion was taken. See *Newcastle Commission Report* (hereafter *NC*), Vol. 1 (1861), 178.
24. *Ibid.*, Vol. 6 (1861), 6.
25. M. Arnold, *Reports on Elementary Schools 1852-1882* (London: Wyman & Sons for HMSO, 1980), 3.
26. *Ibid.*, 19-20.
27. *Reports of the Committee of Council on Education* (hereafter *RCCE*) (1858-9), 178-80.

28 *NC*, Vol. 6 (1861), 199–204.
29 *RCCE* (1861–2), 126–7.
30 *NC*, Vol. 5 (1861), 384–6.
31 *Ibid.*, Vol. 6 (1861), 256–8.
32 *Ibid.*, 290.
33 *Ibid.*, 6–7.
34 'Returns of Particulars of All Schools for the Poorer Classes of Children in the Municipal Boroughs of Birmingham, Leeds, Liverpool and Manchester', *PP* (1870), LIV, 127–8.
35 H. Mann, 'National education', *Transactions of the National Association for the Promotion of Social Science*, Bristol Meeting, 1869 (London: Longman, Reader and Dyer, 1870), 366–8.
36 Anonymous, 'What is the proper use for board schools?', *The School Guardian* (23 September 1876), 635.
37 Anonymous, 'For what class of children are our board schools intended?', *The School Guardian* (18 March 1876), 177.
38 *The School Guardian* (23 September 1876), 625.
39 *RCCE* (1873–4), 190.
40 See W. E. Marsden, 'Education and the social geography of nineteenth-century towns and cities', in D. A. Reeder (ed.), *Urban Education in the Nineteenth Century* (London: Taylor and Francis, 1977), 62–3.
41 *RCCE* (1875–6), 369–70.
42 *School Board Chronicle* (9 November 1872), 390.
43 *The School Guardian* (18 March 1876), 177.
44 *School Board Chronicle* (28 July 1883), 78 and 87.
45 See W. E. Marsden, 'Residential segregation and the hierarchy of elementary schooling from Charles Booth's surveys', *The London Journal*, Vol. 11 (1985), 127–46. Also W. E. Marsden, *Unequal Educational Provision in England and Wales: The Nineteenth-Century Roots* (London: Woburn Press, 1991), 157–72.
46 Cross Commission, *Second Report of the Royal Commission on the Working of the Elementary Education Acts*, PP (1887), XXIX, 739 and 746–7.
47 'The Higher Grade Schools in England, Their Origin, Growth and Present Condition' (First Morant Memorandum (1897)), reproduced in full in E. Eaglesham, *From School Board to Local Authority* (London: Routledge and Kegan Paul, 1956), Appendix A, 189.
48 Hurt, *Elementary Schooling*, 14.
49 *School Board Chronicle* (11 January 1873), 251.
50 Cross Commission, *Second Report*, 129.
51 *Hansard*, Vol. 354 (1890–1), col. 1902.
52 *RCCE* (1879–80), 346–7.
53 Cross Commission, *Third Report of the Royal Commission on the Working of the Elementary Education Acts*, PP (1887), XXIX, 401.
54 Letter from Education Department to London School Board dated 5 July 1881, printed in *School Board Chronicle* (16 July 1881), 31.
55 *Minutes of the London School Board* (School Management Committee), 23 July 1891, 578.
56 See Marsden, 'Education and the social geography', 59–62.

57 C. F. G. Masterman, 'The English city', in *England, a Nation: Being the Papers of the Patriots' Club* (London: Brinsley Johnson, 1904), 46–7.
58 See, for example, Anonymous, 'The danger of deterioration of race from the too rapid increase of great cities', *Transactions of the National Association for the Promotion of School Science*, Sheffield Meeting, 1865 (London: Longman, Green, 1866), 427.
59 R. E. Park, *Human Communities: The City and Human Ecology* (Glencoe, IL: Free Press, 1952), 261.
60 See W. E. Marsden, *Educating the Respectable: A Study of Fleet Road Board School, Hampstead, 1879–1903* (London: Woburn Press, 1991).

6 Compulsion, work and family: a case study from nineteenth-century Birmingham

Christine M. Heward

The introduction of compulsion

In the historical development of societies and governments, the introduction of universal compulsory school attendance is always a social and educational development of major importance affecting all families with children. The change in the emphasis in children's lives from a range of economic activities, including paid employment, to a settled period of regular school attendance represents a change in the way childhoods are valued from an economic investment to an emotional one, the process of 'sacralisation' in Zelizer's terminology.[1] Despite their interest, the effects on families of the introduction of compulsory school attendance have been largely ignored by historians. Only a few detailed studies of these problems exist and they are mostly North American.[2]

This essay presents some of the findings of a study of the decline of juvenile labour and introduction of compulsory school attendance in a particular locality, the Jewellery Quarter in Birmingham, England. This area was chosen because of its very high rates of juvenile employment and the extent and quality of its records, which include authentic testimony from children themselves about their lives in the period immediately before compulsion was introduced.

The essay begins with an outline of the background of state legislation, followed by a brief discussion of the methodology adopted for the study and a summary of the local background. The main body of the essay presents evidence about how families in the locality experienced the changing relations of home, school and work in the period under review. Because of the nature of the local economy, wages were low and irregular, juvenile employment high and many families were partly dependent on the wages of the older children. Changes in the local economy, the control of juvenile labour and the introduction of compulsory school attendance placed even greater strains on the already overstretched budgets of families with only one low, irregular wage and several young, dependent children. Parents had to pay fees for their children's education and the strategies they adopted to cope with their new responsibilities caused numerous problems for the school board officers, whose task it was to enforce the policy of compulsory school attendance for the first time.

National legislation

In England in the second half of the nineteenth century, further rapid industrialisation and urbanisation were being met by growing regulation by the state. Attempts to control juvenile and child labour had begun in 1833 and proceeded piecemeal with separate control of each trade and industry. Work in mines and the larger textile factories was controlled in the 1840s. Further regulation followed in the 1860s and 1870s, when employment of children under the age of eight was prohibited and a wider range of industries controlled.[3] Initially, compulsory school attendance was not introduced nationally. It began to be introduced in some urban areas after the 1870 Education Act, which made it possible for areas with an inadequate supply of schools to elect a school board to remedy this deficiency. School boards could levy rates to pay for their schools but all schools charged fees except in areas of extreme poverty, where a free school could be provided. School attendance could be made compulsory but since it was not free, compulsion posed problems for many families.

In 1876 a new Act extended compulsion and prohibited the employment of children under the age of ten. In 1880, school attendance was made compulsory for children between the ages of five and ten.[4] Despite these measures, enforcement was often lax. In rural areas, there was a high seasonal demand for juvenile labour by local landowners, who dominated school attendance committees, school managers' committees and magistrates. Irregularity, poor results and early leaving were persistent problems in many schools. Agricultural workers' wages were particularly low. The problem posed by school fees for large families on such low wages and the seasonal demands for juvenile labour in many trades contributed to continued irregular attendance and early leaving.[5]

Most of the larger urban areas had considerable deficiencies of school provision and elected school boards soon after the 1870 Education Act. A number of these school boards pursued vigorous policies, building schools and introducing and enforcing attendance. The problems they encountered after compulsion was introduced were considerable. Urban populations at this period contained large sections living in poverty, who were also very mobile. In a number of areas, there were opportunities for juvenile labour and in others, few good schools. For all these reasons, especially poverty, sending children to school was not a very high priority for some families. Parents often taught their children the rudiments of literacy themselves at home or sent them to a local dame school, when the demands of local labour markets and exigencies of domestic budgets permitted. For the poorest families, finding suitable jobs for their children was more important than sending them to school.[6]

Methodology and sources

Reconstructing the effects of the introduction of compulsory school attendance upon the poorer sections of the working classes presents a number of problems. Apart from the accumulating corpus of autobiographies and diaries, there is little authentic evidence of family life among the working classes. Despite the fact that in the middle of the nineteenth century nearly half of the population was under the age of twenty-one, children and juveniles remain, like women, 'hidden from history'. Investigating these problems thus demands a methodology which can exploit every method and source to the full. Quantitative and archival methods have, therefore, been used 'interactively', feeding into each other to check, corroborate and extend the findings. The richest sources of evidence giving details of home, school and work of every individual for wealthy and poor alike is the decennial census.

In 1851, the householders' schedule said: 'Against the children above 5 years of age, if daily attending school, or receiving tuition under a master or governess at home, write "Scholar" and in the latter case add "at home".'[7] The same instruction was given in 1861 and 1871, with the exclusion of the instruction about 'under five' and 'at home'. A picture of education in the twenty years before compulsion can thus be gained from the census evidence. The census enumerators' returns also contain information about age, occupation and birthplace and the household to which he or she belonged for every child except those who had been born and had died in the intercensal period. The reliability of the census is considered to be very high and ways of processing and analysing it are well established.[8]

In order to provide an intensive study of the effects of compulsion in the Jewellery Quarter, a cluster sample was taken. Seven streets in the Jewellery Quarter were chosen and the census enumerators' returns for 1851, 1861, 1871 and 1881 were coded into machine-readable form and analysed. The composition of the sample is shown in Table 6.1, which shows the declining population caused by the move to the suburbs led by the middle classes.

An excellent collection of rate books has been preserved in the Birmingham Reference Library, showing properties in street order with the names of owners, rateable values and estimated rentals. After 1870, the names of occupiers are also given. As far as possible, the rate book information has been linked with that in the census. An address has a social status. Social

Table 6.1. *The sample streets*

Households	1851	1861	1871	1881
Vyse Street	69	90	89	85
Northwood Street	172	150	187	157
Water Street	122	104	86	70
Cox Street	77	82	96	66
St Paul's Square	61	33	31	33
Caroline Street	70	68	60	42
Mount Street	107	95	116	35
Total	678	622	665	488

Source: Christine Heward, 'Home, school and work: changes in growing up in the Birmingham Jewellery Quarter, 1851–1881' (MA dissertation, Warwick University, 1985).

Table 6.2. *Mean rateable values of the sample streets* (Expressed in shillings)

Households	1851	1861	1871	1881
Vyse Street	385	414	608	510
Northwood Street	143	148	148	159
Water Street	151	126	124	116
Cox Street	147	136	148	156
St Paul's Square	301	446	639	596
Caroline Street	413	432	518	525
Mount Street	235	218	214	188

Source: Heward, 'Home, school and work.'

class was assigned by ranking the mean rateable values of the streets. Higher rateable values indicate large properties at desirable addresses and low values indicate mean properties in undesirable slum areas. As Table 6.2 shows, ranking the mean rateable values gives a consistent picture with the same three streets at the top, Mount Street in the middle and the same three streets at the bottom. The quantitative study has shown changes in the incidence of working, going to school and staying at home in the population, in the period immediately before and after compulsion was introduced for two social class groups.

The archival study of Parliamentary Papers and local sources has made use of a uniquely valuable source, the 200 interviews conducted with children at work in the Jewellery Quarter in 1863 by J. E. White, a barrister, for the Children's Employment Commission.

105. Henry Aston age 11. Think I am 11. Mind machinery pliers for drawing tubes. Work from 6 til 5½. Breakfast here, dine at home. Work with uncle he reckons for me get 4s. a week, and sometimes 1d. or 1½d. of it for myself.

Do not go to Sunday or night-school now perhaps I shall. Father says he shall buy me some clothes, and I shall go to night-school and all.[9]

Other official inquiries concentrate on the views of opinion leaders. This unparalleled evidence from the children themselves may be dismissed as lurid tales collected by earnest men committed to reform, who wished to shock and shame public opinion into enforcing a change. The evidence collected in the Jewellery Quarter is fresh, liberally interspersed with intimate details of family and work, dialect words and local usages.

The value of the Children's Employment Commission lies in the detailed evidence given of home, school and work for families in the Jewellery Quarter. Much of it is in their own words, expressing their point of view.

The majority of the households in the Jewellery Quarter lived in overcrowded conditions in back to back houses round court-yards, sharing a communual yard, water supply and privy.[10] In the period under review, many families also worked at home, exacerbating the problem of lack of space and disposal of waste. In the 1860s the pearl button makers were facing severe problems because of competition from factory-produced linen buttons and the loss of the American market with the Civil War. One such family, visited by Mr White in the course of his inquiries, were the Lanes who lived 'in great poverty' in New Summer Street. Their court-yard had two open drains and was full of refuse and pieces of pearlshell. William Lane, his wife Rebecca claimed, had been in the trade thirty-three years and was almost the oldest master alive. There had been 700 in the trade, but it was reduced to less than half, the others having 'died, gone for soldiers, in the workhouse or scattered about'. Of the eight or nine they had employed, there were now only two women and her daughter. Bringing up children in such conditions presented many problems. Emma Lane, Rebecca's granddaughter, began work at the age of ten 'sorting blanks up in the attic'. She went on to the lathe at the age of eleven. Despite the fact that she had learned it well, by the age of twelve she could only make 1s 6d a week. She had been to school for a short period, when she was nine, but she was dismissive of her schooling, having 'forgot all my reading. Never did any writing or figures. They used to try to learn me, and I learned as well as I could ... I was one as never took much notice, and I'd not go in till near 10 and came out at half past'.[11] John C. Holley has shown that semi-skilled workers' families used short-term strategies, including sending children out to work.[12]

The study combines archival and statistical evidence about the changing social and economic structure with the testimony of parents and children about how they experienced it, within conceptual frameworks focusing on household economies.[13]

The town of Birmingham

The history of Birmingham is one of very distinctive social and economic development and traditions, based on the hundreds of small workshops of skilled craftsmen in the metal trades. Its cultural, educational and political heritage was based on the strength of leading dissenting families, who in 1869 launched a national campaign for universal free, compulsory education, which resulted in the 1870 Education Act. Birmingham, therefore, played a leading part in the introduction of compulsory school attendance nationally and was one of the foremost towns in its initiation and implementation.[14]

The town of Birmingham had early established itself as a leading centre in the manufacture of multifarious small metal goods, many requiring skilled craftsmanship. It became known as the 'Town of a Thousand Trades' and the 'Toyshop of Europe' after the thousands of metal trinkets made in its hundreds of small workshops from Tudor times. By the nineteenth century, there were four leading manufactures, of buttons, guns, jewellery and brass, and a host of others including japanned goods, edge tools, pots and pans, pins, glass, percussion caps and cartridges and all types of wire products. Many trades, like buttons, were very diverse. Plainer goods, mainly metal and cloth buttons, were made in huge quantities in factories by means of hand presses operated by women and girls. Specialist work, box wood, horn, glass and pearl buttons, was all made in small workshops by craft methods of production, characterised by a minute division of labour. Some trades, especially jewellery and guns, were fragmented into a large number of different specialist crafts, and goods were taken from one workshop to another by errand boys, who carried very heavy loads in the gun trades. These two trades were concentrated in particular localities, the Jewellery Quarter in St Paul's, to the north-west of the town, near to the Assay Office, established in 1773, and the gun trade round the Proof House. Domestic workshops were the foundation of the town's industrial organisation and prosperity. Samuel Timmins, editor of a monumental survey of industry in the area, described the process:

Beginning as a small master, often working in his own house, with his wife and children to help him, the Birmingham workman has become a master, his buildings have increased. He has used his house as a workshop, has annexed another, has built up in the garden or the yard, and consequently a large number of the manufactures are most irregular in style.[15]

In the third quarter of the nineteenth century, there was only a small number of factories in the town and most people worked in small workshops, many with family, kin or neighbours, producing small metal goods by means of hand stamping machines or presses or by craft methods. The linchpin of the commercial organisation of the town was a group of factors who financed and co-ordinated production, selling the output to merchants. The small workshops were linked in an elaborate network of interrelated production but they also competed for work from the factors.

The labour market in Birmingham was very large, free and highly mobile, varying from the most highly skilled craftsmen like gem setters and engravers to women and juveniles, taking in outwork. Almost all workers in Birmingham were paid on piecework rates. Differentials were very high. Skilled craftspeople in buoyant trades like jewellery could command high wages, whereas those in declining trades and the semi-skilled earned very much less and outwork was often paid at sweated rates. Earnings in some trades, like jewellery and buttons, were also subject to seasonal variations in trade and the vagaries of fashion. Hours also fluctuated with trade. Workers on piecework in small workshops controlled their own hours, often working extremely long hours for four or five days and resting for two days. In Birmingham, the demand for juvenile and women's labour was high because it was cheap and the minute division of labour created suitable jobs especially for boys.

Small children were often taken to work by their parents, siblings or neighbours as 'helps'. This practice was particularly common in the button factories, where the young children sat opposite the women and girls operating the hand presses to feed in the raw materials. Child 'helps' had several advantages for poorer families. In trades like the button trades, where piecework rates were low, a higher rate of production and earnings was possible. Taking children to work also enabled wives to work and kept the children out of mischief.[16]

Juvenile labour

The consequence of the prevalence of piecework, low and irregular wages and high juvenile employment was that many families were dependent upon the wages of their older children. The period when there was only one wage and several young dependent children was one of very great strain. At this stage in the family cycle there was great pressure to get the older children out to work. Older children also minded the younger ones so that wives could work, and wives and children took in outwork.

The quantitative study shows the great significance of children in households in working-class streets and the extent of the problem posed by

Table 6.3. *Household composition*

	1851		1861		1871		1881	
	Middle class	Working class	Middle class	Working class	Middle class	Working class	Middle class	Working class
Single persons and married couples	4.5	8.0	10.0	12.0	4.0	8.0	16.0	16.0
Married couples or widows with children	21.0	49.0	22.0	55.0	19.0	49.0	34.0	51.0
Households with servants	41.0	7.5	30.0	2.5	44.0	7.5	18.0	2.5
Households with boarders or lodgers	4.0	16.0	7.0	15.0	2.0	16.0	9.0	15.5
Households with kin or visitors	9.0	14.0	11.5	10.5	8.0	14.5	9.0	13.5
Households with two more of kin, servants, boarders, lodgers, visitors	20.5	6.0	19.5	5.0	23.0	5.0	14.0	3.5
Number of cases	200	478	191	431	180	485	160	328

Source: Heward, 'Home, school and work'.

dependent children in such households. Table 6.3 shows that in all four census years at least half of the households in working-class streets were married couples or widowed parents with their children, and only 43 per cent in 1851, 33 per cent in 1861, 43 per cent in 1871 and 35 per cent in 1881 had non-nuclear members.

In households in the middle-class streets the position was nearly reversed. In 1851, 75 per cent, in 1861 68 per cent, in 1871 77 per cent, in 1881 50 per cent had servants, boarders, lodgers, visitors or kin. While there were no significant class differences in household size, servants were a very important discriminator between the households of the two social classes. A fifth of the households in the middle-class streets had at least two different non-nuclear members, except in 1881. Households in middle-class streets were, therefore, much more heterogeneous than those in working-class streets, which were overwhelmingly nuclear. Children were a larger and more significant part of households in working-class streets, whereas non-nuclear members were more significant in middle-class streets.

The implication of these differences for domestic economies was that children were the most important group of dependants for households in working-class streets, whereas households in middle-class streets had a greater variety of dependants in terms of age and relationship to the

Table 6.4. *Economic composition of households*

	1851 Middle class	1851 Working class	1861 Middle class	1861 Working class	1871 Middle class	1871 Working class	1881 Middle class	1881 Working class
Mean number of dependants aged 13 and over	3.4	2.4	3.1	2.6	3.0	2.3	2.7	2.4
Mean number of dependant children	1.3	1.3	1.2	1.4	1.0	1.32	1.1	1.32
Ratio of dependants under the age of 13 to household size	0.12	0.22	0.19	0.24	0.15	0.23	0.16	0.23
Ratio of adult dependants to household size	0.27	0.21	0.28	0.25	0.31	0.21	0.27	0.21
Number of cases	200	478	191	431	180	485	160	328

Source: Heward, 'Home, school and work'.

household head. These differences are clearly shown in Table 6.4. Medick has argued that in the early phase of industrialisation, families worked as teams in domestic production. The domestic budget depended upon 'the maximal utilisation of the family workforce'. In the early years, children posed a dilemma for such a strategy. As babies, they were not only dependent but also prevented mothers from working. Once old enough, they could work and contribute to the family budget.[17] The pace of industrialisation was uneven. Steam power was still little developed in Birmingham in 1850. The use of juvenile labour in craft production by means of a very complex division of labour was widespread. It seems likely that the demand for juvenile labour in Birmingham was much greater than in most localities where the demand for jobs especially for girls often exceeded supply.[18]

Young people in the Jewellery Quarter did three main kinds of work. First, there was the production of light metal objects by hand- and power-operated machines, pressing, stamping and machine-minding; secondly, there were the industrial processes, where boys worked, plating, brass casting and rolling mills; and thirdly, there were girls' occupations, lacquering, japanning, millinery and dressmaking. The Children's Employment Commission figures in Table 6.5 show the distribution of young people among these occupations.

Much of the work which boys and girls did was repetitive, monotonous and low paid. Hours were long and conditions poor. Boys did a greater

Table 6.5. *Occupations in Birmingham*

Occupations	Males under 20 years	Females under 20 years	Totals
Brass-founding	2,380	— ⎱	3,360
Lacquering and pens	—	980 ⎰	
Other, included wire, gas-fittings, &c.	1,650	—	1,650
Buttons	550	1,300	1,850
			6,860
Jewellers	1,500	800	2,300
Gems	1,750	—	1,750
Iron, screws, &c.,	1,650	680	2,330
Machine and tools	1,050	—	1,050
Steel pins	—	530	530
Plate	510 ⎱	—	730
Tin	220 ⎰		
Errands	1,080 ⎱	—	1,820
Warehouses	740 ⎰		
Millinery, dressmaking, etc.	—	1,090	1,090
	13,080	5,380	18,460

Source: Children's Employment Commission, *3rd Report*, PP (1864), XXI.

variety of jobs than girls. As in other areas, there may have been a shortage of girls' jobs.[19] The commonest job for boys was brass casting, where they were employed by the casters themselves, to prepare the moulds, blow the scum off the top after pouring and run errands. Boys started at 3s 6d. to 4s 0d and earned 6s 0d to 8s 0d at the age of fourteen or fifteen. Brass casting had the reputation of being 'the worst job in Birmingham'. Because of the effects of heat, dust and fumes upon their chests and lungs, casters did not expect to live after forty. William Mountford began work as a boy in brass casting, working for a neighbour, who 'lived next door to we and had been bad a long time, used to spit blood and choke. He died about 36, the nighest I could guess', he told Mr White. The work did not suit William, who felt giddy and coughed a great deal. He left casting after a fortnight and went to work as a packer in the same factory as his father.[20]

Girls' work was confined to a narrower range of trades: millinery, dressmaking, pen making, percussion cap making, japanning and lacquering. The latter two trades involved applying colourless or black varnish to metal articles like trays and bedsteads. The articles were then placed in stoves to dry them. The heat of the stoves was intense and the work hot, dirty, smelly and dangerous. Much of it was done in small domestic workshops. In 1863, Fanny Boyne and Ellen Bond worked together in the lacquering room at Mr Toy's stamping and piercing shop in Regent's Parade in the Jewellery Quarter. Mr White described it as 'low and extremely hot, containing three lacquering stoves and hot places, one of them very large ... most of the work being done on the heated surface'.

Ellen was then thirteen years of age, the youngest in the lacquering room. She lacquered 'photographic plates sitting close beside the stove'. Fanny was fourteen and she saw to the fires, the job Ellen had done before Fanny started at Mr Toy's. Both girls found the work hot, tiring and debilitating. They complained of aching bodies, headaches, sore throats and frequent colds. All the girls caught colds, Fanny said, because 'its sweating in the room and going out in the cold air gives it them'. She always put a cloak and hat on in the summer and a thick cloak in the winter to go home.[21] Wages for older girls and women in lacquering and japanning were 8s to 10s a week.[22] By working, even for such low wages, Fanny and Ellen enabled their families to supplement one low wage with several others, which were equally low and irregular. As John Kimbley, a wire drawer, at Goode's a jewellers in St Paul's Square, told Mr White, 'Father gets such low wages, 10s or 12s or 14s a week and there are nine of us. I get 9s a week, one of my brothers, 19s another 15s and another 6s.'[23]

The importance of work in the lives of children and the changes which were taking place in the period before compulsion was introduced and enforced is demonstrated in the quantitative study of the sample. Table 6.6 shows that boys in working-class streets generally started work earliest in all three census years indicated. Boys in middle-class streets also went out to work in great numbers but started work later than their working-class peers. Except for the boys in middle-class streets in 1851, 90 per cent or over of boys were at work in the sixteen- to twenty-year-old age group. The table underestimates the number of girls from working-class streets at work. Servants, who were working-class girls living in middle-class streets, have been excluded. Undoubtedly, some girls would have left the working-class streets to become servants. However, we do not know how many in total or how many from the other groups had left home to seek work. Girls from working-class streets also went out to work in great numbers, starting work later than their brothers. Middle-class girls differed from all the other groups. The majority did not go to work as frequently, their lives being more home-oriented. The quantitative study shows that for the families in the sample, work was determined by social class and gender, thus confirming the conclusions from the study of the local economy and the Children's Employment Commission.

The table also shows that the age of starting work was postponed between

Table 6.6. *Percentage of children at home, school and work before compulsion*

Age	At work	At school	At home	No. of cases
		1851		
		Middle-class boys		
0–5	0	27	73	66
6–10	4	74	22	50
11–15	51	40	9	43
16–20	77	9	14	43
		Middle-class girls		
0–5	0	25	75	75
6–10	7	77	16	44
11–15	10	68	22	31
16–20	33	3	64	36
		Working-class boys		
0–5	0	16	84	194
6–10	11	60	29	150
11–15	72	16	12	130
16–20	96	2	2	104
		Working-class girls		
0–5	1	15	84	200
6–10	13*	48	39	123
11–15	48*	20	31	143
16–20	80*	2	18	120
		1861		
		Middle-class boys		
0–5	0	19	81	65
6–10	0	72	28	43
11–15	31	52	17	29
16–20	90	7	3	30
		Middle-class girls		
0–5	0	28	72	58
6–10	0	71	29	41
11–15	9	56	35	45
16–20	26	3	71	31
		Working-class boys		
0–5	0	18	82	187
6–10	9	45	46	130
11–15	60	10	30	103
16–20	94	0	6	108
		Working-class girls		
0–5	0	14	86	171
6–10	7*	41	52	140
11–15	39*	18	43	102
16–20	67*	0	33	96

Table 6.6. (cont.)

Age	At work	At school	At home	No. of cases
		1871		
		Middle-class boys		
0–5	0	15	85	48
6–10	0	78	22	40
11–15	33	45	22	40
16–20	93	0	7	40
		Middle-class girls		
0–5	0	23	77	44
6–10	6	46	48	35
11–15	17	63	20	30
16–20	39	9	52	44
		Working-class boys		
0–5	0	11	89	171
6–10	2	35	63	121
11–15	63	16	21	129
16–20	98	0	2	101
		Working-class girls		
0–5	0	9	91	181
6–10	0*	38	62	133
11–15	39*	20	40	109
16–20	82*	2	16	114

Note: * This underestimates the percentage working because servants are *not* included.
Source: Heward, 'Home, school and work'.

1851 and 1871 for all four groups in the sample. The decline of child labour was part of a series of changes which were taking place in the local economy in the third quarter of the nineteenth century. The balance of the four leading industries changed. Jewellery expanded rapidly and divided into two sectors, cheap jewellery, made in small factories employing forty to fifty people, which were built on the northern fringe of the Jewellery Quarter, and the expensive items, which continued to be made in small workshops by skilled craftspeople. The brass trade also expanded with the development of the railway, gas supplies and improved sanitation. Guns and buttons both contracted and wage rates in these trades were depressed. Workshops began to give way to factories and steam power was increasingly used in the pen, screw and pin factories. This depressed the small workshops using older technologies, especially craft methods, which could only survive in high-value goods like jewellery. The effects of the great depression after 1876 were also very uneven, being worst in the gun trade, and this emphasised the changes further.[24]

The Workshops Act of 1867 restricted the employment of women and juveniles in workshops employing less than fifty people. It was not enforced by the Factory Inspectors but by local sanitary authorities, some of whom were slow to take up their powers. Children under the age of eight could not be employed, those between eight and thirteen were employed half-time and were required to go to school. Women and juveniles could not be employed after 6.00 p.m. Because married women had to get their children off to school in the morning, they could neither go to work early nor stay late and were forced into outwork.[25] The prohibition of child labour increased the cost of juveniles over the age of thirteen.

The changes produced a rise in wages and standards of living but this was very unevenly spread. It was highest among the skilled jewellery crafts, where 'it is a poor workman who makes only 25s, 30s to 50s being considered more the average wages'.[26] The rises in other trades were more modest. W. J. Davis, secretary of the Amalgamated Society of Brassworkers, told the Select Committee inquiring into the working of the Factory and Workshops Acts in 1875 that brass workers had gained a 15 per cent rise, but the 'rise in provisions has taken the whole of that away'.[27] The rise in women's wages had not been as great as those of men and boys; in many trades they had remained static. Some trades were in decline and wages and standards of living fell. As we have already seen from the example of the Lanes, the pearl button workers were in acute distress. John Watson, secretary to the Pearl Button Makers' Society, told Mr White in 1863 that the society had negotiated a rise of a farthing (¼d) a gross with the factors, but two-thirds of their former trade had been lost because of the American Civil War: 'pearl button makers are in the same case as people in many other trades. They are so poor that children must be sent to work as soon as they are able to earn anything.'[28]

The changes in the local economy which took place during the period when compulsory school attendance was introduced, therefore, helped some families to cope with the strain of dependent children upon domestic economies, but it was exacerbated for others.

One of the children who clearly touched Mr White's heart was Emma Clark, who was ten or eleven years old in 1863 and worked as a 'help' in a button factory. She and her younger sister took home 1s 6d each to add to their parents' wages. Her father was a pearl button worker and her mother worked in a percussion cap factory.[29] Percussion caps were used for priming guns. The work was dirty and extremely dangerous because of the instability of the compound used to fill the caps. The frequent explosions and high death rates in the percussion cap factories in Birmingham had fuelled agitation for greater control of juvenile and women's labour. The work was low paid and the trade had been greatly affected by the decline in the gun trade. For families in this trade, the decline and control of child labour and the introduction of compulsory school attendance posed very real problems. Sending children to a day school regularly was beyond their means. Indeed, education was a low priority, after rent, food, clothing and fuel.

Educational traditions among the working classes in the Jewellery Quarter were based on family instruction, self-improvement and Sunday schools. For them, education was a life-long pursuit in which a variety of means was used as and when they could take advantage of them. Education was not confined to childhood or to schools. Family instruction by parents and older siblings was common among the children interviewed by Mr White in 1863. Esther Bubb, who sometimes 'made her eighteen pence' at Ludlow's Percussion Cap Factory in Legge Street, told him how her father supervised her brother hearing the younger children 'say and spell'. The family Bible was very important in the Bubb household for it contained 'us names in, when we was born'. Both her father and brother read from it to the rest of the family, although its seems that her mother was illiterate.[30]

Groups of workmates also gathered together in break times for recreation and self-improvement. Libraries were provided by certain firms which encouraged these traditions among working people. Reading and writing for the working classes was associated as much with family recreation, religious experience and political organisation as with school knowledge. Education was therefore pursued as a life-long activity in many different situations. Older people were sometimes reluctant to join classes in which younger people might witness their struggles to make sense of the printed word. Among those interviewed by Mr White, the Quaker First Day Schools in Severn Street had an excellent reputation for teaching adults. One woman learned to read in a year there, much to her employer's astonishment. Carrying on the traditions of family instruction, she was 'learning' her husband.[31]

Most children, like Emma Lane, did have a brief period at school before they started work. The quantitative study shows that school attendance fluctuated widely during the period under review and that between seven and nine was the most popular age for sending children to school in the working-class streets. Table 6.7 shows that school attendance among children from the middle-class streets remained very stable and that of the children from working-class streets appears to decline markedly in 1871. While starting work had been postponed in the period, this does not appear to have resulted in a rise in school attendance. The most dramatic feature of the table is the large rise between 1851 and 1871 in the number of children from working-class streets who were at home. These figures may not indicate a large decrease in school attendance, which fluctuated widely, depending to a considerable extent on the state of trade. Attendance was

Table 6.7. *Percentage of children at home, school and work before compulsion*

	Age				
	5–6	7–8	9–10	11–12	13–14
			1851		
			Boys		
Middle-class streets					
At home	31	23	22	12	10
At work	—	—	9	29	65
At school	69	77	69	59	25
	no. = 16	no. = 22	no. = 23	no. = 17	no. = 20
Working-class streets					
At home	43	30	24	16	9
At work	3	4	24	60	79
At school	54	66	52	24	12
	no. = 63	no. = 64	no. = 50	no. = 57	no. = 56
			Girls		
Middle-class streets					
At home	21	8	25	10	9
At work	—	7	8	16	67
At school	79	85	67	74	24
	no. = 19	no. = 13	no. = 24	no. = 19	no. = 21
Working-class streets					
At home	40	45	38	35	23
At work	—	10	24	39	61
At school	60	45	38	26	16
	no. = 57	no. = 49	no. = 45	no. = 66	no. = 56
			1861		
			Boys		
Middle-class streets					
At home	36	38	21	20	25
At work	—	—	—	—	33
At school	64	62	79	80	42
	no. = 22	no. = 13	no. = 19	no. = 10	no. = 12
Working-class streets					
At home	58	42	43	38	20
At work	—	2	21	42	78
At school	42	56	36	20	2
	no. = 50	no. = 57	no. = 53	no. = 45	no. = 41
			Girls		
Middle-class streets					
At home	41	22	39	35	21
At work	—	—	—	9	37
At school	59	78	61	56	42
	no. = 17	no. = 18	no. = 18	no. = 23	no. = 19

Table 6.7. (cont.)

	Age				
	5–6	7–8	9–10	11–12	13–14
Working-class streets					
At home	61	58	47	49	37
At work	—	—	22	32	46
At school	39	42	31	19	17
	no. = 54	no. = 66	no. = 45	no. = 43	no. = 46

1871
Boys

	5–6	7–8	9–10	11–12	13–14
Middle-class streets					
At home	22	25	23	25	11
At work	7	—	—	12	50
At school	71	75	77	63	39
	no. = 14	no. = 20	no. = 13	no. = 16	no. = 18
Working-class streets					
At home	62	65	57	30	14
At work	—	—	6	39	80
At school	38	35	37	31	6
	no. = 45	no. = 48	no. = 49	no. = 51	no. = 56

Girls

	5–6	7–8	9–10	11–12	13–14
Middle-class streets					
At home	53	60	35	25	11
At work	6	—	10	8	42
At school	41	40	55	67	47
	no. = 17	no. = 5	no. = 20	no. = 12	no. = 19
Working-class streets					
At home	61	61	65	47	39
At work	—	—	2	21	53
At school	39	39	33	32	8
	no. = 49	no. = 62	no. = 79	no. = 53	no. = 39

Source: Heward, 'Home, school and work'.

always low in February when many outdoor workers like brickmakers, bricklayers and labourers were unemployed because of the weather, and industrial workers were laid off because of stock taking. June was the best time of year for school attendance.[32]

Sending a number of children to school regularly represented a very considerable cost for parents. First of all, it was a 'double cost' in the sense that parents had to do without their children's wages. Secondly, parents had to pay school pence. Thirdly, the costs of schooling had to be found during the period when family budgets were under the greatest strain. Schools in

Table 6.8. *Results of the Birmingham Education Society survey, 1868*

	⅔	No.
At school at the time of the inquiry	38	17,023
At work at the time of the inquiry	14	6,337
Neither at school nor work	48	21,696
Could read and write	30	13,380
Could read only	12	5,482
Could neither read nor write	58	26,194

Source: Birmingham Education Society, *1st Annual Report* (Birmingham, 1868).

Birmingham charged 3d or 4d a week in the period before compulsion.[33] Only the Ragged School at Bishop Ryder's Church in Staniforth Street was free. 'Respectable' working-class parents generally did not wish their children to mix with the 'street arabs', nor did they willingly accept the stigma of being ragged. Parents had therefore to find a fourth cost, their children's clothing, if they were to be sent to school regularly. Clothes were potent symbols of poverty and respectability. Many children told Mr White that they did not go to school because they had no suitable clothes.[34] Schools were part of a social hierarchy and the way their pupils dressed was an important indicator of their social and moral standards and standing in the community. Sending children to school, therefore, required a regular and relatively high wage, which many families in the Jewellery Quarter and other working-class districts in Birmingham did not have at this time.

This conclusion is supported overwhelmingly by the results of the survey carried out by the Birmingham Education Society in 1867 (Table 6.8). They canvassed 754 of the 1,027 streets in the borough of Birmingham, omitting the 273 'of a class that does not require visiting'. They visited 45,056 children between the ages of three and fifteen.

The Society's purpose was to enable children to go to school by paying the fees of those who could not afford them, through a system of means tested orders. They therefore inquired very fully into the domestic budgets of the families they canvassed, and whether or not parents wished their children to go to school.

In order to show the effects of poverty on school attendance they calculated the rent, and income left after rent, of three sorts of families: those who did not need the Society's help, those who did and those in dire need, the widows (Table 6.9). They picked random samples of these cases from their returns.

This evidence shows quite clearly that the families who did not need the

Table 6.9. *Results of the Birmingham Education Society survey, 1869*

300 families aided by the Society	
Total number of persons	1,842
Average income per head per week, after deducting rent	1s 1¼d
Rent per head per week	0s 5¼d
Total number of children of all ages	1,322
Number of children at school	31
Number at work above 15 years old	334
Neither at work nor school above 15 years	28
Number at work below 15 years old	79
Number neither at work nor at school between 3 and 15 years old	440
Under 3 years old	410
300 families not aided by Society	
Total number of persons	1,970
Income per head per week, after deducting rent	1s 10¼d
Rent per head per week	0s 5¼d
Number of children of all ages	1,400
Number of children at school	240
Number at work above 15 years old	341
Number at work below 15 years	76
Neither at work nor at school, above 3 years old	461
Number under 3 years of age	282
80 families with widowed heads	
Total number of persons	494
Average income per head per week, after deducting rent	0s 10¼d
Rent per head per week	0s 5¼d
Total number of children of all ages	414
Number of children at school	4
Number at work under 15 years old	90
Number at work above 15 years old	64
Neither at work nor school above 15 years old	18
Number neither at school nor at work between 3 and 15 years old	174
Under 3 years of age	64

Source: Birmingham Education Society *2nd Annual Report* (Birmingham, 1869).

Society's aid had higher incomes per head, a larger number of their children at school and a lower number of children under the age of three to support than those who did need the Society's help. The widowed heads present a picture of abject poverty, extremely low income per head and fewer children at school.

In the Society's view, their evidence showed, 'for the most part, the very poor have their energies and attention too fully engaged in obtaining bread, to think of sparing anything towards their children's schooling. In very many poor families, where sickness and infirmity exist, the Society's aid is absolutely indispensable if the children are to be taught at all'.[35]

The 1870 Education Act

As a result of these and other demonstrations of the ineffectiveness of educational provision and the rapidly changing balance of political forces at this period, the leading members of the Birmingham Education Society founded the National Education League (NEL) early in 1869. They were all members of the extreme radical wing of the newly powerful Liberal Party and they were all dissenters, with the exception of George Dixon, the mayor of Birmingham and one of its Members of Parliament. In October 1869, the League launched a national campaign for universal, free, compulsory elementary schools, supported by a local rate, a policy which commanded wide support in the country and strong opposition in the House of Commons.[36] The League's leading spokesmen were George Dixon in the House of Commons and Joseph Chamberlain outside it. Chamberlain was then a young and ambitious radical Liberal, for whom the League was a springboard from local to national politics.

The leaders of the League were vigorous in their pursuit of popular support. Working men's auxiliaries were formed and trades councils and trades unions were encouraged to affiliate to it. Working men never held office in the League, however, nor were they selected as candidates in the early school board elections. For the dissenting leaders of the League, the principal issue was denominational supremacy. They wished to limit the power of the Church of England National Society by ensuring that control over all schools was vested in a publicly elected body, which they believed they, as the majority in the town, would dominate.

At meetings of groups like the Working Men's Auxiliary, the most important issue was that the new schools should be free. Working-class leaders believed that many children were not at school because their parents could not afford the school fees and that the number not at school was so large that compulsion was the only way to solve the problem, but it could only be introduced if the schools were free.[37]

In the event, the Education Bill published in February 1870 was a bitter disappointment to the League and its supporters. Strenuous efforts were made on the floor of the House of Commons by George Dixon and his colleagues in the NEL to amend the Bill to provide for free compulsory school attendance. Both clauses were heavily defeated, free education by 257 to 32 and direct compulsion by 259 to 92.[38] The size of these votes was a telling indication of the difference between the views of working people, who were to be affected by the Bill, and the legislature in power over them.

The Education Act of 1870 provided for the election of *ad hoc* school boards in districts with a deficiency of educational provision. The boards had the right to levy rates to support their schools and were composed of between five and fifteen members, elected on a unique system, which safeguarded minority interests by allowing voters to plump all their five or more votes for a single candidate. In Birmingham, the Roman Catholic minority used this facility to advantage and their candidate regularly topped the poll.

The school boards had the power to introduce compulsion by passing bye-laws, if they chose. Schools under the control of the school boards had to charge fees of up to 9d a week. Clause 25 of the Act permitted the payment of fees for indigent children from the rates, at either voluntary schools or those under the board's control.[39] Free schools could be built in exceptionally poor areas.

The first school board in Birmingham

The first school board elections in Birmingham took place in December 1870. The League misunderstood the effects of the plumping system and the Church of England Party was in the majority. Joseph Chamberlain and George Dixon had undistinguished positions, Chamberlain narrowly avoiding defeat. As the school board elections were triennial events, the League had to endure three years of impotence in its stronghold, Birmingham. By providing for the payment of fees of indigent children at voluntary schools, by school boards out of the rates, Clause 25 made it possible for rates paid by dissenters to be used to support Church of England schools and the religious instruction they provided. Such an eventuality was anathema to the dissenters on the Birmingham School Board.

Their first year on the Birmingham School Board was spent, not in the immediate and active realisation of the League's aims of providing free, compulsory, unsectarian elementary education, but in opposing the Church Party and voluntary schools from benefiting from the introduction of compulsion and payment of fees of indigent pupils. They employed a wide variety of delaying and filibustering tactics to ensure that voluntary schools did not benefit from the school board rates. Chamberlain answered the critics of these tactics in a speech at Carrs Lane Baptist Chapel on 5 June 1871. He told his audience that dissenters had fought hard and long, earlier in the century, for the abolition of the Church rates. These gains were not now to be reversed. Opposition to rate support of voluntary schools was part of a long heritage of dissenting struggles against state support for the established Church of England. Replying to the charge that the members of the League on the board were now obstructing the very cause they had fought so hard to secure, the education of poor children, Chamberlain declared, 'Much as I love the cause of education, I love the principles of religious freedom more'. Great cheering greeted this ringing statement in the bastion of English dissent.[40]

Working-class leaders were more interested in their children's education than religious principles; and by October 1871, their patience was exhausted. Two deputations waited upon the board, one from the working men's Auxiliary of the Scriptural Education Union and the other from the Birmingham Trades Council. They left the board in no doubt of their disappointment that despite ten months of the board's existence, no more children were at school.[41]

From 1872, the board acquired sites, built new schools, closed inefficient dame schools and introduced compulsory school attendance. Visiting officers were appointed, who took censuses of the school-age population, caught truants in the streets and visited their families. Fee waivers were given to families who could not afford the school fees and persistent offenders were fined between 2s 6d and 5s 0d for further offences.[42]

The problems of parents

Parents in Birmingham had new problems to face in bringing up their children, for visiting officers and teachers began to make inquiries if they did not send their children to school regularly. Boots, babies and illness were the main reasons why parents did not send their children to school, according to a reporter on the *Birmingham Daily Mail* who accompanied a visiting officer on his rounds in November 1874. Boots, said the writer, were 'the unsolvable equations of the domestic economy, hard to get, hard to keep and alternating between the pawnshops and the marine store dealer'. Their lack was the most obvious mark of poverty, which kept children at home. Minding the baby and running errands also prevented them going to school. Ill health, dirt and misery combined in a number of cases. In one house, visited by the reporter with the visitor, the children had been ill with fever and were now suffering from the itch. The mother had tumours. When the visitor recommended soap and water she told him fiercely, 'call them dirty, I washed one of 'em all over the day before yesterday'. Mortality and morbidity rates among children in Birmingham were extremely high at this period. The *Birmingham Daily Mail* reporter heard of six deaths in less than twelve visits and 'saw cases of sickness in numbers of children which almost precluded life, not to mention learning'.[43]

Poverty was at the root of most parents' difficulties. One woman told the visiting officer her husband was in prison. She had three children to keep so 'she kept the lad at home to mind the babby'. She and her children were lodgers and paid 1s 6d a week rent. Another mother, found by the officer at the maiding tub, said her husband had given her 30s in a month and 'and if I can pay school fees, rent and keep seven children with that, I'll give in'.[44]

School pence were a very real burden, especially for families with several children and one low and irregular wage. In 1860, a new voluntary school was opened in the Jewellery Quarter. Within a month, the headmistress was visited by a number of mothers, asking that their fees should be reduced from 3d a week to 2d because their husbands were unemployed. After consulting the vicar, the reduction was granted.[45]

In 1873, the Liberals won the second school board election and their working-class supporters held a jubilant procession to their offices after the result was announced. Their euphoria was short-lived, and in 1875 W. J. Davis, secretary of the Amalgamated Society of Brassworkers stood as an independent working men's candidate, to be narrowly defeated by Rev. R. B. Burges, vicar of St Paul's in the Jewellery Quarter and brother of the retiring member of the board.[46]

The Liberals introduced a policy of giving fee waivers only at board schools, where the fees were reduced to a penny in poorer areas. Nonetheless, the difficulties with fees continued. At a debate on free schools in 1875, Joseph Chamberlain reported that a survey of board school teachers showed that the majority of teachers felt the abolition of fees would improve attendance. Teachers 'wasted one day a week in the collection of fees'. If children came for a second week without fees they were sent home. Teachers were thus on the horns of a cruel dilemma in deciding to send children home if they did not bring their school pence. For in doing so, they sacrificed what they and the visiting officers were working hard to attain, the children's education. School pence were a sensitive issue with parents. They did not like free orders because their children were looked down on if they had them. Rather than apply for a free order they sent ½d on account or sent the children without their fees or kept them at home.[47]

Getting all the children in Birmingham into schools and making sure they attended regularly was a formidable task. The Birmingham School Board *Report on Compulsion* in 1878 said somewhat disconsolately, 'while we are employing more men (and they evidently work with as much diligence as ever), yet the attendance increases very slowly indeed, excepting when new schools are opened'.[48] To proceed against all the parents who did not send their children to school was impossible. Only a tenth were summoned before the courts. Attendance improved immediately a new school was opened but after the initial improvement further progress was much slower. Once the children had been got into schools, considerable energy was needed to keep them attending regularly. Chamberlain believed that the explanation of this situation lay in the initial success of the board schools with those within the working classes who could afford to send their children to school. The problem lay in persuading the poorest sections of society to send their children to school regularly.

In reviewing the first seven years of their efforts to introduce and enforce

Table 6.10. *The effects of compulsory school attendance*

Age	At work	At school	At home	No. of cases
		1871		
		Middle-class boys		
0–5	0	15	85	48
6–10	0	78	22	40
11–15	33	45	22	40
16–20	93	0	7	40
		Middle-class girls		
0–5	0	23	77	44
6–10	6	46	48	35
11–15	17	63	20	30
16–20	39	9	52	44
		Working-class boys		
0–5	0	11	89	171
6–10	2	35	63	121
11–15	63	16	21	129
16–20	98	0	2	101
		Working-class girls		
0–5	0	9	91	181
6–10	0*	38	62	133
11–15	39*	20	40	109
16–20	82*	2	16	114
		1881		
		Middle-class boys		
0–5	0	24	76	41
6–10	0	93	7	28
11–15	33	60	7	45
16–20	97	0	3	35
		Middle-class girls		
0–5	0	29	71	41
6–10	0	81	19	31
11–15	17	67	16	30
16–20	54	13	33	46
		Working-class boys		
0–5	0	32	68	126
6–10	0	93	7	88
11–15	54	32	14	81
16–20	97	2	1	68
		Working-class girls		
0–5	0	28	72	126
6–10	0*	91	9	96
11–15	35*	50	15	74
16–20	86*	1	13	85

Note: * This underestimates the percentage working because servants are *not* included.
Source: Heward, 'Home, school and work'.

compulsion, the Birmingham School Board noted that in 1871 Birmingham had a population of 343,000 of whom it was estimated 68,000 children should be on the books of elementary schools and 57,000 in average attendance. There was, then, accommodation for 30,000 and 16,000 in average attendance, only 28 per cent of what it ought to be.

By May 1878, the population had risen to 385,000 and there were 79,000 children between the ages of three and thirteen. On a similar basis as the previous estimate, this would suggest that 65,000 should be in average attendance. School accommodation had increased to 52,171 and attendance to 43,491, 66 per cent of the total. The percentage in regular attendance had more than doubled in seven years. A rapid and marked change was occurring in the lives of working-class children in Birmingham.[49]

This dramatic change is shown in the sample drawn from the Jewellery Quarter. Table 6.10 shows that the percentage of boys and girls from working-class streets between six and ten years old reported to the census enumerator to be at school more than doubled between 1871 and 1881 and the percentage at home plummeted from over 60 per cent to under 10 per cent. The percentage of boys and girls at work between sixteen and twenty years old remained constant. Similar changes took place among the boys and girls in the middle-class streets but the changes were not so large and dramatic as those among children from working-class streets. Middle-class girls remained a somewhat distinct group. While half of the sixteen- to twenty-year-olds were at work in 1881, this was much smaller than the other three groups. They were further distinguished by their longer length of schooling and larger percentage at home between the ages of sixteen and twenty. Boys were destined for work in both social classes. The boys from middle-class streets stayed at school longer and were older when they started work. Working-class girls stayed at school longer than their brothers and started work later. Of the sixteen- to twenty-year-olds, 86 per cent were at work in 1881. The table shows that for the first time a settled period of school attendance was a feature of children's lives among all four groups. For the first, time, the majority of children had systematic instruction in the three R's rather than picking up the rudiments of literacy by a variety of means.

This change increased the responsibilities of parents, especially among the working classes. They adopted a number of strategies to cope with these changes. They sent their children to school irregularly and bargained with the visiting officers, teachers, school managers and school board officials about the children's absence and school pence. They continued to move their children from school to school and to move their homes. Children combined school attendance with working, selling newspapers and flowers, carding buttons and hooks and eyes and chopping wood at home or working as van or errand boys for shops. The introduction and enforcement of compulsory school attendance took children from work, but more often from their homes and put them into school, but it did not provide a roof over their heads, food in their bellies, clothes for their backs or pay their school pence. Parents in the area investigated had to do that from wages which were often low and irregular, rising very unevenly in the period when compulsory school attendance was introduced and enforced. For many families, it proved a mixed blessing indeed.

These conclusions, from a case study of the introduction of compulsion in the Birmingham Jewellery Quarter, have important implications for historical studies in education. They demonstrate the insights into previously neglected educational issues which can be gained by using broader methodological strategies and placing educational problems within their wider social and economic context.

The impact of compulsion upon the poorest sections of society has hitherto remained obscure, due to the paucity of sources. The present study has shown that this problem can be overcome by combining quantitative and archival methods. The evidence suggests that an understanding of the historical development of school attendance among the poorest families requires an investigation of changing social and economic contexts as well as educational institutions. For poorer families, sending children to school depended upon domestic budgets. Keeping a roof over the family's head and feeding and clothing them were more pressing needs than schooling. After the introduction of compulsion, the problems of providing for families with several children of school age with only one low and irregular income were exacerbated. The study shows the importance of understanding the costs of education for the domestic budgets of the poorest families. *Punch*, always an astringent social commentator, understood only too clearly that schooling filled the heads of the children of the poor but left their bellies hungry.[50]

> THE SCHOOL-BOARD VICTIM
>
> 'Mother', how my head is aching,
> In a strange and painful way.
> See what sad mistakes I'm making
> In my exercise today.
>
> All the irksome words are whirling
> Underneath my listless glance;
> And the rows of figures curling
> Round like demons in a dance.
>
> I was cold and wet and weary,
> Hungry too, at school today.
> Why is learning all so dreary,
> Is there never time to play.'

Compulsion, work and family

So the School-Board victim crying,
Bowed her little aching head,
and her Mother watched her, sighing
For to-morrow's daily bread.

Oh ye men of small discerning
On official red-tape nurst,
Though there's good no doubt in learning
We must feed the children first.

NOTES

1 Viviana Zelizer, *Pricing the Priceless Child: The Changing Social Value of Children* (New York: Basic Books, 1985).
2 David Rubinstein, *School Attendance in London 1870–1904: A Social History* (Hull: University of Hull, 1969); David Hogan, *Class and Reform: School and Society in Chicago, 1880–1930* (Philadelphia, PA: University of Pennsylvania, 1985); Selwyn Troen, Popular education in nineteenth century St. Louis', *History of Education Quarterly*, Vol. 13 (1978), 23–40.
3 Frederick Keeling, *Child Labour in the United Kingdom: A Study of the Development and Administration of the Law Relating to the Employment of Children* (London: P. S. King & Son, 1914), xi–xxvii; *Report of the Commissioners Appointed to Enquire into the Working of the Factory and Workshops Acts* (Cmd 1443) (1876), 213–17.
4 Frank Smith, *A History of English Elementary Education 1760–1902* (London: University of London, 1931); Gillian Sutherland, *Policy-Making in Elementary Education 1870–1895* (Oxford: Oxford University Press, 1973).
5 Flora Thompson, *Lark Rise to Candleford: A Trilogy* (London: Oxford University Press, 1951); Pamela Horne, *Education in Rural England, 1800–1914* (Dublin: Gill and Macmillan, 1978); Philip Gardner, *The Lost Elementary Schools of Victorian England* (London: Croom Helm, 1984).
6 John Burnett, (ed.), *Destiny Obscure: Autobiographies of Childhood, Education and Family from the 1820's to the 1920's* (London: Allen Lane, 1982), 135–40.
7 B. I. Coleman, 'The incidence of education in mid-century', in E. A. Wrigley (ed.), *Nineteenth Century Society: Essays in the Use of Quantitative Methods for the Study of Social Data* (London: Cambridge University Press, 1972).
8 Richard Lawton (ed.), *The Census and the Social Structure: An Interpretive Guide to the 19th Century Censuses for England and Wales* (London: Frank Cass, 1978); E. A. Wrigley (ed.), *An Introduction to English Historical Demography from the Sixteenth to the Nineteenth Century* (London: Weidenfeld and Nicolson, 1966); Wrigley (ed.), *Nineteenth Century Society*.
9 Children's Employment Commission, *3rd Report*, PP (1864), XXI, 74, para. 105.
10 Kathleen Dayus, *Her People* (London: Virago, 1982), is an eloquent description of childhood in a court in Camden Drive, in the Jewellery Quarter in the Edwardian period.
11 John C. Holley, 'The two family economies of industrialism: factory workers in Victorian Scotland', *Journal of Family History*, Vol. 6 (Spring, 1981), 57–69.
12 Children's Employment Commission, *3rd Report*, PP (1864), XXI, 103, paras. 394–6.

13 Michael Anderson, *Family Structure in Nineteenth Century Lancashire* (London: Cambridge University Press, 1971); Joan Scott and Louise Tilly, *Women, Work and Family* (New York: Holt, Rinehart and Winston, 1978); Hans Medick, 'The proto-industrial family economy: the structural function of household and family during the transition from peasant to industrial capitalisation', *Social History*, Vol. 1 (1981), 291–334; Holley, 'The two family economies of industrialism'; James H. Treble, *Urban Poverty in Britain 1830–1914* (London: Batsford, 1979); Burnett, (ed.), *Destiny Obscure*.
14 G. C. Allen, *The Industrial Development of Birmingham and the Black Country 1860–1927* (London: Allen and Unwin, 1928; E. P. Hennock, *Fit and Proper Persons: Ideal and Reality in Nineteenth Century Urban Government* (London: Edward Arnold, 1973); Asa Briggs and Conrad Gill, *A History of Birmingham*, 2 vols. (London: Oxford University Press, 1952); Dennis Smith, *Conflict and Compromise. Class Formation in English Society 1830–1914: A Comparative Study of Birmingham and Sheffield* (London: Routledge and Kegan Paul, 1982).
15 Samuel Timmins (ed.), *Birmingham and the Midland Hardward District* (London: Robert Hardwicke, 1866), 377.
16 Children's Employment Commission, *3rd Report* PP (1864), XXI, 95, para. 315; Timmins (ed.), *Birmingham and the Midland Hardware District*, 377.
17 Medick, 'The proto-industrial family economy'.
18 Raphael Samuel, 'The workshop of the world: steam power and hand technology in mid Victorian Britain', *History Workshop Journal*, Vol. 3, (1977), 6–73; Maxine Berg, 'Women's work, mechanisation and the early phases of industrialisation', in R. E. Pahl, (ed.), *On Work: Historical, Comparative and Theoretical Issues* (Oxford: Blackwells, 1988); Eric Hopkins, *Birmingham: The First Manufacturing Town in the World* (London: Weidenfeld, 1989); H. Cunningham, 'The Employment and Unemployment of Children in England c1680–1851', *Past and Present*, Vol. 126 (1989), 115–50.
19 Cunningham, 'The employment and unemployment of children'.
20 Children's Employment Commission, *3rd Report* PP (1864), XXI, 80, para. 160.
21 *Ibid.*, 117, paras. 524 and 525.
22 Timmins (ed.), *Birmingham and the Midland Hardware District*, 285.
23 Children's Employment Commission, *3rd Report* PP (1864), XXI, 199, para. 551.
24 Allen, *The Industrial Development of Birmingham and the Black Country*.
25 *Report of Factory and Workshop Commissioners*, 338 (6659–66).
26 Timmins (ed.), *Birmingham and the Midland Hardware District*, 452.
27 *Report of Factory and Workshop Commissioners*, 239 (4689).
28 Children's Employment Commission, *3rd Report* PP (1864), XXI, 102–3, para. 392.
29 *Ibid.*, XII, 95, paras. 312–13.
30 *Ibid., 1st Report*, PP (1863), XVII, 110.
31 *Ibid., 3rd Report*, PP (1864), XXI, 105, para. 411.
32 *Ibid.*, XXI, 161, para. 758.
33 *Report on Schools for the Poorer Classes in Birmingham, Leeds, Liverpool and Manchester* – 'Special Report by H.M.I. J. G. Fitch on Birmingham and Leeds', PP (1870), LIV, 17–122.
34 Children's Employment Commission, *3rd Report* PP (1864), XXI, 70, para. 59, 77, para. 128.

35 Birmingham Education Society, *1st Annual Report* (Birmingham, 1868), 10.
36 Francis Adams, *History of the Elementary School Contest in England* (Bath: Cedric Chives, 1970), 197.
37 *Birmingham Daily Post*, 11 May 1870.
38 Smith, *A History of English Elementary Education*, 289.
39 James Murphy, *The Education Act 1870: Text and Commentary* (Newton Abbot: David and Charles, 1972).
40 Speech of Mr Joseph Chamberlain on the Payment of the Fees for indigent children attending Denominational Schools, Carr's Lane chapel, June 5th, 1871 (Birmingham: Osborn, 1871), pp. 4–5.
41 *Birmingham Daily Post*, 21 December 1871.
42 *Birmingham Daily Gazette*, 5 July 1872.
43 *Birmingham Daily Mail*, 27 November 1874.
44 *Birmingham Daily Mail*, 18 October 1873.
45 St Paul's School, Camden Drive, Log Book entry, 19 October 1869.
46 *Birmingham Daily Gazette*, 14 October 1875. *Birmingham Daily Gazette*, 18 October, 1875.
47 Birmingham School Board, *Report of a Debate on Free Schools, June 18, 1875* (London: Simpkin Marshall, 1875) 5.
48 Birmingham School Board, *Report on Compulsion as Applied to School Attendance in Birmingham* (Birmingham: Cornish, 1878), 4–5.
49 Birmingham School Board, *Report on the Work Achieved by the Board 1877–83* (Birmingham: Cornish, 1883), 40.
50 *Punch, or the London Charivari* (1 December 1883), 262.

7 Understanding irregular school attendance: beyond the rural–urban dichotomy

Ian Davey and Kerry Wimshurst

An important feature of recent Australian historiography, as elsewhere, has been an increasing awareness and interest in the theoretical presuppositions which underpin the empirical research. Much of this has been generated by younger historians who have been influenced by recent developments in Marxist, feminist and post-structuralist theory. They have attacked much of the recent work in social history for its celebration of the quotidian and its neglect of power relations; they have drawn on the critiques of Castells and others of the Chicago School's ecological approach to urban sociology to cast doubt on the theoretical legitimacy of a specifically urban history; and in the history of education they have argued for an analysis which recognises the centrality of class and gender relations in the establishment and development of public education systems.[1] As well as generating controversy within the field, these critiques have led to a healthy questioning of categories of analysis, the reinterpretation of conventional historical sources and the search for new ones to throw light on issues not easily explored in traditional sources. In the following case study, the influence of these developments will be obvious. We argue that the urban–rural dichotomy implicit in much historical writing about education is an inadequate conceptualisation. We conclude with a brief comment on the imposition of the dependency model of childhood through the educational reforms of the early twentieth century.

The issue we wish to investigate is the persistence of *irregular* patterns of attendance among students long after public schooling was made free and compulsory. It was, we believe, one of the most critical problems confronting educational reformers in the late nineteenth century in England, North America and Australia and of greater significance than non-attendance although the latter has received much more attention from educational historians. Its effects on the new, hierarchically structured school systems were considerable as irregular attendance confounded attempts to grade the pupils by age and forced teachers to 'waste time' repeating lessons for the benefit of those who had been absent. Its effect on the children's school careers was equally dramatic as success in school was predicated upon the assumption of full-time, permanent attendance and repeated failure to gain promotion was the fate of those who did not conform.[2] The continued persistence and widespread incidence of irregular attendance, then, raises some important questions about the organisation of public schooling and its centrality to the lives of the first generation of compulsory school-goers. The analysis of these questions requires us to move far beyond the history of schooling itself and the familiar saga of school authorities battling with recalcitrant parents whose supposed apathy and neglect made them oblivious to the benefits of state education. From the perspective of the system builders, irregular attendance might have been a nagging problem to eradicate that necessitated the establishment of appropriate coercive machinery. From the point of view of the parents, both urban and rural, its status was entirely different. Irregular attendance was the product of a complex process of accommodation between the parents' desire to educate their children and the customary practice of controlling the use of their children's time and labour in accordance with the demands of the family economy.

Before exploring the incidence of irregular attendance, we wish to make some important conceptual and methodological points about child labour. First, nineteenth-century child labour is usually associated with the full-time exploitation of young children in industries such as the textile mills of Lancashire or the bouts of seasonal work, especially at harvest time, common to most agricultural areas. We contend that this model of contrasting urban and rural work rhythms needs to be revised because in the urban areas outside of England, and in the second half of the nineteenth century in particular, the full-time employment of children under the age of thirteen was quite rare. Second, there has also been a tendency to associate urban child labour with the grinding poverty of the day labourers and widows. Without negating its importance to the survival of the very poor, we believe also that most working-class and petty-bourgeois parents relied on the casual and seasonal labour of their children, particularly in times of family crisis. Moreover, we suggest that this need persisted well into the twentieth century. In short, we argue that small masters, shopkeepers and skilled workers as well as labourers and widows organised their family economies along similar lines to small farmers and agricultural labourers and relied upon their children's labour in particular seasons or when illness affected one or both of the parents.

This raises an important methodological point. In earlier research on the relationship between school and work in nineteenth-century Ontario, Canada, Davey argued that although irregular attendance was widespread in both rural and urban areas, the causes were different.[3] In farming areas, he suggested, the age and sex-specific seasonal absenteeism which characterised schooling was rooted in the demands of the family economy whereas in urban areas irregular attendance stemmed not so much from the large-scale employment of young children as from the lack or loss of jobs by parents. Essentially this formulation, embodying the rural–urban dichotomy was derived from the analysis of the manuscript census records for one urban area, Hamilton, which indicate that virtually no children under the age of thirteen were employed in the city although industrialisation resulted in a dramatic rise in the proportion of youths who worked. This we now believe to be largely an artefact of the method of census enumeration. The census records those who were working and who were not working in the same way as it records children who were in school and were not in school. As a result, it fails to capture the experience of those who existed in the grey world between school and work – the irregular attenders and casual labourers who were both in school and working during the course of any one year. The census is a very blunt instrument of analysis indeed, especially in the period after the establishment of compulsory schooling when the enrolment of those subject to compulsion approaches universality.

The reformulation of the relationship between school and work we are suggesting builds upon Wimshurst's earlier analysis of street children in turn of the century South Australia which includes the examination of the information contained in the admission registers of a large primary school established in Hindmarsh, a working-class suburb of Adelaide.[4] Importantly, the registers include information on the school careers and quarterly attendance rates of all students as well as on their age, sex, parent's occupation, residence and previous school experience. Using the information on quarterly attendance, Wimshurst focused on the sizeable minority of boys who attended school on a part-time basis and whose attendance rates clustered around the minimum legal requirement for children between the ages of seven and thirteen of thirty-five days per quarter out of an approximate fifty-five days. In essence, he argued that their irregular attendance and visibility on the streets of Adelaide stemmed from their need to labour casually and was not the result of widespread truancy despite what the urban child-saving authorities claimed. The most interesting aspect of his analysis involved a comparison of urban and rural children in which he examined the excuses for non-compliance with the attendance requirements proffered by parents in the Barossa Valley, a viticultural and mixed farming region to the north of Adelaide. The conclusion was that the same relationship between child casual labour and irregular attendance operated in both urban and rural areas.

The critical point in the argument is the existence of a minimum attendance requirement which was a feature of the Act establishing the state school system in South Australia in 1875 and which remained in force in various forms until the institution of full-time compulsory attendance forty years later in 1915. As in Ontario, the initial provision for a minimum attendance requirement was made with rural children in mind. School and child-saving authorities tended, reluctantly, to accept casual labour absenteeism in farming areas while concentrating their fight against urban irregular attendance which they interpreted as truancy. Hence, in South Australia the requirement in the rural areas remained thirty-five days per quarter from 1878 to 1915 while in the urban areas it was tightened in 1905 to make attendance compulsory for four out of every five days per week. The reasoning behind this distinction between rural and urban attendance requirements was the child-savers' association of street visibility with idleness and crime – a connection which radically underestimated the extent and character of juvenile labour in Adelaide in the period.

The analysis we present here rests on a much more comprehensive data-bank than was available to Wimshurst. It includes the computer-assisted analysis of the quarterly attendance rates of all students – male and female – who attended the Hindmarsh Primary School in the period 1884 to 1899 coupled with information gathered from interviews with fifty people who grew up in the suburb at the turn of the century.[5] Similarly, it includes the computer-assisted analysis of all cases of 'noncompliance', totalling 319, heard by the rural Angaston Board of Advice in the period between 1892 and 1906, rather than the sample originally examined by Wimshurst.[6] As well, it includes the consideration of a vital new source of information: the occupational background of those residents of Hindmarsh who signed a petition to parliament in 1911 opposing government attempts to make attendance compulsory for five days a week. Almost 3,600 South Australians signed this petition, of which 222 representing 199 families came from Hindmarsh. We have identified 167 of these families in the city directories enabling us to build up an occupational profile of those who supported the minimum attendance requirements then in force.[7]

Before exploring the dimensions of irregular attendance, it is important to emphasise that in the late nineteenth century South Australia remained predominantly rural; its economy was built around wheat and sheep. Yet, in 1891 over 42 per cent of the population lived in Adelaide, the capital, and the proportion who resided there rose to over 50 per cent in 1921 by which time industrial capitalism had begun to transform the state's economy. Hindmarsh, situated between the city centre and its port, has been a centre of manufacturing from its establishment and in the late nineteenth century had the largest concentration of industry in the city. It contained a wide range of manufactories, of which brickmaking, tanning and the city gasworks were the most important, and had a population of just over 8,000 in 1891. Skilled workers represented the largest single element in the suburb's occupational structure, reflecting the relative small size of most firms in the area. The suburb also contained a large number of the labouring poor and destitute who were attracted by the cheap housing. Local affairs were presided over by a closely knit compact of manufacturers and businessmen who continued to live in the area. From 1878, Hindmarsh's educational landscape was dominated by the large neo-gothic structure of the Hindmarsh Public School which was established following the passing of the 1875 Act. It was designed to house 1,000 students in its graded classes and infant department although for many years after its establishment, and even after elementary schooling was made free in 1891, it had considerable difficulty filling its classrooms. It was forced to compete with numerous small private and denominational schools which in the late nineteenth century played an important part in the education of the suburb's children.

As the accompanying table of quarterly attendance rates at the Hindmarsh Public School in 1884 and 1899 illustrates, irregular attendance at the school was exceptionally high (Table 7.1). Attendance rates varied seasonally, being lowest in the summer quarter and highest in the autumn and winter when the percentage of students attending for fifty days or more rose substantially. In both years the proportion of children who failed to attend for the thirty-five compulsory days rarely fell below 20 per cent in any quarter, meaning that approximately 150 of the 750 children on the rolls were not in school the required number of days. As well, some 2 to 6 per cent of students did not attend at all in each quarter, further inflating the rates of absenteeism. Importantly, the absentees spanned the occupational structure although the children of labourers and especially widows were more likely to fail to meet the compulsory requirement. Equally important, overall there was a tendency for absenteeism to be highest among the girls in all occupational groups although widows were more likely to keep their sons out of school.

Given the relative ubiquity of irregular attendance among children from all occupational backgrounds and its persistence long after elementary schooling was made free in 1891, it is unlikely that extreme poverty provides a sufficient explanation. Nor was it just the result of sickness. We investigated this possibility by comparing the quarterly attendance rates in pairs of years in the 1890s in which one was a year when the local Board of Health reported an epidemic outbreak and the other a 'normal' year. Certainly, epidemics had a dramatic effect on attendance rates as, for example, during the winter term of 1893 when an outbreak of measles emptied the school and 73 per cent of the boys and 77 per cent of the girls failed to attend for thirty-five days compared to 14 per cent and 19 per cent in 1892. Yet, as the latter proportions and those for 1884 and 1899 indicate, epidemics only exacerbated an underlying tendency towards irregular attendance which was most pronounced in the summer quarter: in both 1892 and 1893 about

Table 7.1. *Quarterly attendance rates, Hindmarsh Public School, 1884, 1899*

		Occupation											
		Merchant/ manufacturer %		White-collar worker %		Skilled worker %		Labourer %		Widow, etc. %		All students[a] %	
Days attended		M	F	M	F	M	F	M	F	M	F	M	F
Summer	*1st quarter*												
1884	1–34	38	54	44	45	36	49	44	49	53	55	41	50
	50+	–	–	–	–	2	–	2	–	–	–	1	–
1899	1–34	17	22	20	20	17	24	21	32	36	17	22	24
	50+	22	22	20	24	19	19	19	7	–	8	16	17
Autumn	*2nd quarter*												
1884	1–34	22	28	18	38	23	26	21	31	32	25	23	29
	50+	39	20	30	16	27	20	34	22	25	15	31	18
1899	1–34	9	11	13	25	20	19	14	12	25	13	19	17
	50+	33	21	35	36	28	25	29	14	13	22	26	23
Winter	*3rd quarter*												
1884	1–34	12	17	12	31	16	29	18	20	15	27	16	24
	50+	54	33	37	19	43	26	46	24	50	12	44	24
1899	1–34	32	16	14	12	17	20	13	35	29	17	19	21
	50+	45	26	46	44	43	38	38	21	18	42	39	34
Spring	*4th quarter*												
1884	1–34	–	19	10	39	12	24	12	25	43	19	13	25
	50+	42	16	33	16	36	24	35	18	20	8	34	19
1899	1–34	31	19	15	35	28	25	32	35	37	24	28	26
	50+	27	8	31	31	20	21	15	20	7	38	20	21

[a] Includes students not in occupational categories listed.
Source: Admission Registers, Hindmarsh Public School, 1884, 1889.

one quarter of the boys and one third of the girls failed to meet the compulsory thirty-five days of the school year in the summer months. This is not to deny that in each quarter endemic illnesses associated with late nineteenth-century life accounted for some absenteeism. Rather, it is to suggest that a full explanation requires a much more complex argument.

The analysis of the cases of non-compliance heard by the Angaston Board of Advice in the viticultural and mixed farming area of the Barossa Valley, 45 miles north of Adelaide, provides us with an insight into the underlying causes of irregular attendance. Under the terms of the 1875 Act, one of the few responsibilities of local Boards of Advice was to investigate cases of non-compliance. The *Minute Book* for Angaston contains information on the child's name, age, parent's occupation, attendance in the offending quarter and the one preceding it, plus the teacher's and parent's explanation and the Board's subsequent action. Investigation of these cases reveals some important points which are germane to our discussion of the Hindmarsh data. First, the same seasonal rhythms of attendance are evident as fully 56 per cent of the cases of non-compliance occurred in the summer quarter yet 68 per cent of the offenders had attended for the minimum required time in the preceding quarter. Second, there was a considerable discrepancy between the excuses offered by parents and teachers. The former gave child illness as the sole reason in 37 per cent of the cases and child working in only 18 per cent, although various combinations of child or parent illness and child working brought the casual work proportion up to 35 per cent. Conversely, teachers suggested illness was the cause in only 3 per cent and work in fully 54 per cent. Family poverty was proffered as an excuse in less than 2 per cent of the cases by both parents and teachers. Third, important age, sex, social class and seasonal differences are apparent in the parental excuses. Illness is given as the principal cause more often in the case of younger children, girls, farmers' children and in the winter months. Child labour was the more likely explanation among older children, boys, the children of skilled workers and widows and in the summer months in which 80 per cent of the excuses involving work were concentrated. Finally, transient work patterns which took the children from the area as well as attendance at small private and denominational schools were also important factors which resulted in the student's failure to meet the specific requirements of the local state school.

The picture that emerges from this discussion of non-compliance in the Barossa Valley is one in which families wanted their children to attend school as often as possible although they relied on the seasonal and casual labour of their children. The minimum attendance requirement allowed them two to three weeks leeway during each quarter for casual work but unforeseen and often traumatic circumstances in the offending quarter could combine with these casual activities to disrupt normal patterns of part-time school and work. The role of child labour both inside and outside the home is nicely illustrated by some actual examples of parent's excuses:

Father was away looking for work. He did not send any money home so I was obliged to find work for the boy.

Mother ill and boy was kept home to do housework.

Family removed 4 miles away to grub land for Mr S. and boy was assisting.

Illness in family and obliged to keep Bertha home to help with grapes.

She was working to obtain clothes for herself.

Away ploughing with father for one month.

Working in store with parents for two weeks, kept to pick olives for one week and helping dentist sometimes.

I have a farm 17 miles away and the whole family were living there the harvest time.

I have three children going to school and I require one at home so I send them alternate weeks.

There is some evidence of a sexual division of labour in this work with boys helping in the field or parent's trade and girls often confined to the domestic sphere although, as the above excuses suggest, the family profile did not always allow for such a clear-cut division. Older children worked at home, in the fields or for wages as circumstances dictated. In short, children from about age ten were expected to work as required and, importantly, this need appears to have been recognised by the teachers and the local school authorities.[8] The teachers, as we have seen, were much more likely to explain absenteeism as a result of work and the Board of Advice was most inclined to accept the excuse of casual labour in the summer months and almost invariably excused all cases involving parental illness. They were much more critical of child labour in the winter months when attendance at school was expected to improve. As local businessmen and farmers, the Board officials knew the seasonal demands for labour and the circumstances of many of the families and while occasionally cautioning parents, they very rarely prosecuted them.

If we return to the working-class suburb of Hindmarsh, there is some evidence that the local teachers and the Board of Advice were reluctant to prosecute as well. 'We regret', they reported in 1900, 'that so many cases should so continually come before the board which are caused by the want of parental control over their children, and in others, parents' absolute neglect of duty.'[9] Yet, in the 1890s the most cases they sent to court was 7 out of 178, in 1896. This was at a time when fully 30 per cent of the boys and 35 per cent of the girls who had attended the school for less than two years failed to meet the thirty-five-day requirement in at least one half of the quarters they were in the school. Among those who were in the school for three years or more, only 15 per cent of the boys and 12 per cent of the girls managed to satisfy the requirement in all quarters. In fact, even some of the inspectors of schools were not too concerned about irregular attendance if, as in the rural areas, it involved work. For instance, in 1905 one inspector, while expressing the hope that the tightening of the urban attendance laws would improve the situation, went on to state that: 'I still hope that at no distant date there will be no limit to the number of attendances a child shall be compelled to make, and that *while children are not profitably or usefully employed* they shall attend school regularly until they are fifteen years of age.'[10]

The tacit acceptance of the need for child labour in urban areas apparent in these comments and the Board's inaction indicate that those familiar with local conditions in the cities realised that irregular attendance was not just a result of parental neglect. Despite the rhetoric of the major child-saving organisation in the city, the State Children's Council, two Education Department inquiries into the incidence of truancy in the 1890s concluded that the problem was almost negligible in South Australia. Virtually all children subject to compulsion were enrolled in schools, state or private, and the overwhelming majority of children accosted on the streets by truant officers were found to be complying with the minimum requirement.[11] It seems clear that parents wanted to send their children to school but, in a period when prolonged attendance was only of tangential relevance to future job prospects, these children attended only when not required to work or help at home. Usually, parents could accommodate these demands for child labour within the minimum attendance requirements but in particular seasons and in times of family crisis the demands of the family economy took precedence. That is, the reasons for non-compliance given by the parents in the rural Barossa Valley – seasonal employment, transient work patterns, illness and poverty – were just as potent determinants of family fortunes in the city and resulted in the same patterns of school attendance.

If we accept that the maintenance of the family economy was of central importance to parental decision-making, then the social class and gender-specific features evident in the attendance patterns in urban schools at the turn of the century are more easily understood. First, the relative ubiquity of irregular attendance among the children of all occupational groups in a working-class suburb like Hindmarsh can be explained by the size and organisation of production in Adelaide in the period before the advent of large-scale industrial capitalism. The urban economy was centred upon commerce and small family-owned workshops as the annual reports of the Chief Inspector of Factories reveal.[12] There were literally hundreds of workshops and sweatshops employing less than six people and many of the parents who appear as merchants and masters in the school registers were in charge of them – the large manufacturers and merchants sent their children to the elite private schools rather than the local state school. Although not destitute like the widows, or subject to the vicissitudes of wage labour like the labourers and skilled workers, these small producers and shopkeepers were often as dependent on their children's labour as farmers in the rural areas, especially in periods when illness affected one or both of the parents. Second, older children, especially girls, were often kept at home to mind younger children and do domestic chores in order to allow the mother to go out to work. Almost certainly, this aspect of the sexual division of labour in the family economy explains the fact that girls were much more likely than boys to attend for less than thirty-five days. They were also much more likely to attend one of the numerous small 'inefficient' private schools which continued to flourish in Hindmarsh throughout the period and which were much more flexible in their attendance requirements. Parents used these small private schools as child-minding centres for their young children and as alternatives to state schools for their older children if and when they required their help. As late as 1908, the inspector of schools in the area commented that 'a careless or neglectful parent who resents the efforts of the school visitors [the truant officers] may remove his child to a private school, and be thenceforth free from what he regards as an annoying interference with his rights. There his children may attend as he pleases.'[13]

Whatever the strategy adopted by the parents, their children's school attendance in the period was governed by the relationship between the demands of the family economy, the availability of work and their strong belief in their customary right to control, at least partially, the use of their children's time. This was true of urban as well as rural dwellers and of petty-bourgeois as well as working-class families. It is most clearly borne out by an examination of the occupational backgrounds of those who fought to retain some flexibility in the attendance requirements, such as those who petitioned parliament in 1911 to show their 'disapproval of the proposed alteration in the Education Act, namely the compulsory attendance of five days per week'. What is most striking about the Hindmarsh petitioners is the wide variety of occupations represented. The 167 families we identified were drawn from 51 different occupations and 15 female-headed households (most likely widows). While the majority were skilled workers, labourers and transport workers like carters and carriers, twenty-eight were merchants and shopkeepers and twenty were masters in such trades as brickmaking, building and baking. Other occupations represented were civil servants, clerks, travellers and storemen and this indicates the breadth of support for the minimum attendance requirements. The diversity of occupations represented and the large number of signatures gathered in other parts of Adelaide and outlying towns suggest that the degree of community support for the existing arrangements went far beyond the 'careless and neglectful' parents so often cited as the cause of irregular attendance by the Education Department inspectors.

A year later, the Board of Advice in Thebarton, a working-class suburb adjacent to Hindmarsh, strongly opposed any alteration to the urban minimum on the grounds that children were usefully occupied in casual work when not in school and that parents maintained close supervision of their children's activities.[14] In 1913, a Royal Commission on Education recommended the same because such provisions were a service to a large number of families.[15] Such widespread opposition was to no avail, though, as in 1915 the Labor government introduced full-time compulsory attendance, increased the leaving age to fourteen and restricted the number of hours children could work outside of school time. The twentieth-century model of the dependent child had triumphed.

We have not dwelt on the issue of casual labour and irregular attendance because we wish to romanticise nineteenth-century forms of child labour or to deny some exploitation of children by both parents and employers. Rather, we wish to suggest that a form of organisation of the family economy common to both the country and the city became defined as a specifically urban problem and generated a solution which has had dramatic consequences for the twentieth-century child. This form of organisation involved a combination of work and school for older school-age children who were expected to assume some responsibility for the maintenance of the family economy. In consequence, the transition from child to adult was blurred as children adopted adult roles from an early age. Moreover, because the nexus between school and work had not been forged with any precision, most children left school as soon as they were legally able to do so and found jobs through family connections or networks of acquaintances and an intimate knowledge of the local labour market. The fact that their irregular attendance at school had meant that most failed to reach the compulsory standard at the end of Class Four before they left was not important as they knew that success in school was not critical for future work chances for the overwhelming majority of them. As the oral evidence we have collected indicates, in the urban areas at least, few children entered permanent jobs immediately upon leaving school; most continued to work casually and seasonally for three or four years, changing jobs frequently.[16] They found casual or 'dead-end' labouring jobs relatively easily because the decline of apprenticeship and the increased demand for unskilled work associated with deskilling in the transition to industrial capitalism had added a range of factory and commercial jobs to the traditional street and domestic jobs available. Their visibility on the streets, their independence and their 'precocity' fashioned a youth culture in turn of the century Adelaide which, through the operation of the minimum attendance requirements, reached down into the school-age population.

Despite the widespread reliance of parents on this casual labour, the uncontrolled entry of urban children into the permanent workforce began to be defined as a 'crisis of youth' as the decline of apprenticeship and the opening up of alternatives to domestic service meant that these customary arrangements to control the transition to adulthood in the cities were increasingly ineffective. An influential coalition of Labor politicians anxious to protect the interests of skilled workers, bourgeois philanthropists concerned about the 'moral dangers' of the 'fatal liberty of the streets' and professional educators wedded to an expansion of the school system increasingly focused on the institutional hiatus which gave rise to the youth problem. As one assistant inspector-general of schools noted as early as 1902:

Nothing could be more beautiful than the tone and discipline of our fourth and fifth class children as long as they attend school, but when for months, and, in hundreds of cases, for years they have no regular employment to go to, they drift into mischievous habits and idle loafing. A boy of, say, from 12 to 15 years must either have lessons or some regular occupation and how to keep him at one or the other is one of the most serious problems the state has to solve.[17]

The reformers buttressed their case for the need to regulate youth by reference to the new psychological theories of Stanley Hall and others and argued that the magnitude of the problem meant that it could not be left to the plethora of voluntary welfare and youth associations which had sprung up to deal with it. Their solution was to use the state's control over schooling to extend systematically the period of institutionalised dependency for children. The 1915 Education Act marked an abrupt change in the customary arrangements as the state unambiguously asserted its power to determine the nature of childhood experience.[18] Full-time schooling was made compulsory and the leaving age was raised. As well, the foundations of mass secondary education were laid in a manner which was designed to ease the transition from school to permanent work more efficiently through the establishment of class- and gender-specific vocational educational programmes. In the future, 'the business of childhood was to be schooled'.

NOTES

1 See, for example, the special issue of *Australian Historical Studies*, Vol. 23 (1988), 'Making the bicentenary'; and Verity Burgmann and Jenny Lee (eds.), *A People's History of Australia since 1788*, 4 vols. (Melbourne: McPhee Gribble/Penguin, 1988). For the history of Australian education, see particularly Pavla Miller, *Long Division: State Schooling in South Australian Society* (Adelaide: Wakefield Press, 1986), and R. J. W. Selleck and M. Theobald (eds.), *The Family, School and State in Australian History* (Sydney: Allen and Unwin, 1990).
2 See Ian Davey, 'Growing up in a working-class community: school and work in Hindmarsh', in P. Grimshaw, C. McConville and E. McEwen (eds.), *Families in Colonial Australia* (Sydney: Allen and Unwin, 1985), 163–72, for an analysis of age-grading, and failure rates at the Hindmarsh Primary School, Adelaide, in the late nineteenth century.
3 Ian E. Davey, 'The rhythm of work and the rhythm of school', in N. McDonald and A. Chaiton (eds.), *Egerton Ryerson and his Times* (Toronto: Macmillan Canada, 1978), 221–53. For an interesting recent commentary on Davey's account, see Bruce Curtis, *Building the Educational State: Canada West, 1836–1971* (London, Ontario: Falmer Press and Althouse Press, 1988), Chap. 5.
4 Kerry Wimshurst, 'Child labour and school attendance in South Australia, 1890–1915', *Historical Studies*, Vol. 19 (1981), 388–411. On South Australian attendance patterns, see also Davey, 'Growing up in a working-class community', and Miller, *Long Division*, Chap. 4. For a comparative discussion of school attendance patterns in Hamilton, Ontario, and Hindmarsh, South Australia, see Ian Davey, 'Patterns of inequality: school attendance and social structure in nineteenth century Canada and Australia', in J. Hurt (ed.), *Childhood, Youth and Education in the Late Nineteenth Century* (Leicester: History of Education Society, 1981), 1–30.
5 The analysis of the Hindmarsh data is made possible by two grants from the now defunct Education Research and Development Committee, a Commonwealth granting body. The first, in 1978, funded the establishment of the Hindmarsh Project by Davey which is designed to investigate the relationship between class, gender and schooling in a late nineteenth-century working-class community and is based on a computer-assisted analysis of the 8,000 entries in the Hindmarsh Primary School admission registers (located in the South Australian Public Records Office) between 1878 and 1899. The project has also been supported by the University of Adelaide and we would like to acknowledge the help of Mr Bill Pearce of the University of Adelaide Computing Centre, in particular, in the analysis of the data. The second, funded in 1979, was a joint project of Davey, Dr Ray Broomhill and Ms Susan Marsden involving interviews about the family, school and work experiences of fifty people who grew up in the Hindmarsh area.
6 See the Schedules of Non-Compliance contained in the *Minute Book* of the Angaston Board of Advice 1892–1915, Government Record Group, 18/70/S.A. Public Records Office.
7 This petition is located in the South Australian House of Assembly Archives, Nos. 44 and 47, tabled by W. Peake, 8 August 1911.
8 For a more detailed discussion of child labour in nineteenth-century South Australia see Ian Davey, 'Growing up', in Eric Richards (ed.), *The Flinders*

History of South Australia: Social History (Adelaide: Wakefield Press, 1986), 371–402.
9 *Annual Report of the Minister of Education for 1900* (Hereafter *Annual Report*), South Australian Parliamentary Papers (SAPP) No. 44 (1901), 28.
10 *Annual Report . . . 1905*, SAPP, No. 44 (1906), 13 (emphasis added).
11 See Wimshurst, 'Child labour', 389.
12 See, for example, the *Annual Report of the Chief Inspector of Factories* for 1899 which indicates that inspectors visited 292 premises employing fewer than six people (and, therefore, not compelled to lodge official returns) with a total labour force of only 676. *South Australian Votes and Proceedings of Parliament*, 1900, Vol. 3, Pt 2, No. 64.
13 *Annual Report . . . 1908*, SAPP, No. 44 (1909), 13.
14 *Annual Report . . . 1912*, SAPP, No. 44 (1913), 50.
15 Royal Commission on Education, *Final Report*, SAPP (1913), Vol. 3, No. 75, 12.
16 See Davey, 'Growing up in a working-class community'.
17 *Annual Report . . . 1902*, SAPP, No. 44 (1903), 15.
18 See Miller, *Long Division*, Chaps. 5–8. For an interesting commentary on the imposition of the dependency model of childhood in the United States, see Viviana Zelizer, *Pricing the Priceless Child: The Changing Social Value of Children* (New York: Basic Books, 1985).

8 Redoing urban educational history

Barbara Finkelstein

Introduction

This essay is an exploratory historiographical foray into the city as both an education-generating setting and an educational entity in its own right.[1] It reflects a personal conviction that historians of education have been less theoretically sophisticated, psychologically imaginative, culturally aware and humanly sensitive than the subject either requires or warrants. It is a plea to think of cities and the evolution of urban education as the product of human agency, human attempts to mute the force of circumstance, impose meaning on life and cope with the effects of diversity, heterogeneity and size. It is a plea to analyse educational evolution sensitively, as people have created, experienced, transformed and reacted to it. It is a plea to look at the city as Robert Park, the great urban sociologist has suggested, as a place that 'magnifies, spreads out and advertises human nature in all its various manifestations'.[2]

This sort of interest has been only marginal in the awareness of urban educational historians. As a group, they have reconstructed a broad, if incomplete, vision of urban educational development that proceeds in this way: the growth and character of urban education represented a response to ideological and material transformations taking place over the course of the nineteenth and twentieth centuries. The popularisation and extension of schooling to an ever larger number of people over time represented the emergence of specialised institutions which could prepare people for labour in an industrial market place, and for civic participation in emerging nation states. Schools were places designed to complete a transition from agrarian to industrial modes of production, to ready people for contractual rather than status-based relationships, for impersonal rather than personal modes of association, for labour in factory and line, rather than in field and in craft. The popularisation of schools, newspapers, the penny press and magazines in the nineteenth century, and of radio and television in the twentieth, complete a transformation in modes of cultural transmission which elevated, if it did not substitute, the authority of public authorities, professional experts and industrial leaders for the traditional authority of family, church and neighbourhood.[3]

As large and elegant as this current portrayal appears to be, it emerges from a tradition of historical inquiry that brings the urban educational experience only partially into view. Like the reformers whom they study, historians of urban education have typically portrayed the city as an incubus of social tension on the one hand, or as a haven of intellectual opportunity on the other.[4] They have favoured the study of elites. They have focused on structural features of urban life. They have typically emphasised the centralising tendencies of modern educational arrangements and linked education to the evolution of economic, political and intellectual macro-structures. As they have discovered social history, they have lost track of its human dimension. As a result, historians have yet to do justice to the complexity and richness of urban educational experience.

The emphasis on elites informs the historiography of urban education in subtle ways. It provokes and simplifies analyses of the motivations of reformers and takes effects of education reform for granted. It reveals the evolution of high rather than folk culture, of large educational traditions rather than small ones. It leads to the recovery of an urban educational past that reveals what was consciously intended rather than what might have occurred, what was taught rather than learned. It accounts for the popularisation of schooling as a by-product of the interests of a relatively small group of middle-class moral reformers in the nineteenth century, and of scientific and/or administrative progressives in the early decades of the twentieth century. For all its pretensions to the contrary, a subtle form of Whiggism continues to inform the doing of urban educational history.

A second characteristic of urban educational history is a tendency to locate its origins and principal features exclusively in the centralising tendencies of modern life – the emergence of nation states, the expansion of industrial networks and the popularisation of literacy. Indeed, historians of education have focused almost exclusively on the analysis of macro-structures.[5] The evolution of families, churches and indigenous neighbourhood organisations, the analysis of child-rearing practices and norms within localities, even the intersection of school and family life have been virtually ignored. Thus, we lose a fundamental element in our understanding of urban educational development – the whole of small cultures and traditions.

A third characteristic of the work of urban educational historians has been a focus on what Clifford Geertz calls 'the hard surfaces of life – the political, economic, stratifactory realities into which people are born and in which they lead their lives'.[6] Whether they have explored 'urban education in the aggregate', adopted ecological approaches focusing on particular social and educational networks, historians of education have studied educational structure rather than behaviour, drawing conclusions from an analysis of structural variables: density, size and heterogeneity. Even those who have reconstructed social networks aim to reveal structural rather than behavioural meanings of urban education experience.[7] Hence, we learn much less than we need to know about the qualities of urban consciousness and the uses to which people might put education, not only in the pursuit of power and status, but in the pursuit of dignity and meaning as well.

With some striking exceptions – one thinks immediately of the work of Daniel Calhoun, David Hogan, James Sanders, Ian Davey and Michel Doucet, Ronald D. Cohen and Raymond A. Mohl, Vincent P. Franklin, David Reeder, Barbara M. Brenzel and Neil Sutherland among others – historians have recovered a truncated urban educational history, revealing a limited range of goals, processes and structural developments.[8] They have barely begun to explore the city as an educational setting or, as Daniel Calhoun has put it, as a 'kind of automatic teaching environment – poorly and chaotically programmed, but effective for all that'.[9] They have not as yet incorporated the study of ordinary people, nor typically explored the impact of urban environments on processes of child-rearing and on the work and roles of the family and church as educational institutions.[10] Only a handful attempt to link the study of urban educational history to the study of human development, of modes of human association and communication, or processes of identity formation.[11] They have only just begun to focus on education in the forming of human community.[12] As Donald R. Warren has suggested in an insightful observation characterising and criticising the state of urban educational history in the United States: 'we are only beginning to appreciate the impact of the texture of urban life on the schools, other educational forms, and other institutions. We need historical appreciation of the extent to which cities represent not problems, but qualitatively different resources for thinking and imagining.'[13]

Such an appraisal requires historians to go beyond the study of structure, beyond the analysis of macro-politics and economics, beyond the study of the work of elite planners, to include the study of experience, of small face-to-face social contexts and processes, the consciousness of reformers and the educational experience of ordinary people. To bring these dimensions of urban educational experience into view, historians of education will need to conceptualise cities as cultural and psychological as well as material and intellectual environments. They will need to analyse the work of educational elites in psycho-social as well as structural terms. They will have to view education as something experienced as well as planned – a process of interaction between learners and teachers.[14]

To call psychological and cultural aspects of urban educational development into view is not to suggest that they are more important than material conditions, though they are surely more interesting. It is to balance perspectives and, through the balance, to deepen the conceptual apparatus with which to bring a more complete and true-to-life urban educational history into view. It was, after all, the sensitivity to psychological and cultural realities that led creative social theorists like George Simmel, Louis Wirth and Robert Redfield to recognise 'urbanism as a way of life', and to see the city as a distinctive socio-cultural, psycho-social environment, creating distinctive modes of cultural transmission. And it is an emphasis on the psychological that will also enable historians of education to construct questions and identify educational indices which can bring learning as well as teaching into view, distinguish between educational intention and educational outcome, illuminative bases for comparative study and recover the past as humans lived and experienced it and without losing an awareness of the factors beyond the control of individuals and groups.

What follows is a presentation of promising approaches to the recovery of a fuller, more complex and true-to-life urban educational history. It is intended to reveal possibilities and directions, rather than elaborate a complete research agenda. It is organised to reflect the state of the field. The first section, called 'Cities and the discovery of children as learners', presents ways of infusing cultural and psychological dimensions into traditional historiographical concerns: the origin and development of mass schooling, the study of education as a vehicle of social control, the role of education as an instrument of social change. The next, 'Cities and the nurture of Community', takes up approaches which can bring previously neglected aspects of urban educational history into larger view: learners and learning as one example; the role of education in the forming and transforming of community as another. The last section, 'Urban education and the nurture of human potential', aims to reveal new themes to be explored. It includes some uses to which educational history might be put in studies focusing on the evolution of human consciousness and human potential, the nurture of political sensibility, the forming of identity and the nurture of creativity and intelligence.

Cities and the discovery of children as learners

The origins and expansion of schooling

The origins and expansion of popular schooling has invited study and explanation from several generations of educational historians in Europe and North America. The corpus of work suggests in an unequivocal manner that education became a mass, bureaucratically organised, politically meaningful, deliberately conceived instrument of political authority, cultural transmission, moral and social regulation during the nineteenth and twentieth centuries beginning in North America, Great Britain, parts of Western Europe and extending gradually over the course of the two centuries to Eastern Europe, Japan, China, Africa and the Middle East. The popularisation of schooling, is, by definition, an aspect of modernisation processes all over the world. It has proved to be an irresistible, and apparently irreversible, invention of social and political planners throughout the world. And yet, the relationships of cities or urban settings to all of this is not at all clearly joined.[15]

What, if anything, in the urban environment might account for the extraordinary expansion of educational institutions, and the orgies of educational planning that initiated and formed it? It might be useful to take leaves from the books and articles of Richard Sennett, John Higham, Thomas Bender, Daniel Calhoun and Robert Wiebe, and recognise the city as a special kind of myth-inducing, myth-building environment, giving special saliency to the role of ideas, and special kinds of power to educational mythmakers.[16] Indeed, there is reason to believe that the psychological and cultural characteristics of urban environments would galvanise three distinct tendencies. It would hone, sharpen and refine the educative sensibilities of social planners and urban inhabitants generally. It would give particular salience to the kinds of social and political arrangements built on tacit consents. It would galvanise social planners and opinion leaders into action.

Cities and the nurture of educational sensibilities

The effect of urban conditions on the quality of educational reform thought has been an implicit theme in the work of urban educational historians. Daniel Calhoun called attention to the city as a nursery of educational sensibility as he analysed the motives of American moral reformers in the early nineteenth century. The cities, by virtue of their uncontrolled growth, heterogeneity and diversity, enriched the missionary spirits of Protestant elites, revealing opportunities to extend and intrude 'bookish culture', universally and uniformly among urban inhabitants.[17] Emphasising both a conservative quality and an urban sensibility in the ideas of progressive educational reformers in Gary, Indiana, Ronald D. Cohen and Raymond A. Mohl recognised self-serving motives as well as imperial dispositions.[18]

Extending these themes, other historians have characterised the ideas of urban educational reformers as essentially conservative visions, forged in the cities, and constructed over time. Though they have not explicitly imagined the city as a forge from which new and elaborate educational visions would emerge, they have amply demonstrated the reality of the links. They are clearly elaborated in the work of Charles Strickland, Jane Silverman Mulligan, Jacques Donzelot, Elizabeth Badinter and Nancy B. Weiss as they explore the discovery of infancy as a distinct stage in the life-span, and the invention of mothers as educators in nineteenth-century cities in the United States, France and Canada alike.[19] It is similarly embedded in works by Barbara M. Brenzel, Joseph F. Kett, Steven Schlossman, Joseph Hawes, Robert Mennell, and Patricia Rooke and Richard Schnell as they document the discovery of adolescence and the invention of delinquency among English, Canadian and American urban reformers.[20] It is an important element in the work of Michael Zuckerman, Nancy B. Weiss, Christopher Lasch and David J. Rothman who analyse educational myths arising from the heads of twentieth-century reformers that would give scientific definition to social myths defining the educational roles of parents.[21]

If cities presented imperial opportunities on the one hand, and struck fear into the hearts of educational reformers on the other, they also inspired and shaped the commitments of a new and emerging urban inhabitant – the young man on the make. For these young men the city represented a kind of mythic Circe, calling them away from tradition, restraint and obligation, luring them toward new possibilities, freedoms and opportunities. As the work of Peter Dobkin Hall, Lawrence A. Cremin, Joseph F. Kett, Michael B. Katz, Vincent P. Franklin, Judy Jolley Mohraz, Selma Berrol and Maxine Seller suggests, cities represented places of escape, liberation and self-cultivation for generations of young men–Protestants and Catholics, native-born and immigrant, black and white, rich and poor.[22] Cities were places to which they fled to escape the constraints of family life, to maintain and/or enhance their social positions, to develop and expand networks of social and intellectual affiliations and to increase their commercial prospects. For these groups of educational reformers and opinion leaders, cities inspired the building of intellectual and social networks to replace ones they had left behind. They would turn cities into intellectual and cultural clearing-houses, collecting worldly information, organising it, storing it and making it available through newspapers, magazines, museums, libraries, mechanics' institutes and other mediating agencies which they worked to build and develop.[23]

Marvin Lazerson, Michael B. Katz, David Tyack and Elisabeth Hansot, and Ian Davey have emphasised the call of cities upon the ambitions and hopes of an emerging middle class of technocrats and professionals.[24] As Lazerson put it: 'the complexities of industrialism and urban life' provided rich soil for the flowering of administrative dispositions and managerial tendencies in an emerging middle class who, he suggests, 'would create and seize upon opportunities to introduce the values of continuity and regularity, functionality and rationality, administration and management' into education planning processes.[25]

The myth of the vulnerable child

The myth-generating quality of city life is an explicit focus in recent work being done by the few urban educational historians who pay close attention to the evolution of childhood as well as education. David Reeder, exploring the responses of hundreds of Edwardian and Victorian urban educational planners, characterised the depth of the city's hold on their imaginations. They visualised the city as a kind of monster, 'devouring children, dragging them down into its commercial entrails, burning up their idealism and finer instincts and processing their minds and characters in all sorts of undesirable ways'. Conditions in nineteenth-century English cities apparently nurtured what was to become an increasingly compelling mythic construction: the myth of the vulnerable child.[26] The work of Lloyd DeMause, Lawrence Stone, Elizabeth Badinter, Dominick Cavallo, Barbara Finkelstein, Allison L. Prentice and Susan E. Houston, Neil Sutherland, Marvin Lazerson and W. Norton Grubb all suggest that the myth of the vulnerable child was deeply embedded in the visions of educational reformers in Canada, the United States, England and France by the beginning of the nineteenth century.[27]

In their explorations of government involvement in child-rearing and education, Barbara Finkelstein and Jacques Donzelot suggest that the myth of the vulnerable child acquired a new dimension enabling educational planners to imagine whole new tutorial environments, or, as Jacques Donzelot calls them, 'tutelary complexes'. To the myth of the vulnerable child Finkelstein discovered another – the myth of children as learners.[28]

Although we need many more biographical studies focusing on the effects of the city on the mentalities of educational planners, there is reason to believe that the discovery of children as learners acquired new social and political dimension in the presence of urban transformations.[29] Barbara Finkelstein argued in this way in a study exploring the schooling of American childhood in the century from 1820 to 1920. As they experienced the cities in the midst of industrialisation and in the process of assimilating immigrant strangers, urban educational reformers developed an acute awareness of the effects that home, church and neighbourhood had on the content and quality of educational fare being made available to children. Carrying the myth of vulnerable childhood around in their heads, they developed an acute sensitivity to urban disorder, and began to envision children as learners, vulnerable to the force of circumstance and subject to multiple influences. Thus, they transformed an older notion of childhood vulnerability into a disposition to build and organise learning communities for the young: specialised educational settings in which their moral and cognitive capacities would be tended.

Out of a deep sense of moral and political concern, a profound fear of social disorder and an awareness of childhood vulnerability, they began to advocate the construction of an array of overlapping educational environments, to be located in churches, homes, factories and in publicly sponsored schools and asylums – wherever children were to be found. In the rough and tumble of urban growth, American educational reformers had become acutely conscious of the structures of experience, i.e., the networks of association, circles of acquaintance, structures of authority, qualities of intellect and the character of the activities which influenced children as they grew up.[30]

There is reason to believe that visions of children as learners, and of schools as appropriate environments, would resonate with the visions of less powerful and less imperial urban inhabitants. For the cities were places which honed the educative consciousness and energies of parents as well as planners. Explorations of the educational roles of immigrant families has been only superficially unexplored. Nonetheless, there is work suggesting that cities provided firm psycho-social bedrock for the flowering of the twin myths among urban parents as well as urban planners, among certain ethnic minorities and immigrant groups, as well as ethnic minorities and immigrants as well as native-born, English speaking elites.[31] Cities were places which, as Robert A. Levine and Merry I. White have demonstrated, would effectively transform the structure and meaning of inter-generational relationships.[32] Cities would, among other things, give particular salience to the economic concerns of parents, as well as the educational visions of planners. They would strain the capacity of families, churches and other traditional authorities to remain educationally useful on the one hand and educationally authoritative on the other.[33]

What little work there is exploring the history of immigrant education experience suggests that the myth of the vulnerable child and the discovery of children as learners would speak as meaningfully and sensitively to the concerns and realities among ethnic minorities as it would for the fears and status–anxieties of elite planners. The vision of the vulnerable child, subject to unholy influence and social temptation, and of the child as learner in need of tutorial enclosure, were twin components in the building of parochial as well as public schools in certain urban localities in the United States.[34] They were important elements in the decision of certain immigrant parents to commit their children to asylums and industrial schools, and well before the passage of school attendance statutes and effective enforcement procedures.[35] The discovery of children as learners drove black urban dwellers in the 1920s and 1930s to cities in order to transform what had been deeply embedded commitments to the acquisition of literacy into political action in support of public education.[36]

Indeed, the commitment to universal schooling originated in the psychosocial as well as material realities of nineteenth-century cities. In Great Britain, English-speaking Canada and the United States, the appeal for universal schooling would organise what people had in common – vulnerable children and tutorial dispositions. The twin visions, childhood vulnerability and tutorial walls, would create an 'ideological template' of such compelling power that it would become the scaffolding on which universal public education could be mounted.

Levine and White put this observation into structural language when they suggest that educational mobilisation occurs in societies when the visions of planners and child-rearing commitments of inhabitants are complementary. These conditions set in motion 'processes that motivated an investment of time, space, attention, and money in teaching and learning at both microsocial and macrosocial levels and especially to ideological commitments.'[37]

Though we need to develop our knowledge of daily educational realities among all classes of families in urban settings in many nations of the world before we accept this or any other global explanation for the discovery of universal schooling, there is reason to believe that the commitment to universal schooling formed a basis for solidarity in a complex urban environment. Taken together, the twin myths of childhood vulnerability and the child as learner could harmonise the commitments of diverse people, enabling both planners and planned for, elites and immigrant minorities, rich and poor, black and white, to view schooling as in the best interest of children.[38]

Not so much a by-product of consensus on the one hand, or conflict on the other, but of psycho-cultural, psycho-social realities of urban life, the discovery of universal schooling proceeded simultaneously with a need to give order, coherence and common sense to basic human processes – raising children, learning to labour, transmitting culture and the like.

Cities and the nurture of community

Yet another reason to attend to the psychological and cultural as well as material aspects of urban educational history is to illuminate previously unrecognised or unacknowledged educational processes occurring in cities. As they explain the emergence of specialised institutions for the young and very young, historians of education have typically described them as the products of centralising tendencies of modern life – the emergence of mass culture, the building of nation states, the industrial transformation of society.

They have adopted a variety of descriptive and explanatory modes, which, in one way or another, neglect to recover the psycho-social context of urban environments. Some have proceeded as though cities were little more than cradles of mass culture, places from which national rather than local ideologies would be organised and disseminated. They interpret the flowering of educational institutions in the nineteenth and twentieth centuries as nothing more, nor less, than attempts to standardise and diffuse national culture, 'to centralize ... the nerve centers of information and influence', and in the case of the United States, to transform Protestant, republican and capitalist dispositions and beliefs into national cultural standards and child-rearing norms.[39] Some explain the emergence of institutional complexes as a product of humanitarian concern and benevolent sentiment, emphasising the promises rather than the realities, the benefits rather than the costs, the aspirations rather than the realities of extended schooling.[40] Other historians proceed as if cities were nothing more than specialised working environments requiring schools that would prepare the rising generation for labour in factory and line. For these historians, the emergence of specialised education institutions was an inevitable outcome of a need for docile, able and disciplined workers. As handmaidens of industrial development, schools would provide the regulatory wherewithal to impose an 'urban discipline'.[41] To put it another way, schools represented the emergence of tutorial environments which would institutionalise commitments to reason and rational planning in human affairs. They were the regulatory apparatus enabling planners 'to bring madness under the unbending control of reason', and bring childhood under the command of rules and regulations that would disorganise folkways and organise industrial habits. For these historians, the orgy of institution-building which characterised the nineteenth and twentieth centuries represented attempts to bring children under the command of rules and regulations and the authority of clocks, and fines, rather than under the personal authority of more traditional environments. In short, modern educational institutions were the products and instruments of industrial transformation.[42]

No matter which emphasis they have taken or which cities they have studied, historians of education typically account for the emergence of tutorial settings with reference to large rather than small traditions, trans-local ideologies rather than folk beliefs and sentiments, mass rather than local cultures.

The discovery of cities as unique environments for the flowering of educational forms and processes emerges directly from recent work being done by historians and anthropologists exploring the evolution of community. Cities are places where, as Richard Sennett has observed, the likelihood of running into strangers is multiplied, and the need for psychological as well as physical boundaries between groups assumes special significance.[43] They are places where 'local social patterns and translocal ideologies co-exist, where little traditions and great traditions, folk culture and mass culture flourish simultaneously'.[44] They are places distinguished not only by size, heterogeneity and diversity but by the choices which become effectively available as individuals and groups encounter divergent ways of knowing, believing, feeling and labouring. They are places where domestic culture and work culture diverge. They are places, as Thomas Bender has observed, where culture becomes bifurcated, split into public spheres, and where individuals and groups must make sense of multiple and divergent realities.[45]

Among their other characteristics, cities are confusing, especially for newly arriving immigrants, and those whom cities displaced or threatened. Thus, they are places providing fertile soil for the cultivation of what Clifford Geertz calls 'integrative structures, bringing local communal units of life, primordial groups, into relations with a national civil state'.[46] Cities would inspire the construction of education myths of such compelling power that they would induce harmonies of interest among diverse and sometimes contentious people living in close proximity. They were places which have honed the capacities of groups to mute and transform the force of economic, political, and psychological circumstance. Not only have they provided rich ground, as John Higham has observed, for the cultivation of ideologies and social forms built on consent either tacit or explicit, but they have taxed and extended the adaptive capacities of cultural groups.[47] Cities thus generate felt needs for the deliberate nurture and protection of community.

This is a promising line of inquiry for historians of education. It organises an approach to educational history that goes beyond the study of centralising tendencies and ideologies, regulatory dispositions and social strains to include the study of local and folk customs, small ideologies and the adaptive, i.e., educational, capabilities of hitherto neglected educational groups and agencies – urban families, local churches, ethnic newspapers and even local public and denominational schools.[48]

Understood in this way, the study of community will necessarily involve the study of educational processes through which people come to share in a universe of meaning. It involves the study of mentalities, of what people learn about who they are 'in small social units, primary circles of identity, values, associations and goals' as well as in large, so-called secondary units.[49] It involves the systematic exploration of the capacity of families, churches, informal associations and schools, not only to reflect and define economic opportunity and political power, but to nurture a sense of community identity – to create boundaries between groups, and to forge social bonds, evoke loyalty, compel allegiance, exact commitment and organise meaning. It requires close attention to what John Bodnar has called 'enclaves', and others have called 'purified communities', 'havens', 'utopian retreats' and 'communities built on the shared experience of family life and toil ... cut off from social and political influence'.[50]

Looked at in these ways, the multifarious events and occurrences that define the history of urban education emerge as attempts by one or another group to preserve, protect, nurture, rebuild or transform community. The possibilities of this kind of study are elaborated in detail in an article by Barbara Finkelstein exploring new sorts of conceptual scaffolds, source materials and methodological perspectives on which to mount community studies.[51] In it, she suggested that the emergence of tutorial enclosures might best be understood as a history of conflict between increasingly diverse groups for control over the network of relationships enclosing the young, and for the power to censor, filter and define significance. It emphasised the work of schools as structures of persuasion rather than of regulation or of opportunity. It linked them to their local settings as well as to national or state ones. It focused on relationships between parents and children, teachers and students, employers and employees as important funnels for the construction and transformation of community. It redirected the focus of study to incorporate the ways individuals and groups adapted and/or transformed as well as reacted or succumbed to the educational fare being made available to them. The article suggested ways to shift the focus of study to include analyses of the interior cultures of individuals and groups, to explore the uses to which they might have put the educational fare being intruded upon them. The article called for a renewed respect for the possibilities of biographical studies, whether they reflect the lives of individuals, or of families over time. It called for systematic studies of immigrant educational as well as economic experiences. It should have called, but did not, for the systematic use of material artefacts to reconstruct the character of educational experiences in household, neighbourhood and school. In fact, the limitations and possibilities of this approach are explicitly addressed in Thomas J. Schlereth's remarkable volume *Material Culture in America*.[52] In it, he provides guides for the 'reading of landscapes', finding meaning in artefacts, exploring household technologies, explicating monuments and myths, folk art and artefacts. While there are only a few historians of education who have made good analytic as well as ornamental use of photographs, etchings and paintings, the few who have reveal their utility as guides for the reconstruction of educational life in small settings.[53] The article should also have called, but did not, for the elaboration of sophisticated modes of literary and linguistic analysis that have been put to such good use by historians exploring daily life and social events as reflections of evolving mentalities.[54]

Urban education and the cultivation of human potential

Yet another value of incorporating the psychological dimension into the study of urban educational history is to uncover previously unacknowledged effects of urban education on a variety of mentalities, social dispositions and political inclinations. There are only a handful of educational historians who explore the effects of urban life on the nurture of individual creativity, intelligence and cognitive style. Relatively few focus on the forming of political sensibilities, class consciousness and gender identity. A mere handful explore the city as a specialised environment nurturing national and global perspective. Daniel Calhoun is one of the few educational historians who has explicitly recognised the city as a unique environment for the cultivation of individuality and of particular mental, social, political and economic qualities in its inhabitants.[55] It is an implicit and undeveloped theme in the work of Finkelstein which explores the consciousness-raising and/or consciousness-constraining aspects of various educational settings in which individuals and groups learned to read and write. Here, the city emerges as a differentiating educational environment – particularly odious and constraining for children of ordinary people who typically learned to read and write in schools; particularly broadening and expansive for the children of the well born who acquired literacy in smaller, protected domestic enclaves.[56] The effect of the city on the consciousness of its inhabitants is an unintended focus of Ellen C. Lagerman's work which explores the effect of mentors on the development of social and intellectual consciousness of five progressive reformers in the United States.[57] And it has been an important focus of historians exploring the evolution of feminine sensibilities.[58]

George Simmel, in a classic study of the mental life of cities, described the city as a unique place for the cultivation of individual potential.[59] As Simmel saw them, cities provided individuals with unprecedented opportunities to transform life's determinacies into new forms of expression. Because people lived in relatively dense spaces and, unlike their rural counterparts, lived and worked in geographically separated spaces, they encountered strangers regularly, cities constituted unique environments for the cultivation of individuality and creativity. They were places that enabled the individual to transcend the immediate environment, transform experience and thus cultivate new ways of knowing, feeling, believing, working, doing and expressing themselves.

No pollyanna he, Simmel also saw the darker sides of cities. They were places where interactions between people were constant and unrelenting, where individual consumptive appetites were systematically titillated, senses bombarded with external stimuli. Hence, they were places which could mute the capacity of individuals to create, discriminate and judge, a theme which Daniel Calhoun has developed with considerable sophistication.[60] Cities were also places which gave rise to constraining structures – schools binding the impulse and imagination of the young, and discouraging risk-taking; work environments of unrelenting tedium and meaninglessness.[61]

Less interested in the possibilities presented to the individual than in the ways urban environments might have filtered information, visions of reality and cognitive styles and dispositions, Daniel Calhoun nonetheless calls attention to the selective effects of urban settings. 'What the individual actually experiences [in a city] is a series of interlocking or impinging or nested environments, whose interacting effect on him may be quite different – either more effectively liberating or more effectively binding – from any one setting within the array.'[62] Embedded in this observation is a recognition of the city as a place of variability and multiplicity. Though he did not say so explicitly, he described the city as a place requiring educational intermediaries. The urban environment would transform churches, schools and neighbourhoods into specialised educational institutions – serving as interfaces between the individual and society, linking children to the world outside their immediate neighbourhoods, constituting schools that would function as way stations between the increasingly differentiating world of men and women, adults and children, workplace and home, the local and the distant.[63]

With some few exceptions, historians of education have not attached the history of education to the historical study of human consciousness and potential. It is this orientation, more than anything else, I suspect, that led Ian Davey to suggest that 'the most important task facing the British educational historian is the assessment of mass education's role on the formation of the social consciousness of the British people'.[64] It is this orientation that inspired the writing of this essay. More than any other, I believe, it will ultimately deepen our understanding of the meaning of social class, gender, ethnicity and social regulation, not only as categories of analysis, but as lived realities as well. A focus on the processes by which local groups mediate pressures – from developing central governments, industrial planners, social reformers on the one hand; or the producers of mass culture on the other – will enhance comparative studies and cultivate our understanding of the processes of educational transfer. This orientation will lead historians of education to learn rather than argue about the effects of universal schooling on the quality of justice in the world.

NOTES

1 More than a decade ago, Daniel Calhoun advocated the value of such an approach. Daniel Calhoun, 'The city as teacher: historical problems', *History of Education Quaterly*, Vol. 9 (1969), 312–26.
2 Quoted in D. A. Reeder (ed.), *Urban Education in the Nineteenth Century* (New York: St Martin's Press, 1978), 1.
3 This synthesis cannot be found in any one work, but its principal features are developed in the following monographs, articles and collections which, when taken together, exemplify the range of approaches typically used by urban educational historians studying Great Britain and North America: Ronald K. Goodenow and Diane Ravitch (eds.), *Schools in Cities: Consensus and Conflict in American Educational History* (New York: Holmes and Meier, 1983); Diane Ravitch and Ronald K. Goodenow (eds.), *Educating an Urban People: The New York City Experience* (New York: Teachers College Press, 1981); Michael B. Katz, *The People of Hamilton, Canada West: Family and Class in a Mid-Nineteenth-Century City* (Cambridge, MA: Harvard University Press, 1976); William E. Marsden, 'Ecology and nineteenth-century urban education', *History of Education Quarterly*, Vol. 23 (1983), 29–53; Reeder (ed.), *Urban Education in the Nineteenth Century*; Neil Sutherland, 'The urban child', *History of Education Quarterly*, Vol. 9 (1969), 305–11; David B. Tyack, *The One Best System: A History of American Urban Education* (Cambridge, MA: Harvard University Press, 1974); Donald R. Warren, 'Return to old times: rural romanticism in American education history', *Urban Education*, Vol. 18 (1984), 389–96; Marvin Lazerson, *The Origins of the Urban School: Public Education in Massachusetts, 1879–1915* (Cambridge, MA: Harvard University Press, 1971). This vision of urban education history owes often unacknowledged intellectual debts to the grand social theories of sociologists Edward Tonnies, Karl Marx, Max Weber, Emile Durkheim, Louis Wirth, Robert Redfield and Robert Park. Whereas these modernisation theorists were as interested in the evolution of culture and community as they were in the evolution of material processes, or, at the very least, studied them simultaneously, historians of education have not typically been equally concerned with both. Even David B. Tyack, Michael B. Katz, Carl F. Kaestle and Maris Vinovskis, who are fully acquainted with the work of these grand theorists, assume rather than study relationships between material and psychological processes.
4 More optimistic views of urban educational possibilities are revealed in the following works, though none focuses specifically on urban educational developments. Lawrence A. Cremin, *American Education: The National Experience, 1783–1876* (New York: Harper and Row, 1980); Joseph F. Kett, *Rites of Passage: Adolescence in America, 1790 to the Present* (New York: Basic Books, 1977); Peter Dobkin Hall, *The Organization of American Culture, 1700–1900: Private Institutions, Elites, and the Origins of American Nationality* (New York: New York University Press, 1983); R. Freeman Butts, *Public Education in the United States* (New York: Holt, Rinehart, and Winston, 1984).
5 Analyses of this aspect of the work of urban educational historians can be found in Robert A. Levine and Merry I. White, 'Human conditions: the cultural basis of educational development' (summary of a manuscript in progress, 1984);

Marsden, 'Ecology and nineteenth-century urban education'; Barbara Finkelstein, 'Exploring community in urban educational history', in Goodenow and Ravitch (eds.), *Schools in Cities*, 305–21; Patricia T. Rooke and R. L. Schnell, 'Childhood as ideology: a reinterpretation of the common school', *British Journal of Educational Studies*, Vol. 27 (1979), 7–28; Paricia T. Rooke and R. L. Schnell, 'Childhood, family, and schooling', in David Jones *et al.* (eds.), *Approaches to Educational History* (Winnipeg: Faculty of Education, University of Manitoba, 1981), 158–63.

6 Clifford Geertz, *The Interpretation of Cultures* (New York: Basic Books, 1973), Chap. 3, 193–233.

7 Marsden, 'Ecology and nineteenth-century urban education'; W. E. Marsden, 'Education and the social geography of nineteenth-century towns and cities', in Reeder (ed.), *Urban Education in the Nineteenth Century*, 49–75: Ian Davey and Michael Doucet, 'The social geography of a commercial city, ca. 1853', in Katz, *The People of Hamilton, Canada West*, 319–52.

8 Calhoun, 'The city as teacher'; David Hogan, 'Education and the making of the Chicago working class, 1880–1930', *History of Education Quarterly*, Vol. 18 (1978), 227–70; Davey and Doucet, 'The social geography of a commercial city'; Ronald D. Cohen and Raymond A. Mohl, *The Paradox of Progressive Education: The Gary Plan and Urban Schooling* (Port Washington, NY: Kennikat Press, 1979); Vincent P. Franklin, *The Education of Black Philadelphia: The Social and Educational History of a Minority Community, 1900–1950* (Philadelphia, PA: University of Pennsylvania Press, 1979); D. A. Reeder, 'Predicaments of city children: late Victorian and Edwardian perspectives on education and urban society', in Reeder (ed.), *Urban Education in the Nineteenth Century*, 75–95; Barbara M. Brenzel, 'Domestication as reform: a study of the socialization of wayward girls, 1856–1906', *Harvard Educational Review*, Vol. 50 (1980), 196–213; Neil Sutherland, *Children in English–Canadian Society: Shaping the Twentieth-Century Consensus* (Toronto: University of Toronto Press, 1976).

9 Calhoun, 'The city as teacher', 314.

10 For an analysis of the few sources which exist, see: Barbara Finkelstein, 'Family studies', in *Encyclopedia of Educational Research* (New York: Macmillan 1983), Vol. II, 656–70; Barbara Finkelstein, 'Incorporating childhood into the history of education', *Journal of Educational Thought*, Vol. 18 (1984), 21–43. See also Hogan, 'Education and the making of a Chicago working class', 231.

11 Thomas Bender, *Community and Social Change in America* (New Brunswick, NJ: Rutger University Press, 1978). This is a focus developed by historians emphasising the evolution of children and youth. See the essays of Phyllis Vine, Dominick Cavallo and Barbara Finkelstein in Barbara Finkelstein (ed.), *Regulated Children/ Liberated Children: Education in Psycho-Historical Perspective* (New York: Psychohistory Press, 1979).

12 For examples, Finkelstein, 'Exploring community in urban educational history'; David Hogan, 'the market revolution and disciplinary power: Joseph Lancaster and the psychology of the early classroom system', *History of Education Quarterly*, Vol. 18 (1989), 381–419; David F. Labaree, 'Politics, markets, and the compromised curriculum', *Harvard Educational Review*, Vol. 57 (1987), 483–94. See also Carl F. Kaestle, *Pillars of the Republic: Common Schools and American Society, 1780–1860* (New York: Hill and Wang, 1983); Barbara Finkelstein,

'Casting networks of good influence: the reconstruction of childhood in nineteenth century America', in N. Ray Hiner and Joseph Hawes (eds.), *Childhood and Childrearing in History: Handbook and Resources* (Westport, CT: Greenwood Press, 1985); Barbara Finkelstein, 'Perfecting Childhood: Horace Mann and the origins of public education in the United States', *Biography*, Vol. 13 (1990), 6–21; Harvey Kantor and David B. Tyack (eds.), *Work, Youth, and Schooling; Perspectives on Vocationalism in American Education* (Stanford, CA: Stanford University Press, 1982).

13 Warren, 'Return to old times: rural romanticism in American education history', 295. Historians of education would do well to consult the work of urban sociologists who do not examine education specifically, but have reasoned brilliantly about urban community; George Simmel, 'The metropolis and mental life', in Richard Sennett (ed.), *Classic Essays on the Culture of Cities* (New York: Appleton-Century-Crofts, 1969), 47–60; Robert Redfield, 'The Folk Society', *American Journal of Sociology*, Vol. 3 (1947), 293–308; Frederick Tonnies, *Community and Society*, trans, C. P. Loomis (East Lansing, MI, Michigan State University Press, 1956); Louis Wirth, 'Urbanism as a way of life, in Albert J. Reiss, Jr (ed.), *Louis Wirth on Cities and Social Life* (Chicago, IL: University of Chicago Press, 1964), 60–83.

14 Ultimately, the systematic recovery of the social and psychological contexts of urban education should begin to provide answers to the following sorts of questions. Are there forms of human community, i.e., ways of producing, thinking, believing, doing and knowing, which are revealed through the study of education and which might distinguish cities from non-cities, and from each other? Are there educational forms, arrangements, policies, practices which developed in cities, and which distinguish urban educational forms from, e.g., rural or agrarian ones? Are forms of educational authority different in urban areas? Did particular forms of human association, i.e., intergenerational, male–female, teacher–learner relationships arise in cities? If so, did they develop in similar and/or predictable ways across regions, nations, etc.?

15 The limitations in our current understanding are revealed clearly when one sees the sequence and timing of urbanisation and educational expansion. In some countries, urbanisation preceded universal education, in others, it was reversed. In 1860, more than half of the English population lived in cities but education was not required. The apparatus of compulsory schooling emerged first in the United States when less than one third of the population lived in urban centres.

In China, popular schooling and industrial development proceeded with only 20 per cent of the population living in cities. Levine and White, 'Human conditions'; Robert Redfield, 'The cultural role of cities', *Economic Development and Cultural Change*, Vol. III (1954), 53–73.

16 Richard Sennett, *The Uses of Disorder: Personal Identity and City Life* (New York: Random House, 1970); John Higham, 'Hanging together: divergent unities in American history', *Journal of American History*, Vol. 61 (1974), 5–28; Bender, *Community and Social Change in America*; Calhoun, 'The city as teacher'; Robert Wiebe, *The Search for Order, 1877–1920* (New York: Hill and Wang, 1967).

17 Calhoun, 'The city as teacher', 317; See also Kaestle, *Pillars of the Republic*; Paul Boyer, *Urban Masses and Moral Order in America, 1820–1920* (Cambridge, MA: Harvard University Press, 1978); Helen Lefkowitz Horowitz, *Culture and the*

City: Cultural Philanthropy in Chicago from the 1880s–1917 (Lexington, KY: University of Kentucky Press, 1976); Tyack, *One Best System*, 39, put the myth-creating qualities of the urban environment in this way: 'as the villages grew into congested, heterogeneous cities, as conflicting values and strangers on the streets threatened the old patterns of socialization, decentralized decision-making and pedagogical variety struck many educational leaders as anarchy. They sought instead to centralize the nerve centers of information and influence and to standardize the educational process.'

18 Cohen and Mohl, *The Paradox of Progressive Education*, 161.
19 Charles Strickland, 'Families, children, and women: the revolt against the Victorian model' (unpublished manuscript, 1979); Jane Silverman Mulligan, 'The Madonna and child in American culture' PhD thesis, University of California at Los Angeles, 1975, 38–43; Jacques Donzelot, *The Policing of the Family* (1st English edn, New York: Pantheon Books, 1979); Elizabeth Badinter, *L'Amour en plus: histoire de l'amour maternelle, 17 ème–20ème siècles* (Paris: Flammarion, 1980); Nancy B. Weiss, 'Mother, the invention of necessity: Dr. Benjamin Spock's baby and child care', *American Quarterly*, Vol. 29 (1973), 519.
20 Brenzel, 'Domestication as reform'; Kett, *Rites of Passage*; Steven L. Schlossman, *Love and the American Delinquent: The Theory and Practice of 'Progressive' Juvenile Justice, 1825–1920* (Chicago, IL: University of Chicago Press, 1977); Joseph Hawes, *Children in Urban Society: Juvenile Delinquency in Nineteenth-Century America* (New York: Oxford University Press, 1971); Robert Mennell, *Thorns and Thistles: Juvenile Delinquents in the United States, 1825–1940* (Hanover, NH: University Press of New England, 1973); Patricia Rooke and Richard Schnell, 'The child institutionalized in China, Britain, and the United States: a transatlantic perspective', *Journal of Educational Thought*, Vol. 2 (1977), 156–7.
21 Michael Zuckerman, 'Children's rights: the failure of reform', *Policy Analysis*, Vol. 2 (1976), 371–85; Weiss, 'Mother, the invention of necessity'; Christopher Lasch, *Haven in a Heartless World: The Family Besieged* (New York: Basic Books, 1979); David J. Rothman, *The Discovery of the Asylum: Social Order and Disorder in the New Republic* (Boston, MA: Little Brown and Company, 1971).
22 Hall, *The Organization of American Culture*; Cremin, *American Education: The National Experience*, Kett, *Rites of Passage*; Katz, *The People of Hamilton, Canada West*; Franklin, *Education of Black Philadelphia*; Judy Jolley Mohraz, *The Separate Problem: Case Studies of Black Education in the North, 1900–1930* (Westport, CT: Greenwood Press, 1978); Selma Berrol, 'The open city: Jews, jobs, and schools in New York City, 1880–1915', in Ravitch and Goodenow (eds.), *Educating an Urban People*, Chap. 5, 101–16; Maxine Seller, 'The educational experience of immigrant adults', in Donald R. Warren (ed.), *History, Education, and Public Policy: Recovering American Educational History* (Chicago, IL: McCutchan Press, 1978); John Higham (ed.), *Ethnic Leadership in America* (Baltimore, MD: Johns Hopkins University Press, 1978).
23 Cremin, *American Education: The National Experience*; Kett, *Rites of Passage*; Hall, *The Organization of American Culture*.
24 Lazerson, *Origins of the Urban School*; Katz, *The People of Hamilton, Canada West*; David B. Tyack and Elisabeth Hansot, *Managers of Virtue: Public School Leadership in America, 1820–1980* (New York: Basic Books, 1986); Ian Davey,

'Popular education and socialization', *History of Education Quarterly*, Vol. 21 (1981), 373–81.
25 Lazerson, *Origins of the Urban School*, xii. See also David Tyack and Harvey A. Kantor, *Learning to Earn: School, Work and Vocational Reform in California: 1880–1930* (Madison, WI: University of Wisconsin Press, 1988); David F. Labaree, *The Making of an American High School* (New Haven, CT: Yale University Press, 1988). For examples of studies emphasising ethnic and cultural ideology, see Joel Perlmann, *Ethnic Differences: Schooling and Social Structure among the Irish, Italians, Jews and Blacks in an American City, 1880–1935* (Cambridge: Cambridge University Press, 1988); Ira Katznelson and Margaret Weir, *Schooling for All: Class, Race, and the Decline of the Democratic Ideal* (New York: Basic Books, 1985).
26 Reeder, 'Predicaments of city children', 26.
27 Lloyd DeMause, 'The evolution of childhood', in L. DeMause (ed.), *The History of Childhood* (New York: Psychohistory Press, 1974); Phillipe Aries, *Centuries of Childhood: A Social History of Family Life*, trans. Robert Baldick (New York: Alfred A. Knopf, 1962); Lawrence Stone, *The Family, Sex, and Marriage in England, 1500–1800* (New York: Harper and Row, 1977) Badinter, *L'Amour en plus*; Dominick Cavallo, 'The politics of latency: kindergarten pedagogy, 1860–1930', in Finkelstein (ed.), *Regulated Children*; Barbara Finkelstein and Kathy Vandell, 'The schooling of American childhood: the emergence of learning communities', Mary Lynn Stevense Heininger and Harvey Green (eds.), *A Century of Childhood, 1820–1920* (Rochester, NY: Margaret Woodbury Strong Museum, 1984), 65–97; Finkelstein, 'Casting networks of good influence'; Alison L. Prentice and Susan E. Houston (eds.), *Family, School, and Society in Nineteenth Century Canada* (Toronto: Oxford University Press, 1975); Sutherland, *Children in English–Canadian Society*; Marvin Lazerson and W. Norton Grubb, *Broken Promises: How Americans Fail their Children* (New York: Basic Books, 1982).
28 Finkelstein, 'Casting networks of good influence'; Finkelstein and Vandell, 'The schooling of American childhood'; Donzelot, *The Policing of the Family*.
29 There are several biographical studies exemplifying ways to recover the mentalities of educational reformers. As examples, see Katharine Kish Sklar, *Catharine Beecher: A Study in American Domesticity* (New Haven, CT: Yale University Press, 1973); Dorothy Ross, *G. Stanley Hall: The Psychologist as Prophet* (Chicago, IL: University of Chicago Press, 1974); Gregory Nenstiel, 'Jacob Abbott: The evolution of a nineteenth century educator' (PhD thesis, University of Maryland, College Park, 1979); Finkelstein, 'Perfecting childhood'. This orientation is nowhere evident in standard biographies of American educational reformers of the nineteenth and twentieth centuries, though it represents a minor theme in Merle Curti, *The Social Ideas of American Educators* (new and revised edn, Totowa, NJ: Littlefield, Adams and Company, 1961); and Cremin, *American Education: The National Experience*.
30 Finkelstein and Vandell, 'The schooling of American childhood'; Finkelstein, 'Casting networks of good influence'. These themes are elaborated in Barbara Finkelstein, *Governing the Young: Teacher Behavior in Popular Primary Schools in Nineteenth-Century United States* (London and New York, Falmer Press, 1989).

31 This orientation is reflected in the classic work of Timothy L. Smith, 'Immigrant social aspirations and American education, 1880–1950', *American Quarterly*, Vol. 21 (1969), 522–5; and 'Native blacks and foreign whites, 1880–1950', *Perspectives in American History*, Vol. 6 (1972), 311–31. See also Herbert Gutman, *Work, Culture, and Society in Industrializing America* (New York: Vintage Books, 1977); E. P. Thompson, *The Making of the English Working Class* (New York: Vintage Books, 1963), 830–2. For a small survey of literature, see John Bodnar, *Workers' World: Kinship, Community, and Protest in an Industrial Society, 1900–1940* (Baltimore, MD: Johns Hopkins University Press, 1982).
32 This point is well made in Levine and White, 'Human conditions'. See also Hogan, 'Education and the making of the Chicago working class'.
33 Robert Wiebe, *The Segmented Society* (New York: Oxford University Press, 1975; Bender, *Community and Social Change in America*; Finkelstein, 'Casting networks of good influence'.
34 For examples, implicitly documented, see James W. Sanders, *The Education of an Urban Minority: Catholics in Chicago, 1833–1965* (New York: Oxford University Press, 1977); Charles Wollenberg, *All Deliberate Speed: Segregation and Exclusion in California* (Berkeley, CA: University of California Press, 1978); Finkelstein, 'Casting networks of good influence'.
35 Brenzel, 'Domestication as reform'; Finkelstein, 'Casting networks of good influence'; Schlossman, *Love and the American Delinquent*. Court records in New York and Philadelphia consistently reveal these sorts of commitments.
36 Franklin, *Education of Black Philadelphia*; Mohraz, *The Separate Problem*; Smith, 'Native blacks and foreign whites'.
37 Levine and White, 'Human conditions'.
38 Reeder, 'Predicaments of city children'; Finkelstein and Vandell, 'The schooling of American childhood'; Finkelstein, 'Casting networks of good influence'.
39 Kaestle, *Pillars of the Republic*; Tyack, *One Best System*: Cremin, *American Education: The National Experience*.
40 Cremin, *American Education: The National Experience*; Butts, *Public Education in the United States*; Hawes, *Children in Urban Society*; DeMause, 'Evolution of childhood'.
41 Michael B. Katz, *The Irony of Early School Reform: Educational Innovation in Mid-Nineteenth Century Massachusetts* (Cambridge: Harvard University Press, 1968); Katz, *The People of Hamilton, Canada West*; Raymond A. Mohl, *Poverty in New York, 1783–1825* (New York: Oxford University Press, 1971); Kett, *Rites of Passage*.
42 The corpus of work done by Michel Foucault on prisons, sexuality, madness, work, discipline and punishment all reflect the wedding of intellectual history and sociological functionalism. See also Michael Ignatieff, 'Prison and factory discipline: the origin of an idea' (unpublished paper delivered at the annual meeting of the American Historical Association, Washington, DC, 1976); Rothman, *The Discovery of the Asylum*, Chap. 9.
43 Sennett, *Personal Identity and City Life*; Bender, *Community and Social Change in America*.
44 Clifford Geertz, 'The integrative revolution: primordial sentiments and civil politics in new states', in Clifford Geertz (ed.), *Old Societies and New States* (New York: Free Press, 1963); Higham, 'Hanging together'; Higham (ed.), *Ethnic*

Leadership in America. The classic and original treatment of large and small traditions is that of Redfield, 'The cultural role of cities'.
45 Bender, *Community and Social Change in America*. See also Wiebe, *The Search for Order*; Bodnar, *Workers' World*.
46 Geertz, 'The integrative revolution'; Bender, *Community and Social Change in America*.
47 The work of adaptation and the work of ethnic leaders is explored in the variety of essays in Higham (ed.), *Ethnic Leadership in America*.
48 The need for this kind of study is articulated in Sol Cohen, 'The history of urban education in the United States: historians of education and their discontents', in Reeder (ed.), *Urban Education in the Nineteenth Century*, 115–33. In it he summarises efforts of historians like Ronald Cohen and Selwyn Troen to infuse some complexity into the political analysis of schools. See also Rick Ginsburg, Paul Peterson and Carol Peterson, 'The 1917 Otis Law Compromise', *Issues in Education*, Vol. 1 (1984), and various essays in Ravitch and Goodenow (eds.), *Educating an Urban People*.
49 Wiebe, *The Segmented Society*, Preface; Bender, *Community and Social Change in America*, p. 5.
50 Bodnar, *Workers' World*; Kirk Jeffrey, 'The family as utopian retreat from the city: the nineteenth century contribution', *Soundings*, Vol. 55 (1972), 21–41; Richard Sennett, *Families Against the City: Middle Class Homes of Industrial Chicago, 1872–1890* (New York: Random House: Vintage, 1970).
51 Finkelstein, 'Exploring community in urban educational history'.
52 Thomas J. Schlereth (ed.), *Material Culture in America: An Anthology* (Nashville, TN: American Society for State and Local History, 1982).
53 Eugene J. Provenzo, Jr, 'The photographer as educator: the child labor photostories of Lewis Hine', *Teachers College Record*, Vol. 83 (1982), 593–612; Heininger and Green (eds.), *A Century of Childhood*.
54 For a thoughtful analysis, see J. Stephen Hazlitt, 'Education as it was: a view of life in schools', *History of Education Quarterly*, Vol. 15 (1975), 351–61, and analyses contained in Finkelstein, 'Family studies'.
55 Calhoun, 'The city as teacher'; Daniel P. Calhoun, *The Intelligence of a People* (Princeton, NJ: Princeton University Press, 1973).
56 Barbara Finkelstein, 'Reading, writing, and the acquisition of identity in the United States: 1790–1860', in Finkelstein (ed.), *Regulated Children*, Chap. 6, 114–40.
57 Ellen C. Lagerman, *A Generation of Women: Education in the Lives of Progressive Reformers* (Cambridge, MA: Harvard University Press, 1979).
58 Sklar, Nancy F. Cott, *The Bonds of Womanhood: 'Women's Sphere' in New England, 1780–1835* (New Haven, CT: Yale University Press, 1977); multiple works of Carroll Smith Rosenberg.
59 Simmel, 'The metropolis and mental life'; Kurt H. Wolff (ed.), *The Sociology of George Simmel* (New York: Free Press, 1950).
60 Calhoun, 'The city as teacher'; Calhoun, *The Intelligence of a People*.
61 Calhoun, *The Intelligence of a People*.
62 Calhoun, 'The city as teacher', 313.
63 These themes are extended and expanded in the works of Barbara Finkelstein, David Tyack and Clifford Geertz cited above.
64 Davey, 'Popular education and socialization'.

Part 3

Needs and opportunities: policy and theory considerations

9 Theory in educational history: a middle ground

Carl F. Kaestle

Most historians are not very theoretical. There is little in their training, in their favourite historical writing or in their intellectual instincts that inclines them to the sustained use of theory. There are exceptions, of course. Historians who study the attitudes and behaviour of ordinary people face difficult methodological problems, and they sometimes use theory as a handle on their incomplete or indirect evidence. Historians of large social transformations, like industrialisation, or of deviance problems, like insanity, often turn to sociology or psychology for theoretical insights. Others draw on philosophy, economics or anthropology. Still, non-theorists predominate in historical work, especially in America, where pragmatism seems to sanction an indifference to theory.[1] Although the non-theorists can therefore take comfort in numbers, logic seems to favour the theorists. Because all historical writing is selective and interpretive, it is necessarily guided by individual historians' sense of what is important, where to find meaning and how social change and human motivation work. The answers arise partly from the materials, of course. History is, after all, partly inductive. However, the answers also lie in a historian's temperament, convictions, hunches and theories. By paying attention to the best theoretical work in related disciplines, historians can better identify their informal, personal theories. More important, they can shape their understanding of human experience by learning from other disciplines. And sometimes, historical work reflects back in important ways on social theories, confirming, refuting or modifying various theoretical statements.

The word 'theory' is used loosely to mean an idea about how some particular thing works or why some particular event happened. But in the more formal sense, a theory must present more general propositions about causes and consequences, about why things work the way they do. If the propositions are generally true, they will allow us to make predictions about new cases not previously considered. Theories thus strive for predictability. Theory is used here in this formal sense.[2]

Historians deal with two categories of theories, with some overlap: first, theories about historical phenomena, that is, about social structure and social change in different times and places; second, theories about methodology, that is, generalisable propositions about what kinds of inferences we can draw from certain kinds of evidence. Theories about historical phenomena may have implications for historical methodology. They may influence what sort of evidence we look for, what sort of evidence we will accept and what sort of arguments we will make from the evidence. If a historian accepts the Marxist proposition that one's relationship to the means of production is crucial to one's experience, the historian will make a concerted effort to determine historical actors' class consciousness and will make class a prominent part of the explanation of historical events. On the other hand, many methodological theories may be used in the service of different social theories. For example, if an historian accepts Clifford Geertz's theory that ritualistic or everyday behaviour can symbolise the deeper meaning of a culture, she or he will feel free to move from observed behaviour to cultural meaning and will devote much attention to that interpretive leap, but this method does not prejudge or prescribe a particular theoretical view of the world. Similarly, statistical theories about causal inference may be used by historians with very different social theories.

Systematic theories are philosophically satisfying to some historians, but most working historians are not comfortable with a comprehensive system. Used more incidentally, however, theory can be fun, suggestive and enlightening. Historians are scavengers; sometimes they will raid a theoretical system for a revealing concept, leaving the theoretical framework behind. Attention to theory can be a counterbalance against a tendency in historical work to particularism or mere chronicle. However, many historians feel caught in the middle, sceptical about the truth or usefulness of theoretical systems and yet lured by the demonstrated power of some theorists to get beneath the surface, beyond the facts, to structure and meaning.

I shall not attempt a critique of comprehensive theoretical efforts in history. The literature on that subject is already mountainous, and most historians have found that they can get along quite well by ignoring it.[3] Instead, I shall argue in this essay that non-theorists lose much by ignoring theory, that there is a large middle ground between particularism and grand systems and that comparative history has an important place in this middle ground.[4]

Five ideal types of historians will illustrate the ways in which practitioners have resolved the history–theory dilemma. The first type is the producer. Some people who write about history actually aim to construct theory, not just use it. Great social theorists from Marx to Parsons wrote historical work, and some contemporary scholars try to make contributions to theory through their historical analysis. Often, the theory producers were trained in a discipline other than history. For example, Neil Smelser, a sociologist, has applied his structural functionalist framework not only to the early Lancashire textile industry but to nineteenth-century American education, arguing a triangular model of family, economy and education.[5]

Most historians who deal with theory are not producers; they are users. There are basically three kinds of users. First, there are systematic users, scholars who subscribe to some version of a comprehensive theory about human nature and social change, and seek to illustrate its workings in historical studies. Marxist users include Samuel Bowles and Herbert Gintis on the history of American education, and John Foster on the history of English industrialisation. Another systematic user among American social historians is Richard D. Brown, who applied modernisation theory to early American history; and Geertz's 'thick description' has found a champion in Rhys Isaac, an historian of early Virginia.[6]

One problem suffered by systematic users is that the theorists and their interpreters often disagree about what the theory actually is. The history of Marxist scholarship has provided many extended debates about such matters as economic determinism, human agency and inevitability. Modernisation theorists differ about the characteristics of modernity, for example, whether it includes democratisation or not. Once systematic users sort out what their theory is, they still may differ about how to apply it to historical analysis. Eugene Genovese and Elizabeth Fox-Genovese, for example, argue that the activities of pre-industrial bourgeois merchants retarded, rather than advanced, capitalism, a view counter to the usual Marxist interpretation. Francis Schrag argues, counter to most neo-Marxists, that in applying historical materialism to the analysis of education, we should focus on schools' contribution to production, not reproduction, to structure, not superstructure.[7] At their best, of course, systematic users do not expect their theories to tell the whole story before they analyse the untidy historical evidence. Systematic theory offers historians not certain predictions but the appeal of interpretive coherence. Still, the application of such theories presents serious problems that leave most historians sceptical. As a result, there are not very many systematic users among historians. Even if we put the committed Marxists, modernisers, Annalists, Weberians and Parsonians all together (an interesting thought), they are not numerous.

The next species is the eclectic user. This scholar is interested in theory but cannot find a comprehensive theory that is fully satisfying. So the eclectic user puts together different theoretical insights wherever they seem to apply, or wherever they help illuminate a particular historical situation. Sometimes an eclectic historian will be very explicit about eclecticism and even try out different theories on the same set of historical data. David

Tyack explored compulsory schooling from a variety of theoretical perspectives in an essay called 'Ways of seeing'. Later, in *Managers of Virtue*, he and Elisabeth Hansot employed different fragments of social theory for different periods. In explaining seventeenth-century American witchcraft trials, John Demos wrote separate analyses using a biographical, then a psychological and then a sociological perspective.[8]

Such organised eclecticism is unusual. More common is the casual and occasional use of theory practised by the next group, the incidental users of theory. These historians use a proposition from social science theory from time to time because it helps to explain their data, or structure their inquiry or ask the right questions. Sometimes, it must be said, theory just provides footnotes or sanctions for beliefs the historian would have expressed anyway. Often, however, the theory has suggested a way of looking at a particular problem. It is fashionable to call such incidental uses of theory 'heuristic'. Examples include Arthur Mann, who used the sociological concept of 'marginal man' in his biography of Fiorello La Guardia, and Paul Johnson, who used Durkheim's sociology of religion as a guide to revivals in ante-bellum Rochester.[9] Some incidental users flaunt their interaction with social science theory, bringing it into the text and discussing it in their footnotes. Others think that this combination of historical explanation and social science theorising is inappropriate and distracting. In his recent presidential address to the American Historical Association, Bernard Bailyn expressed this arm's-distance relation between social science theory and historical explanation.

> The ultimate purpose of all historical scholarship [is] comprehensive narration. No effective historian of the future can be innocent of statistics, and indeed he or she should probably be a literate amateur economist, psychologist, anthropologist, sociologist and geographer. In the end, however, historians must be, not analysts of isolated technical problems abstracted from the past, but narrators of worlds in motion – worlds as complex, unpredictable as our own.[10]

Some historians wish to distance historical writing even further from theory. This brings us to the last type: the knowledgeable anti-theorist. These are historians who have thought about the use of theory in history and have become outright critics. Here, one might include C. Vann Woodward, who has argued for a revival of graceful, narrative history that will make historians' work accessible and enjoyable to the general public. Like Woodward, other historians believe that history is not a social science and should not be a quest for generalisation but rather a sensitive rendering of particular historical situations. A colleague once told me that the job of the historian was to tell 'true stories about the past'. E. P. Thompson, himself a sophisticated theorist, has recently argued 'the poverty of theory', by which he means that the only theory useful to historians is internal to historical methodology, not borrowed from abstract philosophical or sociological systems. Even such anti-theorists, or course, must know theory in order to reject it.[11]

Although the debates between systematic theorists and anti-theorists are sometimes elegant, most historians who engage theory do so on a middle ground. As an incidental user of theory, I shall use a few personal examples to illustrate this middle position and to underscore the relationship between comparative work and theoretical work. The first example is of a theoretical statement that I found comforting but which did not change my analysis. In the introduction to our 1980 study of Massachusetts education, Maris Vinovskis and I stated our rather commonsensical position on the primacy of economic structures in historical explanation in this way: 'We believe that intellectual discourse, religion, ethnic traditions, and other spheres of social experience play determining roles in human events and are in some regards independent of the productive system and the social relations it generates; yet we believe that social structure and economic conditions provide a bedrock that heavily influences the shape and direction of human activities.' A reviewer selected this as an example of equivocation. Battered but not defeated, I was relieved to find a philosopher arguing a position similar to ours. In *Marxism and the Methodology of History*, Gregor McLennan writes:

Unlike natural science, historical knowledge must in principle be incomplete, because the relations it seeks to analyze are between human beings, who are themselves casual agents ... Structural principles must be complemented by ... notions of individual action, natural causes, and 'accidental' circumstances ... Nevertheless, material and social relations can be long-term, effective real structures that set firm limits to the ... practical effect that accident and agency have.

This statement, and the arguments about philosophical realism that accompanied it, reinforced my prior inclination but provided me with a slightly different and more articulate expression on the issue. Similarly, as Ronald Walters has written, Clifford Geertz has a 'knack for stating precisely lines of interpretation similar to ones historians were pursuing, less rigorously and self-consciously'. Bits of theory, then, can clarify or confirm historians' homegrown theorising. That is what McLennan was doing for me in this case, but it did not change my analysis.[12]

In contrast, my reading on ideology did influence my analysis. I surveyed the treatment of ideology in some of Marx, Mannheim and Gramsci, plus recent commentators like Geertz, Seliger and Plamenatz, in order to understand better the social views of nineteenth-century reformers.[13] The result was a concept of ideology that is inclusive and non-normative, that portrays all people as thinking and communicating in ideological terms sometimes. According to this view, people can participate in more than one coherent ideology at the same time, and they express their ideological commitments not only through formal statements but in everyday behaviour. Ideology is a set of apparently compatible propositions that help justify and interpret social structure and human relations. It is a simplification of reality, but not necessarily a deliberate distortion. This concept shaped my analysis of ante-bellum school reform, in particular a chapter on the native Protestant ideology that supported school reform in America.

At a broader level, historians on the left have influenced me (and other non-radical historians, I suspect) because they hearken to theory more regularly and tend to make the primacy of economics and class an issue in social history. This has made me think more in recent years about what *model* of explanation is embedded in my account of nineteenth-century educational history. Historians' attempts to portray causation and interrelationships often lead to spatial models, which are metaphorical representations of some implicit or explicit theory. They often portray society as a machine, as a living organism, as a drama or as a game. More originally, Lawrence Stone imagined seventeenth-century social structure as the towers of San Gimignano, and Tamara Hareven expressed the relationship between family cycles and the life course of individuals by envisioning fish swimming in schools.[14]

Not all models employ such colourful metaphors, nor do they necessarily embody a predictive theory. They can be merely schemes for organising historical explanation. In analysing nineteenth-century school reform, I developed a model that ordered my causal thinking. I looked first at structural features, like production, demography and ethnic composition, then at ideology, which was not only a justification for existing structures but a plan for moving them in certain directions. Then I looked at social action and reform by dominant groups, and then at reaction by non-dominant groups, both acquiescent and resistant. This is an analytical strand, not a chronological sequence. Within the strand, there are many feedback loops. Ideology can reflect back upon social relations and shape them; the clash of ideologies can modify both the ideologies and the institutions they support; new institutional arrangements become part of new structures generating new ideologies and conflicts. As a model, this began simply as a flow chart. It did not predict what aspects of socio-economic structure and culture were most important, nor what sort of reactions to expect from non-dominant groups. In some sort of dialogue between eclectic theory and my knowledge of the historical evidence, I developed the conviction that social structure and social change were the starting place in explaining educational development, and that the confrontation of the dominant ideology with various sub-cultural and partially dissenting groups provided a conceptual handle on how it all worked out. If I had believed that great ideas and great men were the starting point for educational changes, or that school systems develop in relative independence from social change, I would have needed different models, different metaphors and different middle-range theories.[15]

Models, then, can embody pieces of theory and provide an explanatory approach. They are a good tool for the incidental user of theory. Models can be looser than predictive theories. Although systematic theories are predicated on the notion that we can make generalisations about history, they often run into trouble when several disparate cases are compared. Some causal elements may be more salient in one case than another. In Sweden, for example, religion encouraged state education, and urbanisation was not much of a factor; whereas in England, urbanisation encouraged state intervention, but religious conflict inhibited it. Even when the correlations go in the same direction, it is hard to prove simple causal relationships in historical situations where there are a lot of reinforcing social trends and a lot of static. For example, literacy was high in seventeenth-century New England, and one can make a plausible case that the decisive factor was Calvinist religion. When we look at the period from the 1740s to the 1830s in the American Northeast, sketchy evidence suggests a further take-off in schooling enrolments and literacy. In view of the religious revivals of the 1740s and the early nineteenth century, should we continue with our religious theory? The truth seems to be that rising enrolments and literacy in these later periods were due to rising female education and the creation of decentralised school districts. Both of these proximate causes were fostered by background factors: population patterns, capitalist economic development, republican political ideas and the reviving influence of assertive Protestantism. Further work in the historical sources may refine our understanding of the relative influence of these factors, but a single-factor religious explanation will not suffice. Some theories fit one country better than another, or one period better than another, or one institutional level better than another. Human capital theory applies to education better for the later industrial period than the earlier; social control theory fits elementary education better than secondary; while credentialing and screening theories work better at higher levels than lower. Comparative work across nations, regions, time periods or institutional levels can thus be a proving ground for theory. For the committed systematic user, comparative studies can provide an empirical arena in which to do fine tuning; it may result in revision or reinforcement of a general theoretical position. For the committed particularist, comparative studies may display a welter of complexity and individual experiences that defy generalisation, reinforcing an anti-theoretical stance.

For those of us in the middle ground – those who use theory eclectically or incidentally – comparative studies press us to think about explanatory frameworks and the relative salience of various causal factors in different settings. Having developed a model of educational development for the American Northeast, in which capitalism, republicanism and Protestantism combined to support a reformist ideology, I applied it to the Midwest, finding that region superficially different but fundamentally similar to the Northeast. The American South, in contrast, was economically different. Moreover, both Protestantism and republicanism had an uncomfortable, twisted relationship with slavery in the South. Educational reform generally failed in this region. Thus, both my model and the ingredients of my explanation seemed to fit the different regions and the different results.

In an earlier article I compared the effect of early nineteenth-century charity schooling in England and in America, finding that the raging English controversy over the education of the poor was almost wholly absent in America. Both countries were Protestant and capitalist. The purpose of charity schooling was social stability in both countries, and the institutions were very similar. Why did the wisdom of charity education seem so obvious to American elites, while among English leaders the fear of popular education persisted so stubbornly? In this study, I did not begin with a hypothesis or a model, but the comparative design forced me to think about the relevant differences in the two countries. Class, politics and ethnicity provided the answers. Although American cities contained distressed poor people, and substantial inequality, England had tighter class lines and vastly more poor people; thus Americans had less to fear from their poor. Both countries had spawned republican politics, but they had become a doctrine in the United States, and this provided a rationale for widespread education. Finally, America was more racially, ethnically and religiously diverse than England, even before the heavy immigration that began in the 1830s; American leaders thus turned to formal schooling as a means of behavioural assimilation.[16]

I find comprehensive theoretical viewpoints more limiting than penetrating in historical work, yet I have found the study of theory or models to be intellectually fun and analytically helpful in different ways at different times. The result has been incidental use of theory and a rather loose functionalist framework within which I expect to find conflict as well as consensus, persistent anomaly as well as adjustment, agency as well as oppression. This does not, I believe, preclude clear analysis nor the development of a moral point of view about history. There is lots of room to play with theory on this middle ground, and I recommend it to historians who have not yet resolved the history–theory dilemma in their own way.

NOTES

These reflections were assisted by an evening's discussion with the Comparative Studies group, headed by Neil Smelser, at the University of California at Berkeley. The essay was begun during a year at the Center for Advanced Study in the Behavioral Sciences at Stanford, supported by the National Endowment for the Humanities and the Research Committee of the Graduate School, University of Wisconsin-Madison. The author gratefully acknowledges this assistance, as well as helpful comments by Prof. Francis Schrag at the University of Wisconsin.

1 See J. Henretta, 'Social history as lived and written', *American Historical Review*, Vol. 84 (1979), 1293–322; B. Bailyn, 'The problems of the working historian: a comment', in S. Hook (ed.), *Philosophy and History: A Symposium* (New York: New York University Press, 1963), 92–101; A. Megill, 'Recounting the past: "description," explanation, and narrative in historiography', *American Historical Review*, Vol. 94 (1989), 627–53; and J. M. Kousser, 'The state of social science history in the late 1980s', *Historical Methods*, Vol. 22 (1989), 13–20.

2 See C. G. Hempel, 'The function of general laws in history', in P. Gardiner (ed.), *Theories in History* (Glencoe, IL: Free Press, 1959), 344–56; A. L. Stinchcombe, *Constructing Social Theories* (New York: Harcourt, Brace and World, 1968); and M. Brodbeck, 'Models, meaning, and theories', in L. Gross (ed.), *Symposium on Sociological Theory* (New York: Harper and Row, 1959), 373–403.

3 Dabblers might start with the following works on particular theories: G. McLennan, *Marxism and the Methodology of History* (London: Verso, 1981); T. J. Jackson Lears, 'The concept of cultural hegemony: problems and possibilities', *American Historical Review*, Vol. 90 (1985), 567–93; P. H. Hutton, 'The history of mentalités: the new map of cultural history', *History and Theory*, Vol. 20 (1981), 237–59; H. White, 'Foucault decoded: notes from underground', *History and Theory*, Vol. 12 (1973), 23–54; R. Walters, 'Signs of the times: Clifford Geertz and historians', *Social Research*, Vol. 47 (1980), 537–56; A. D. Smith, *The Concept of Social Change: A Critique of the Functionalist Theory of Social Change* (London: Routledge and Kegan Paul, 1973); and R. Bendix, 'Tradition and modernity reconsidered', *Comparative Studies in Society and History*, Vol. 9 (1967), 292–346. A useful anthology is Q. Skinner (ed.), *The Return of Grand Theory in the Human Sciences* (Cambridge: Cambridge University Press, 1985).

4 R. Merton endorsed 'theories of the middle range' in his *Social Theory and Social Structure* (New York: Free Press, revised edn, 1957), 5–10, where he in turn credited T. H. Marshall of the University of London.

5 N. Smelser, *Social Change in the Industrial Revolution* (Chicago, IL: University of Chicago Press, 1959); N. J. Smelser and S. Halpern, 'The historical triangulation of family, economy, and education', in J. Demos and A. S. Boocock (eds.), *Turning Points: Historical and Sociological Essays on the Family* (Chicago, IL: University of Chicago Press, 1978), 288–315.

6 S. Bowles and H. Gintis, *Schooling in Capitalist America: Educational Reform and the Contradictions of Economic Life* (New York: Basic Books, 1976); J. Foster, *Class Struggle and the Industrial Revolution* (New York: St Martin's Press, 1974); R. D. Brown, *Modernization: The Transformation of American Life, 1600–1865* (New York: Hill and Wang, 1976); and R. Isaac, *The Transformation of Virginia, 1740–1790* (Chapel Hill, NC: University of North Carolina Press, 1982).

7 E. Fox-Genovese and E. D. Genovese, *Fruits of Merchant Capital: Slavery and Bourgeois Property in the Rise and Expansion of Capitalism* (New York: Oxford University Press, 1984); and F. Schrag, 'Education and historical materialism', in E. Robertson (ed.), *Philosophy of Education 1984: Proceedings of the Fortieth Annual Meeting of the Philosophy of Education Society* (Normal, IL: Philosophy of Education Society, 1985).
8 D. B. Tyack, 'Ways of seeing: an essay on the history of compulsory schooling', *Harvard Educational Review*, Vol. 46 (1976), pp. 355–89; D. B. Tyack and E. Hansot, *Managers of Virtue: Public School Leadership in America, 1820–1980*, (New York: Basic Books, 1986); and J. P. Demos, *Entertaining Satan: Witchcraft and the Culture of Early New England* (New York: Oxford University Press, 1982).
9 A. Mann, *La Guardia: A Fighter against his Times* (Philadelphia, PA: Lippincott, 1959); and P. Johnson, *A Shopkeeper's Millennium: Society and Revivals in Rochester, New York, 1815–1837* (New York: Hill and Wang, 1978).
10 B. Bailyn, 'The challenge of modern historiography', *American Historical Review*, Vol. 87 (1982), 1–24.
11 C. Vann Woodward, 'A short history of American history', *New York Times Book Review* (8 August 1982), 3, 24; and E. P. Thompson, *The Poverty of Theory and Other Essays* (London: Monthly Review Press, 1978).
12 C. F. Kaestle and M. A. Vinovskis, *Education and Social Change in Nineteenth-Century Massachusetts* (Cambridge: Cambridge University Press, 1980); M. B. Katz, 'Hardcore educational historiography', *Reviews in American History* (December 1980), 509; and McLennan, *Marxism and the Methodology of History*, 233–4.
13 See C. F. Kaestle, 'Ideology and American educational history', *History of Education Quarterly*, Vol. 22 (1982).
14 L. Stone, 'Social mobility in England, 1500–1700', *Past and Present*, Vol. 33 (1966), 17; and T. K. Hareven, *Family Time and Industrial Time: The Relationship between the Family and Work in a New England Industrial Community* (New York: Cambridge University Press, 1982), 6.
15 C. F. Kaestle, *Pillars of the Republic: Common Schools and American Society, 1780–1860* (New York: Hill and Wang, 1983).
16 C. F. Kaestle, '"Between the scylla of brutal ignorance and the charybdis of a literary education": elite attitudes toward mass schooling in early industrial England and America', in L. Stone (ed.), *Schooling and Society: Studies in the History of Education* (Baltimore, MD: Johns Hopkins University Press, 1976).

10 Approaches to urban education in the USA and the UK

David Coulby

The historical approach and the context of practice

As a speculative and theoretical piece rather than one of detailed historiography, this essay considers how urban education can best be conceptualised so as to evaluate the contribution of historical approaches to the subject. Informing its analysis are two presuppositions which can be stated briefly by way of introduction.

The first of these is that cities are sites of social conflict and inequality which educational institutions play a (sometimes crucial) role in ameliorating, exacerbating or reproducing. The second presupposition is that there is an intimate relationship between theory and practice because much theory and research attempt to assist the understanding of the practice of urban educational institutions. This means that theory and research should not only be predicated on what is learned from practice but should, at the best, aspire to inform, question or influence the work of practitioners. In more conventional formulation, this could be seen as a firm position on the need for 'relevance' of the most informed kind among scholars.

The essay begins by considering this question of the interplay of theory and practice. It suggests that an exclusively historical approach to urban education is likely to be limiting. It then goes on to consider other approaches to the subject. Social theory approaches are examined briefly. After considering one comparative approach which reflects on the state of the field of comparative education and rejects the value of historical study, a different international approach is advocated. The strengths and possibilities of historical approaches are then reconsidered. There is no attempt here to limit urban educational study to a 'one right way'. An international approach would need to draw on the strengths of social theory and of historical analysis. However, it is maintained that urban educators cannot ignore the wider context of cities and must see their work as drawing from and contributing to practice.

Whilst it is easy to be sceptical about the influence of theory on practice, such an influence cannot be denied. It may not lead to the ends at which theorists had aimed and practitioners may be fickle in the espousal of various causes, but some influence certainly exists. Furthermore, many theorists, although cautious about their impact on practice, see it as their task not only to reflect and analyse urban schooling but to seek to participate in its development.

In the UK and even more in the USA much of the work done by urban educationists is historical in its orientation. Published works range from broad canvases[1] to much more tightly constrained studies of a particular area or a particular school. Interesting and informative historical accounts can now be found of a single school in Sheffield[2] or of school policies in Detroit between 1836 and 1842.[3] Given the amount of data now available from schools, school boards and local education authorities, there appears to be no reason why such studies should not proliferate almost endlessly, thereby providing rewarding and harmless employment for busy urban educationists.

It is possible that some of the resulting studies may seem remote from the exigencies of those working in urban educational institutions. The issues confronting urban schools in the 1990s continue to generate intense conflict at macro- and micro-levels. Many of the conflicts, against a background of relatively shrinking financial resources, continue to centre on how to deal with inequalities and prejudices.

To take the example of London, against considerable central government opposition which indeed ultimately contributed to its demise,[4] the former Inner London Education Authority announced in 1983 major initiatives to counter educational disadvantages on the basis of class,[5] race,[6] gender[7] and handicap.[8] These initiatives led to debate, sometimes conflict and often significant changes in practice in over a thousand urban schools. The belief in equality and in the urban school as a vehicle in that direction continues to generate educational debate and struggle in many cities of the UK and the USA. Against this background, an exclusively historical approach to urban education may be perceived as a retreat from politics, indeed from policy. Historical approaches may be seen to permit urban educationists the leeway of distancing themselves from the struggles of the present. There would then be a risk that they would be regarded as having little to contribute to the concerns of policy-makers and practitioners.

This is not to assert that history has no 'relevance' to the present nor that it is not an important aspect of urban educational studies. It is merely to contest a too rigid restriction of what is conceived to be history in relation to urban education. As a discipline, history *per se* is not tightly constrained, it certainly does not exclude economic, political or social forces; its terms of reference are rarely limited to events in only one nation state. But for urban educationists adopting an historical approach, these wide issues can all too often be overlooked in the fascination of researching specific topics in specific areas at a specific time. Where this happens, the resulting studies can seem remote not only from current practice and conflicts in urban educational institutions but from the wider field of history itself. Of course, urban education cannot be ahistorical but neither can it be exclusively historical. This is particularly important where the historical approach itself may be narrowly conceived in terms of data collection and description without significant social, political and economic contextualisation. In order to have relevance to the intensity of current debates and in order to do full justice to history itself, urban educationists need to adopt approaches which take account of the context within which urban educational institutions operate.

Theory and practice in urban education often have high degrees of overlap. The theory itself may be produced by teachers, heads and central and local administrators. Teachers, schools and local authorities may explicitly espouse the work of a particular theorist. An initiative in one institution may be evaluated by its originators and this evaluation have a significant impact on a wide area of theory. People ostensibly outside the system may perform or commission research and polemic which has a practical impact. Pressure groups for black people or the handicapped or middle-class suburbanists, teachers' unions, wider social movements such as environmentalism or unilateralism may all lead to educational writing which has varying degrees of influence on urban schools.

Considering the types of writing which have been most influential, historical studies have played a minor part. Large government reports (which may include a small element of history), cohort studies and elegant polemic would seem to be the kinds of writing which influence the debate on urban educational institutions if not the practice within them. It is more difficult to point to instances where specific policy decisions have been made in the light of historical analysis. Perhaps historical approaches cannot aspire to this type of 'relevance'. On the other hand, historical studies can be particularly forceful in framing the wider debate. Grace's work on social control in the UK[9] is a good example here. It is unlikely that this work has led to the reorganisation of pastoral care in many schools but it is certain that it has helped many teachers to reflect critically on the wider implications of their role. The inspiration of critical reflection is a task not without relevance, though its influence on policy decisions may be indirect.

In the next three sections three approaches to urban education are identified. They derive from social theory, from comparative and international education and from history. The advantages and disadvantages of these approaches are briefly considered by focusing on the works of selected authors. Castells and Althusser are chosen to represent the social theory approach since they exemplify the analysis of wider economic, political and social forces which operate in cities and schools. By contrast, Holmes, who represents one possible comparative approach, is seen to disregard these forces. A different international approach is suggested. This is based on the international division and movement of capital, labour and knowledge. Grace is chosen as a strong and recent advocate of the historical approach. The final section considers whether urban education as a field of study is necessarily confined to cities and then goes on to attempt a preliminary summation of the three identified approaches.

Approaches derived from urban social theory

Social theory might provide an attractive approach for urban educationists since it is often concerned with specifically urban issues. Social theory with a specifically urban focus has had at least two separate important manifestations: the first culminated in the Chicago School; the second is European and was in many ways brought to a focus by the fierce repression of demonstrations by workers and students on the streets of Paris in May 1968.

In neither instance is education an important research topic. The first manifestation concentrated on demographic movement, social differences and sub-cultures; the second on the economic structures and political control of cities. In looking to this area for an approach to urban education, it is necessary to apply theories to issues which were rarely addressed by the original theorists.

Park and his colleagues of the Chicago School developed a theory of the social organisation and growth of cities based on an analogy with ecological balance.[10] Burgess, for instance, developed a dynamic model of urban growth in terms of extension, succession and concentration.[11] Cities were seen to have different 'natural' areas within them where certain types of human activity and social life could thrive: these could be transformed as the city, like an organism, grew outwards. The ecological framework prompted an interest in how these 'natural' areas retained or lost their stability and balance. This led to a concentration on the norms and institutions whereby urban social order could be maintained.[12]

Although this theoretical position has not been overtly espoused by educators or educationists, it does have a familiar ring. Policies such as compensatory education or educational priority areas have been based on the similar notion that specific areas of the city suffer from social, if not moral, decline. The concept of isolated areas of cities being subjected, as if by nature, to cultural or educational deprivation has not, in the UK, been proved to be a firm foundation on which to base policy.[13]

More generally, recent critiques of the Chicago School have pointed to its limitations. Castells insists: '1. That there is no cultural system linked to a given form of spatial organisation; 2. That the social history of humanity is not determined by the type of development of territorial collectivities; 3. That the spatial environment is not the root of a specificity of behaviour and representation.'[14]

The links between social class, lifestyle and spatial location in cities cannot be assumed to be 'natural' or self-determining. They are part of larger urban processes and need to be studied alongside them. The human ecology approach largely ignores the importance of elements such as political and economic power in the shaping of urban space. The ecology metaphor tends to conceal the decisions of city-wide importance which can be taken by active human agents.

Castells himself may be taken as a representative of that recent European urban social theory which has found much of its inspiration in Marx. Castells uses the concept of contradiction to apply to conflicts (of both interest and action) between the bourgeoisie and the proletariat or between different factions within each class. He stresses that urban contradictions are a spatial intensification of the consequences of a socio-political structure linked to the capitalist mode of production. For Castells, the process which underlies the shaping of cities is the reproduction of labour power, that is the maintenance of a large, mobile, skilled workforce: 'in advanced capitalist societies the process which structures space is that which concerns the simple and extended reproduction of labour power: the ensemble of the so-called urban practices connotes the articulation of the process with the social structure as a whole'.[15]

He condemns ecological approaches which reduce social and economic injustices to a limited and 'natural' urban difficulty:

The consequence of this way of approaching the question is that the solution to the conflicts and contradictions implied becomes technical not political. Planning (rational, neutral and scientific) should replace social and political debate about the decisions which are the basis of the concrete manifestations of the problem. In reality this approach has corresponded throughout history to the ideological practice of the dominant classes.[16]

Castells here points to the dangers for policy-makers in too narrowly constraining a subject such as urban education. An exclusively historical approach could be seen to divert debate and policy away from central urban issues.

The state is crucial to Castells' theory in that it has taken on the role of funding many facilities of collective consumption and has thereby interfered significantly in the urban system. State investment and spending relieves private capital of the need to make expenditure on either the urban macro-structure (roads, ports, etc.) or on the facilities necessary for the reproduction of labour power (housing, schools, etc.). But one of the effects of state expenditure is that the level of urban collective consumption becomes a political issue and an area of potential conflicts. When such conflict occurs, it is likely to be directed against the state rather than against particular capitalist interests. In the cities of the UK and the USA, politicised urban collective consumption has led to rapidly increasing public expenditure. Attempts by the state to reduce this expenditure, along the lines of contemporary government policy in both the UK and the USA, leads, for Castells, to the compounding of the urban crisis: 'the crisis of state intervention on the crisis of the reproduction of the labour force'.[17]

For Castells, this crisis depends on the activities of urban social movements. It seems possible that his research interests have led him to overestimate the importance of these. Nevertheless, his account of the 'statisation' of expenditure provides a resonant context for urban educationists, both those concerned with the history of the growth of state schooling and those involved with the policy issues that face schooling systems where revenues have been cut. Certainly, among those urban social movements which can be identified today are those protesting against deteriorating fabric and provision in urban educational institutions and teachers and lecturers struggling to maintain their relative levels of pay. Whether such movements constitute an element in an urban crisis is rather more open to doubt.

Castells himself makes very few specific references to education. However, theorists working within the same paradigm have been concerned with education. Althusser is an appropriate example of these since there are strong theoretical links between his work and that of Castells.

In discussing the role of education in the reproduction of capitalism, Althusser acknowledges the importance of the material base but goes on to incorporate a concept of ideology: 'the reproduction of labour power requires not only a reproduction of its skills, but also at the same time a reproduction of submission to the rules of the established order'.[18]

He suggests that in order to maintain its power and to preserve the position of those capitalist interests which it represents and reflects, the state has developed two sets of apparatuses, the repressive state apparatuses (police, armed forces, etc.) and the ideological state apparatuses. Althusser identified various ideological state apparatuses including the religious, the family, the educational, the political, the trade union, the communications and the cultural. He asserts that education has now replaced religion as the most important of these apparatuses: 'the ideological state apparatus which has been installed in the *dominant* position in mature capitalist social formations as a result of violent political and ideological class struggle against the old dominant ideological state apparatus is the *educational ideological apparatus*.[19] Were it to be adapted to take account of the ways in which schools, teachers and pupils resist the pressure to conform to ideological structures, Althusser's approach might have attractions for urban educationists. First, it provides a context within which to place current debates about social control, hidden curricula, the return to basic skills, testing and competence, the stress on vocationalism, etc. Secondly, this context is linked to a wide range of social theory which is specifically concerned with the urban.

This brief overview of some of the theoretical work of Castells and Althusser is both selective and partial. Castells, for instance, following his research interest in urban social movements, has subsequently shifted his whole stance in a more pluralistic direction.[20] Nor are these views being offered uncritically: Castells' insistence on structures can verge on the deterministic,[21] Althusser presents a one-sided view of the processes of schools, and does not substantiate his theoretical clarity by an examination of a specific school system and its articulation with the dominant political and economic structures in any specific nation state. Although part of the Marxist tradition, Castells, in particular, shows very little interest in history. His research investigations are largely of contemporary phenomena. Urban social theorists nevertheless offer a potential approach to urban education which emanates not from history but from a lively tradition of social theory. Interestingly, little attempt has been made to link their theories with the works of urban educationists.

There are, of course, writers on education who link themselves to a Marxist tradition. Examples of such work have proliferated on both sides of the Atlantic.[22] The missing connection is between the specifically urban focus of the social theory and those writers working in urban education. Urban sociologists, such as Castells, offer a theoretical view of cities within which urban educationalists could investigate the role of urban educational institutions. The theoretical view need not determine the investigation nor the analysis. Indeed, it is possible to find urban theorists whose frame of reference is more derived from Weber than Marx.[23] The point is that by contextualising themselves within wider theories of urbanisation and urbanism, urban educationists might be able to avoid those restrictions of perspective which are associated with, for instance, an exclusively historical approach.

Comparative and international approaches

The potential to examine issues, patterns and policies within the setting of different cities in different nation states might make a comparative approach an attractive one for urban educationists. One English writer, Holmes, has attempted to develop a systematic comparative approach which he sees as being of relevance to urban education. Holmes suggests that a scientific approach to initiating a comparative inquiry is to identify a 'problem', to hypothesise potentially successful policy 'solutions' and, where possible, to compare predicted outcomes with the observed results of the policy. In looking at the results of policy, data from countries where suggested policies have been adopted may be helpful. For Holmes, problems are seen as resulting from asynchronous change. Holmes classifies data into four different categories: normative patterns, institutional patterns, patterns of mental states and patterns of the environment. It is asynchronous change between these four categorisations that, according to Holmes, generates 'problems'.[24] He sees urban education as particularly concerned with 'problems' brought about by demographic change. Urban institutions are seen as failing to adapt to meet the educational needs of often rural, immigrant people with different norms.[25] Holmes' approach then is problem-solving and is linked to a philosophy of science which prefers hypothetico-deduction to induction and which considers it more productive to hypothesise outcomes than to search for causes. The contrast with historical approaches is evident.

Indeed, comparative education in both the UK and the USA has been deliberately shifted away from history. Much of early comparative education consisted of a loose assembly of historical narratives from various countries. It is this approach which Holmes, as well as empirical American scholars, are concerned to eschew. Holmes' infatuation with Popper makes him cautious of lapsing into 'historicism'. This rather loose concept is used to cover a range of evils popularly connected with Marxism. Indeed, historicism almost seems to be confused with history *per se*, in Holmes' usage, so determined is his refusal to acknowledge the importance of the past or of causality.

Holmes' approach manages to avoid simultaneously the strengths of social theory approaches and of historical approaches. The criteria for selecting what will be taken as 'problems' are so crude that they can completely overlook those issues where there has been no apparent change. As enduring social phenomena, poverty, exploitation and injustice are not the kinds of 'problems' to which Holmes' approach would draw attention. The stress on 'solutions' to 'problems' necessitates a restrictive frame of reference which results in wider social structures remaining unexamined. The predilection for cautious piecemeal social engineering serves to move academic and policy debate away from wider and more complex social, economic and political issues. Habermas' remarks on Luhmann are to the point here: 'This theory represents the advanced form of a technocratic consciousness which today permits practical questions to be defined from the outset as technical ones, and thereby withholds them from public and unconstrained discussion.'[26] Holmes' approach, then, not only has little to offer to urban educationists, it may actually distract attention away from the necessity to develop a bolder and more fruitful comparative analysis.

Urbanisation is now an international phenomenon. Comparative urban educationists may respond to this phenomenon in two ways. The first, traditional, method would be to discuss similar issues or policies in two or more cities. Such comparisons are not without value provided that they are focused on contents and policies and not on the technique of the comparison itself. Without such a focus, comparative approaches can be solipsistically obsessed with method or can degenerate into the increasingly esoteric. Cities and policies may be compared without any criterion of selection beyond the satisfaction of academic research.[27]

A second approach, which is as yet nascent, might consider the international relations of urban education. Such an approach would not be concerned with the activity of comparison *per se*; it would draw on information from various cities and nation states in order to reveal the international forces which are operant in urban educational systems. As a starting point, such an approach might consider the importance of various kinds of international movement: the movement of people, capital, produce, knowledge and culture.[28]

The twentieth century has brought unprecedented urbanisation as a result of widespread national and international demographic movement. People have moved to New York from Europe, the southern states of the USA, Puerto Rico, Mexico and Cuba. People have moved to London from Russia, Jamaica, Kenya, Bangladesh and Vietnam. Many of the cities of the USA and the UK contain a bewildering variety of people and cultures. Urbanisation in the third world is often from within a nation state to a primate city. Some of these cities, like Mexico, Cairo and Jakarta, are very large and still expanding rapidly. Whilst educational implications in first world cities might concern issues of cultural and linguistic diversity, in the third world cities difficulties might be encountered in resourcing and organising even the most minimal educational provision.

The relations between nation states and between cities seem to be dominated by the buying, selling and sometimes use of military technology. This trade is part of a more general pattern of movements of capital and profits, especially between the first and third worlds. International financial transactions and the operations of transnational corporations have developed a pattern of dependency which has crucial implications for urban education.[29] A new international division of labour seems to be emerging where the subordinate classes are principally but not exclusively located in the third world and the dominant classes are principally but not exclusively located in the first world. The role of urban educational institutions in explaining and reproducing this pattern can only be understood in international terms.

Within the international market for products, the control of knowledge, especially technical and specifically military knowledge, can be a key element in the success of a nation state or city. This knowledge is often generated in and transmitted through institutions of higher education. Educational processes cannot be separated from the international patterns of technological and military trade. Cultural artefacts such as books, magazines, films, TV programmes, pop music, styles of dress and types of sporting activity can be important trading commodities. They also serve as important legitimations for the existing international political and economic order. They transmit an idealised first world lifestyle which tends to shape the aspirations of people throughout the world. They provide the cultural concomitant of political and economic dependency. It is in the context of this internationalisation of culture that urban schools attempt to reproduce the values of their particular nation states.

Cultural movements, like demographic and economic movements, do not take place in only one direction. Whilst manufactured mass culture may be moving primarily from the metropolitan centres of North America and the European Community towards the cities of the third world, other cultural forces – musical, gastronomic, artistic, religious – are moving in the opposite direction.

An alternative comparative approach to urban education could then be developed within a framework of the international movements and countermovements of people, capital, produce, knowledge and culture. Such an approach would have at least three advantages. First, it would take account of wide social, political and economic forces within the contexts where they are increasingly tending to operate, that of international relations. Secondly, given the continuing rapid urbanisation of the third world, such an international approach could be firmly centred on the study of urban areas. Thirdly, in view of the role of educational institutions in generating and transmitting knowledge, of the importance of educational and cultural legitimations for the existing political and economic order and of the importance of technical knowledge to the process of industrialisation,[30] education is actually a crucial element in understanding the emerging pattern of international relations.

The development of history as a field of study may be taken as a parenthetical example of this process. It is not only that ethnocentric interpretations of world history are still prevalent in Europe and North America, nor even that these interpretations can be exported to the third world via publications and the career trajectories of professional historians. Such crudities can be resisted. However, the notion of what constitutes historical research, its formulation, evaluation and dissemination is also largely controlled by the elite institutions of Europe and North America. These definitions of the nature of the subject of history may prove limiting or inappropriate for elaborating the hidden histories of the third world.

Historical approaches

Historical approaches to urban education have been more prevalent in the USA than in the UK. The conflicts within urban educational history in the USA hardly substantiate anxieties about an exclusively historical approach. At their best, the American studies whether 'revisionist' or 'apologist' have revealed the 'relevance' of history to contemporary debates and conflicts. In neither case have the issues of social and racial stratification or the role of the state been overlooked.[31] The very fact that the dispute has occurred and the vigour with which it was conducted indicate that the assumptions behind various historical approaches to urban education have been brought forward for scrutiny. Nevertheless, Grace suggests that the debates about urban educational history and those about contemporary urban policy have been carried out to a large extent separately: 'The historical studies of urban schooling and the textbooks on urban education appear to have co-existed but not to have connected in any important degree.'[32]

Grace is a strong advocate of the importance of historical approaches to urban education. He suggests that students need to examine the ways in which contemporary urban education institutions are the products of history. In terms of the debate in the USA, he suggests that students need to examine the arguments put forward by protagonists on both sides. He is particularly concerned that issues concerning the historical role of schools as agencies of social control and cultural domination be discussed. He suggests that such investigation would lead to an understanding of the current role of schools. By revealing what schools used to do, the argument implies, the approach can lead to an understanding of what they are currently doing. He suggests that people's statements were much more explicit and vigorous in the past.

Whilst accepting the main argument of Grace's important paper, two points need to be noted. First, it is far from impossible to find in contemporary materials 'the confident expressions of intent by the providing classes and the robust statements of resistance from the receiving classes'.[33] In both the UK and the USA, providers and receivers remain fairly forthright in their expressions. The recent unsuccessful attempt to introduce religious education into state schools in the USA provided many examples of plain speaking by both protagonists and antagonists of the change. In the UK, the early rhetoric of the Manpower Services Commission (now Training

Agency) with its stress on 'skills', particularly 'social skills', is not too difficult to penetrate. Indeed, the government's own language with its encouragement to teachers to teach about the value of the contribution of commerce and industry to our national life might represent a direct continuation of nineteenth-century plain speaking. This is not to suggest that nothing can be gained from examining nineteenth-century commentators. The point is that this might help to connect with the fact that many current statements are equally outspoken and extreme.

Secondly, if an historical approach is to be adopted it needs to be one which can stress discontinuity as much as continuity. There have been major changes in the urban educational history of both the UK and the USA and these cannot be ignored in the stress on continuing structures and conflicts. To take an example from Grace himself, in his discussion of the revisionists and apologists he suggests that: 'What a proper historical location of the urban problem would reveal is that the race question in the city is a dramatic present manifestation of an historical complex of issues to do with class, with domination and with exploitation in metropolitan cities.'[34]

Certainly, there is a link between class struggles and the social and economic position of black people in the cities of the UK and the USA. However, to stress this continuity may be to overlook the element of racism which, in its present form, is an important factor in schooling, in, for instance, London. The inequalities and oppression to which black people in London are subjected, and in which schools play their part, cannot be understood exclusively in terms of social class. Racism also needs to be examined. Of course, racism also has its history – the connection with nineteenth-century imperialism is particularly relevant here – and this could be used to analyse the phenomenon and its connections with both social class and urban schooling.[35]

Whilst sharing Grace's view of the importance of historical approaches to urban education, it is necessary to stress that they are not the only method of analysing the relevance of social economic and political forces to urban schooling. This can be done at least equally well by the social theory or international approaches referred to in earlier sections of this chapter. The final section briefly suggests which approaches need development and what possibilities there are for conjunction.

Concluding discussion

The argument so far has assumed that urban education is concerned with education in cities. It is worth questioning this apparently obvious assumption, in that some approaches to urban education seem to confuse it with education *per se*, with education in all regions whether urban, suburban or rural. Urban education as a field of study began in the USA in the late 1950s. At that stage, it was little more than a euphemism for the education of black pupils. Since then the term has gone through several transformations. At present, there is a danger that a study is categorised as urban education purely on the ground that the person who wrote it considers her/himself to be an urban educationist.

In social theory, it has been suggested that urban is used as an adjective not to indicate the geographical location under consideration but to suggest that the work in question fits into some wide theoretical or research orientation. Saunders claims that

> Pahl's concern with the role of urban managers and Castells' concern with the provision of collective consumption may both be retained as elements of a distinctive problem for sociological analysis provided that such an analysis is severed from the very different theoretical question of space. To term such a sociology 'urban' is, of course, merely a matter of convention, the application of a convenient label to designate certain specific theoretical problems that have no necessary relation to the empirical analysis of cities.[36]

It is difficult to see how either urban managers or the provision of collective consumption can be separated from the question of space. Both the people and the provision are spatially located. Certainly, there are managers and provisions of collective consumption in rural areas too, but their workings are not as visible nor as open to contest and conflict as those in urban areas. This is to say that the difference is one of concentration rather than of kind. But the difference is highly marked, nevertheless, in social and political terms as well as in the fabric of the visible environment.

Similarly, urban schools have many features in common with schools in other areas but the differences between them can also be marked. The levels of linguistic and cultural diversity, the visibility of extreme poverty, the conflicts evident in daily transactions make urban educational institutions significantly different from most of those elsewhere. Space should not then be removed from the terms of the approaches to urban education. Urban education has, as its subject matter, the workings of educational institutions in cities and the way in which these relate to the wider political, economic, social and cultural forces operant in urban areas. This may mean that certain theoretical approaches are preferable: for instance those that give accounts of conflict and those concerned with inequalities between groups. But these approaches, as far as urban education is concerned, cannot be removed from the subject of cities and the educational institutions which operate within them.

In this respect, the international approach advocated in the third section is particularly attractive in that it encourages the relinquishing of the nation state as the unit of analysis. Although traditional comparative education is still largely conducted in terms of the nation state, an international approach which examines processes of interdependency might concentrate on units both larger and smaller. The movements of people, capital, goods and knowledge between countries needs to be studied not in terms of different individual nation states but rather in terms of international relations. The other potentially rich unit of analysis is smaller than most nation states, namely the city. Demographic movements towards cities make these interesting units of analysis for an international approach. An international approach could then legitimately focus on educational institutions and processes in Bradford or Miami. The education of people from Cuba in Miami or from Pakistan in Bradford may be understood as one aspect of interdependency theory in order to analyse the international aspects of urban educational issues.

It is not the intention of this essay to indulge in pleas for methodological restrictions. On the contrary, the more approaches which are developed for analysing urban education, the more complete our understanding is likely to be. It has, however, been stressed that whatever approach is adopted the wider economic, political and social forces which are operant in cities should not be ignored in discussions of urban education.

Certainly, social theory approaches, historical approaches and international approaches all have their strengths. This paper has emphasised that approaches to urban education should have some impact on practice. The hopefully evident concern for oppression, racism and dependency indicates a particular theoretical (and potentially political) position. This position itself is one notoriously more concerned with practice than with abstract research or theorising. Perhaps, if the business of philosophy is not to describe the world but to change it, it is not sufficient to plead naively for theoretical pluralism.

The threefold categorisation used in this essay might indicate that the three approaches are distinct and watertight. This is, of course, not the case. Social theory illuminates most serious historical approaches to urban education. The limitation here is that urban educationists have strangely not espoused specifically urban social theory. Likewise, social theory would inform the nascent, international approach which would also benefit from an historical dimension. In this case, the difficulty is that social theory still needs to reformulate itself in terms of the international division of labour.[37] An international urban social theory may well be emerging as an important educational literature.[38] In the development of these theoretical areas, the study of urban education, by a wide diversity of approaches, will have a crucial part to play, provided it is informed by a concern for policy and practice.

NOTES

1. D. M. Ravitch, *The Troubled Crusade* (New York: Basic Books, 1983).
2. C. Parsons, *Schools in an Urban Community: A Study of Carbrook, 1870–1965* (London: Routledge and Kegan Paul, 1978).
3. D. L. Angus, 'Common school politics in a frontier city: Detroit, 1836–1842', in R. K. Goodenow and D. Ravitch (eds.), *School in Cities: Consensus and Conflicts in American Educational History* (New York: Holmes and Meier, 1983).
4. C. Jones, 'The break-up of the Inner London Education Authority', in L. Bash and D. Coulby, *The Education Reform Act: Competition and Control* (London: Cassell, 1989).
5. ILEA, *Race, Sex and Class 1: Achievement in Schools*, (London: ILEA, 1983).
6. ILEA, *Race, Sex and Class 2: Multi-Ethnic Education in Schools* (London: ILEA, 1983); ILEA, *Race, Sex and Class 3: A Policy for Equality* (London: ILEA, 1983); ILEA, *Race, Sex and Class 4: Anti-Racist Statements. A Guideline* (London: ILEA, 1983); ILEA, *Race, Sex and Class 5: Multi-Ethnic Education in Further, Higher and Community Education* (London: ILEA, 1983).
7. ILEA, *Race, Sex and Class 6: A Policy for Equality: Sex* (London: ILEA, 1985).
8. ILEA, *Educational Opportunities for All?* (London: ILEA, 1985).
9. G. Grace, *Teachers, Ideology and Control: A Study in Urban Education* (London: Routledge and Kegan Paul, 1978).
10. R. E. Park *et al.* (eds.), *The City* (Chicago, IL: University of Chicago Press, 1967).
11. E. W. Burgess, 'The growth of the city', in J. Raynor and E. Harris (eds.), *The City Experience* (London: Ward Lock, 1977).
12. L. Bash, D. Coulby and C. Jones, *Urban Schooling: Theory and Practice* (London: Cassell, 1985).
13. J. Barnes and H. Lucas, 'Positive discrimination in education, individuals, groups and institutions', in P. Raggatt and M. Evans, *The Political Context* (London: Ward Lock, 1977).
14. M. Castells, *The Urban Question: A Marxist Approach* (London: Edward Arnold, 1977), 111.
15. *Ibid.*, 237.
16. M. Castells, *City, Class and Power* (London: Macmillan, 1978), 6.
17. *Ibid.*, 60.
18. L. Althusser, 'Ideology and ideological state apparatuses', in B. R. Cosin (ed.), *Education, Structure and Society* (Harmondsworth: Penguin, 1972), 245.
19. *Ibid.*, 258.
20. M. Castells, *The City and the Grassroots* (London: Edward Arnold, 1983).
21. P. Saunders, *Social Theory and the Urban Question* (London: Hutchinson, 1981), 106–11.
22. S. Bowles and H. Gintis, *Schooling in Capitalist America: Educational Reform and the Contradictions of Economic Life* (London: Routledge and Kegan Paul, 1976); M. W. Apple, *Ideology and Curriculum* (London: Routledge and Kegan Paul, 1979); M. W. Apple, *Education and Power* (London: Routledge and Kegan Paul, 1982); P. E. Willis, *Learning to Labour* (Farnborough: Saxon House, 1977); S. Castles and W. Wustenberg, *The Education of the Future* (London: Pluto Press, 1979).

23 J. Rex and R. Moore, *Race, Community and Conflict: A Study of Sparkbrook* (London: Oxford University Press, 1967).
24 B. Holmes, *Problems in Education: A Comparative Approach* (London: Routledge and Kegan Paul, 1965); B. Holmes, *Comparative Education: Some Considerations of Method* (London: George Allen and Unwin, 1981).
25 B. Holmes, 'Introduction: education in cities', in J. A. Lauwerys and D. G. Scanlon (eds.), *Education in Cities* (London: Evans, 1970).
26 Quoted in D. Frisby, 'Introduction to the English translation', of T. W. Adorno et al., *The Positivist Dispute in German Sociology* (London: Heinemann, 1976), xxxii.
27 D. Coulby, 'Urban education: the practice and theory of theory and practice', in L. Bash, *Comparative Urban Education: Towards an Agenda* Department of International and Comparative Education (London: Occasional Paper No. 10, University of London Institute of Education, 1987).
28 D. Coulby and C. Jones, 'Urban education and comparative education: some possibilities', in M. McLean, *Education in Cities: International Perspectives* (London: British Comparative and International Education Society/Department of International and Comparative Education, 1989).
29 D. Coulby, 'Dependency theory and education', in C. B. W. Treffgarne (ed.), *Contributions to the Workshop on 'Reproduction and Dependency in Education'* (London: London Institute of Education, 1984).
30 D. Coulby and C. Jones, 'Technologies and curriculum choice', in H. Van Daele and M. Vansteenkiste (eds.), *The Impact of Technology on Society and Education* (Antwerp: Comparative Education Society of Europe, 1985).
31 M. B. Katz, *Class, Bureaucracy and Schools: The Illusion of Educational Change in America* (expanded edn, paperback, New York: Praeger, 1975); D. Ravitch, *The Great School Wars: New York City: A History of Public Schools as Battlefields of Social Change* (New York: Basic Books, 1974).
32 G. Grace, 'Urban education policy, science and critical scholarship', in G. Grace (ed.), *Education and the City: Theory, History and Contemporary Practice* (London: Routledge and Kegan Paul, 1974), 21.
33 *Ibid.*, 36.
34 *Ibid.*, 21.
35 S. Rushdie, 'The new empire within Britain', *New Society* (9 December 1982), 417–19.
36 Saunders, *Social Theory and the Urban Question*, 258.
37 A. Giddens, *A Contemporary Critique of Historical Materialism* (London: Macmillan, 1981).
38 S. Castles and G. Kosack, *Immigrant Workers and Class Structure in Western Europe* (London: Oxford University Press, 1973); F. Frobel et al., *The New International Division of Labour* (Cambridge: University Press, 1980); F. H. Cardoso and E. Foletto, *Dependency and Development in Latin America* (Oxford: University of California Press, 1979).

11 The uses and abuses of comparison in urban educational history

David L. Angus

The deliberate use of comparison in urban educational history remains rare. This collection is evidence of a growing sensitivity to the need for comparison and an invitation to historians to extend their work along this dimension. I want to argue here that, if this development is to be at all fruitful, we need to think much more carefully than we have about the uses and abuses of comparison.

There has been a tendency among those interested in urban history to reflect encouragement or discouragement over the *amount* of research being done in the area. Clearly, this is the wrong standard to apply in assessing the health of urban history. As toilers in a collective enterprise, we are, of course, pleased to be joined by more toilers. But urban history is, or should be, also a *cumulative* enterprise. We ought to feel that with each passing year, we know more than we did before about the social systems of cities. From this vantage point, we are not in very good shape. Sol Cohen once predicted that the breadth of definition of educational history set forth by Bailyn and Cremin would 'lead to diffusion and fragmentation of energy, leaving once again a scarcity of resources for research in urban educational history'.[1] In my view, Cohen was only partly right. Rather than a scarcity, there has been a remarkable expansion of resources, both human and material; nonetheless, the area is certainly characterised by diffusion and the fragmentation of energy. The field is in disarray not because it has been too broadly defined but because it is riven by ideological and methodological disputes and because the toilers seem profoundly innocent of the bases on which valid and cumulative generalisation can be built.

My argument is presented in three sections. First, I want to establish that the use of comparison in urban educational history is not optional, it is an inherent necessity. Whichever way we turn to define the scope or purposes of this endeavour, we encounter the need to utilise comparison. Second, I want to argue that, on the other hand, there are a number of equally legitimate modes of comparison and that we are not to feel terribly constrained in the setting of research agendas. Finally, by considering both actual and possible uses and abuses of comparison, I hope to point the way toward approaches to urban educational history that are both collective and cumulative.

Approaches to urban educational history

It has been suggested here and elsewhere that research in urban educational history is piecemeal and fragmentary, if perhaps no more so than in urban history generally.[2] It is with some risk, therefore, that one tries to identify two or three approaches that might encompass the broad range of ongoing work and serve to focus a discussion of the purposes of the field. Reeder sees two main trends in Britain, the ecological and the neo-Marxist, though early in his essay he also distinguishes between ecological and structural approaches. In Canada, there continues to be a vigorous neo-Marxist flavour to work emanating from the Ontario Institute for the Study of Education, but others are pursuing a 'family strategies' model. Davey and Wimshurst argue that in Australia, the vigour is to be found among those working from a socialist/feminist perspective. Others are tagged with the label of 'mainstream rhetoric', whatever that might be.

In the USA, where the emphasis on quantification got its start and where there may be more crossing of disciplinary boundaries by urban historians, at least three categories are required to encompass the main approaches. First, are the neo-Marxists, the most theoretically sensitive of which are Michael Katz, David Hogan and others who have come under their influence in Canada and in the USA. This 'school' continued to locate much of their research in cities, though, as we will see, not as urbanists. They often use quantitative methods, derive concepts from the social sciences, focus on the experiences of 'ordinary people' and have shown considerable capacity to develop new theory as their work proceeds.

Another large group, perhaps best represented by Maris Vinovskis, Carl Kaestle, David Angus and their students, also use quantification and social science conceptual apparatus, and evidence a powerful interest in the experiences of non-elite groups. Yet, as Kaestle's essay here shows, they have a take-it-or-leave-it attitude toward theory, placing considerably more faith in an incremental approach to building generalisation from carefully crafted empirical work. What is more, they have shown a decided tendency to allow the neo-Marxists to set their research agenda, contributing to the widely held suspicion that quantitative analysis in history is a far more potent tool for destroying social theory than for generating it.

A third group, represented in this collection by Barbara Finkelstein, is distrustful of quantitative methods and of much of the use to which derived theory has been put. This group looks to psychology, psychiatry or anthropology to provide theory wherever it seems needed. They are interested in 'thick description' and in the uniqueness, the 'human dimension', of each case, though they are not averse to making cross-case generalisation where it seems warranted and they are as guilty as everyone else in the persistent habit of speaking in generalisations even where available evidence is limited to one case.

In this schema, as would be true with any simple categorisation, nuances are omitted and some toilers in the field are neglected. What is more, there are a number of affinities across these three categories that will likely not be fully acknowledged. Nonetheless, our intent here is to identify as well as we can what each of these groups is trying to do in urban educational history as a preliminary step to discussing the uses of comparison. In that spirit, I will first look at what I believe to be the common roots of the non-Marxists in a theoretical tradition deriving from Weber and Tonnies, through Simmel and Durkheim, Park, Burgess and Wirth, taking cognisance of the point at which the social psychological variant of this tradition diverges. Then we will turn attention to the emergence of neo-Marxism in the late sixties.

Theories of urbanism

The theory of urbanism sketched out by Louis Wirth in his 1938 essay, 'Urbanism as a way of life' has proved amazingly durable.[3] It came at a time when the ecological approach of Wirth's teachers, Robert Park and Ernest Burgess, was in disrepute and it combined elements of the older rural–urban dichotomies with the social psychology of George Simmel. Wirth started with a clean slate. 'In the rich literature on the city we look in vain for a theory systematizing the available knowledge concerning the city as a social entity.'[4] Wirth's position was that because there were obviously many different 'types' of cities, what was needed was a bare bones definition of 'urban' that would not beg the question of urban variation. He settled for four defining characteristics: population size, population density, social heterogeneity and permanence (Woodstock was an event, not a city). But he also felt that with this definition in place, one could derive an elaborate set of postulates, a system of concomitant variation, that would constitute a theory of 'urbanism' to be 'elaborated, tested and revised in the light of further analysis and empirical research'.[5]

Many of these derived postulates became so well known and so embedded in 'conventional wisdom' that they were accepted as proven. Large population size is associated with spatial segregation along racial, ethnic, class and status lines, the substitution of competition and formal controls for weakened kinship and neighbourhood bonds, impersonality and the segmentation of relationships, the preponderance of secondary over primary contacts, the extreme specialisation and differentiation of family, social and occupational life and, finally, anomie. High population density reinforces some of these associations, such as differentiation and the spirit of competition, but it adds dimensions of its own. It brings about spatial differentiation, dissociating place of work from place of residence, it places a premium on visual recognition and creates a sensitivity to artefacts and a blindness to nature, it encourages a relativistic perspective and an increased tolerance of difference, thus reinforcing secularisation. Heterogeneity of the population brings into being a more complicated class structure featuring heightened social mobility, produces a high turnover rate in group memberships of all types, replaces individuality with social categories and forces such facilities and institutions as public utilities, schools, movies, the radio and the newspapers to be tailored to the *average* person, thus acting as levelling influences.

Here was an extremely large 'package' of ideas and one which would prove to be difficult to untangle and sort out. Shortly before his death in 1952, Wirth was deeply discontented with what had happened to his theory. He worried that the influence of the urban over the rural in America was so profound that it was becoming impossible to test it, that what he thought of as a 'vast continuum' had been misconstrued as a dichotomy, and that much of the theory had come to be seen as established fact.

To set up ideal-typical polar concepts such as I have done, and many others before me have done, does not prove that city and country are fundamentally and necessarily different. It does not justify mistaking the hypothetical characteristics attributed to the urban and the rural modes of life for established facts, as has so often been done. Rather it suggests certain hypotheses to be tested in the light of empirical evidence which we must assiduously gather. Unfortunately this evidence had not been accumulated in such a fashion as to test critically any major hypothesis that has been proposed.[6]

Wirth's legacy was not a well-tested and established theory of the city; it was a sense that empirical research should be ordered by theory, an idea that knowledge of urban life would have to be based on a comparison of variables between places of differing size, and, finally, a research agenda that would keep scholars, both sociologists and historians, busy for years. In one of his last writings he observed,

One looks in vain in the textbooks about urban or rural sociology for a careful, detailed, and reliable comparison of city and country on the basis of: size of family, mortality, marital status, education, ethnic and racial origin, occupation, wealth, income, housing, religion, politics, recreation, stratification, mobility, contacts, associational memberships and participation, consumption, savings, illness, physical defects, mental disorder, delinquency and crime, family organization, marriage practices, sex life, rearing of children, and many other acts on which continuous time series would seem to be indispensable.[7]

It would be a number of years before much progress would be made toward this agenda, and when it came it would be carried out as much by social historians as by sociologists, not only because Wirth was right about the disappearance of the truly rural in the metropolitanising America of the fifties, but also because of the increasing interest in urbanisation as a process rather than in urbanism as a condition and the implication in this that time is an important variable.

In the aftermath of the Second World War, as one after another of the colonies of the Western democracies achieved independence, the primary problem focus in the social sciences became the working out of a theory of social change that could explain (and legitimate) the continuation of Western cultural and economic dominance in the world. Through the efforts of Marion Levy, Bert Hoselitz, Wilbert Moore, Daniel Lerner, David Apter and a host of others, 'modernization theory' was developed. Though the ends of the developmental continuum were now primitive society and modern society, reflecting perhaps a large debt to Redfield's folk–urban continuum, many of Wirth's postulated relationships were woven through various versions of modernisation theory. Even if few modernisation theorists saw urbanisation as the same sort of independent master process that Wirth had suggested, they tended to give a Wirthian flavour to the social and personal concomitants of urbanisation.

In the late 1960s, as urban violence and the new welfare initiatives of the Kennedy/Johnson administrations refocused the attention of social scientists on the 'problems of the cities', a distinctly urban sociology in the Wirthian tradition was still found by some to be viable, if requiring modification.[8] The theory, still not empirically demonstrated, I might add, was described by one of its critics as 'the most widely held image of the nature of social interaction and personal reaction in the urban milieu'.[9] On the eve of 'the new urban history', the Wirthian tradition stood ready for use by a new generation of historians. Its main characteristics were (1) viewing population characteristics as independent variables in the explanation of other social developments, and (2) a tendency to associate urban growth with various forms of deterioration in social and personal life.

The second theoretical tradition standing 'available' to the new urban historians was human ecology. Originating in the work of R. D. McKenzie, Ernest Burgess and Robert Park in 'the Chicago School' of the twenties, ecological approaches to urban and community study were revived in the fifties by Amos Hawley and further refined and modified by O. D. Duncan, Leo Schnore, and Philip Hauser.[10] While Park had divided social life into two levels, the biotic and the cultural, and had limited ecological analysis to a study of the relationship between the environment and the biotic aspects of life, Hawley saw that both the biotic and cultural levels were systematically related to environment.[11] Still, the general direction of explanation for Hawley ran from the environment, or the spatial features of social life, to the cultural and organisational features. Note that in this framework, a city is considered to be a particular socio-cultural *product* of the larger environment, and is thus a dependent variable.

Duncan reintroduced a bit of Wirth into the theory with his concept of the 'ecosystem'.[12] Here, social organisation is considered to be the product of and dependent upon combinations of three other factors: population, environment and technology. With Schnore and Hauser, a fully interdependent model emerges in which all four of these factors are understood to influence each other.[13] The theory now becomes a system of elaborate concomitant variation in which any of its features can become an explanandum. Nonetheless, the distinctive feature of ecological analysis is the emphasis it places on the spatial, environmental contexts of social life. While ecology was once thought to be particularly concerned with macrosociological comparison, its later variants promote as well a micro-social focus. It is therefore a particularly useful theory for those interested in searching for patterned differences *within* the city and for those who view urban life as involving processes of *coping* with environmental and social conditions and constructing new forms of social organisation out of these processes.[14]

The third main theory informing a share of the new urban history is neo-Marxism. This theory is not another variant of urban sociology but rather a theory of political economy, and in that lies one of the sharpest differences with the others we have considered. The problems of cities, what neo-Marxists call 'the urban question', cannot be understood without reference to a more general theory of society. That theory is composed, in classical Marxism, of three elements: a theory of labour-value and exploitation, a theory of the accumulation of capital and a theory of classes and class struggle. All elements of social life are to be understood in terms of their relation to the one central feature of capitalist society, the capitalist mode of production. There are two key *dynamic* aspects of social life: the conflict between capital and labour – the continuous reproduction of the class struggle – and the generation of a series of contradictions that derive from the anarchic character of market competition.

Neo-Marxism makes its most important contribution to classical Marxism at these points. As the total share of populations actually engaged in commodity production as capitalists or as workers has shrunk, a more elaborate theory of social reproduction, as opposed to production, was required. This was provided largely by the Frankfurt School, Habermas in particular, and by the neo-Marxist urban sociologists. It is because of this relatively recent theoretical elaboration that the neo-Marxist understanding of schooling differs so sharply from Marx's own. The second area of theoretical refinement deals with the far more active role of the state in the economy than was anticipated in classical theory. One function of the state is seen as providing sufficient regulation to markets to prevent the constantly emerging contradictions from reaching a crisis stage. The far more important one is the 'management' of general social reproduction.[15]

Where do urban studies or urban history fit into this general scheme? Marx himself saw a dialectic between the city, the actual locus of capital concentration, and the country, still dominated by pre-capitalist production modes. This is now understood as, at most, a feature of very early capitalist development and having nothing to do with the urban question in late capitalist societies. As David Reeder's remarks about neo-Marxist thought in Britain suggest, the exact status of urbanism or urbanisation remains problematic. For many, the city is simply a sort of stage set on which all the basic dynamics of capitalist society are played out on a grand scale. The city is where most capitalists live, where the class struggle is sharpest, where the commodity production is concentrated, where the social reproduction requirements are trickiest to handle, where market contradictions are most obvious and serious, etc. The lack of any theoretical significance for the city has led some neo-Marxists to call for the abandonment of any population constructs in the understanding of late capitalist society.[16] Others are not so sure, and there have been recent attempts to develop new theories of urbanisation, particularly focusing on patterns of land-use and the urban-planning process.[17]

To the extent that urban educational historians in recent years have been cognisant of theory, and this is problematic, as Kaestle's essay shows, I believe they have been influenced by one or more of these three traditions. But just how direct is this influence? Louis Wirth had very little to say about schools, mentioning them only as 'cultural institutions' which, in the city, 'must necessarily operate as leveling influences'. Not much help there. Yet in two other ways, his theory is powerfully suggestive; (1) if urbanism produces social and personal disintegration, might schools be used to counteract these trends? and (2) could it be that population size, density and heterogeneity, in themselves, are concomitantly associated with certain features of schooling, such as attendance patterns, curriculum, organisation, governance, etc.? Both of these questions have been addressed in urban educational history.

An early and excellent example of a Wirthian, linear deterioration model was Henry Perkinson's chapter on 'The city and the schools' in his provocative little book, *The Imperfect Panacea: American Education, 1865–1965*.[18] In a relatively few pages, Perkinson boldly outlines a causal chain which leads from urban growth through a sequence of associated social changes to an explanation of all the more important urban educational developments of the late nineteenth and early twentieth centuries. Beginning neutrally in demography, Perkinson's chain weaves through the family, the economy, immigrant culture, middle-class anxieties and power, compulsion and 'social control' (not his term) and a host of school reforms in governance, organisation, professional identity and pedagogy, and ending only when the rural/urban distinction is itself overwhelmed by the disaster of the Great Depression.

Perkinson's model is a full-blown theory of urban education during the critical years. It accounts for most of the developments that others have seen as important, and it makes considerable use of class conflict and the social control motive, yet it owes everything to Louis Wirth and nothing whatever to Marx. It has also proved quite durable in the sense that many others have invoked all or part of the scheme to explain some particular development or a similar pattern in some city. Better known general works, such as William Bullough's *Cities and Schools in the Gilded Age*,[19] scarcely go beyond it. Yet, it is importantly wrong, because it asserts as fact a host of associations that were for Wirth never anything but postulates and that have subsequently been proved wrong empirically. Urbanisation did not nucleate the family, produce anomie, create concentric circles of deteriorating life quality. Compulsory school laws had little or nothing to do with school enrolments. And on and on.

Much of this we know because of the other type of urban educational research suggested by the Wirthian tradition, the analysis of the statistical association between measures of urbanisation on the one hand and social and educational characteristics on the other.[20] An excellent example of this is the chapter on rural–urban differences in Kaestle and Vinovskis' *Education and Social Change in Nineteenth-Century Massachusetts: Quantitative Studies*.[21] After carefully reviewing all the important theoretical developments on the question of conceptualising rural–urban differences, they settle for the position that only population size and density can be safely used to define community types and that all other alleged concomitants should be left to empirical verification. (They reject Wirth's third component, heterogeneity, but only because they construe it to mean *ethnic* mix and do not want this question to be begged in the analysis.) The result of their analysis is to establish a strong case for important rural–urban differences in school attendance patterns and length of school year. But in exploring these relationships more deeply through multiple regression analysis, they leave Wirth behind and utilise an ecological approach. The difference is that socio-economic and cultural measures are now included *as independent variables* in the analysis. With this method, population size and density are still seen as important predictors of these two aspects of schooling, but such factors as the degree of commercial development (as contrasted to industrial development), the percentage of the population who were foreign-born and the percentage of Catholics are also shown to be significant factors. One could argue that the basic research question is the same in both of these studies, 'what are the educational concomitants of urban growth?' Beyond this, they stand in sharp contrast to one another, Perkinson attempting to derive many complex features of schooling from a single 'cause', Kaestle and Vinovskis focusing on only two aspects and turning to a wide array of explanatory variables just to account for a portion of the variance of those two. Ultimately, the Kaestle and Vinovskis analysis moves beyond the city to suggest that there may be different educational concomitants to urban growth in different *types* of cities and that city types may be constructed out of the relationships of particular cities to such larger social processes as industrialisation, immigration, etc. It should be obvious that, given this agenda, comparison is essential, first, to establish what is distinctively urban, second, to determine what categorical differences between urban places seem to make differences in educational outcomes or features and finally, to determine the strengths of these relationships. The Kaestle and Vinovskis study succeeds because it is carefully and self-consciously comparative; the Perkinson essay fails precisely because it moves at the level of untested theory, avoiding actual comparisons between actual cities, families, school systems.

Others who owe a debt to the theory of human, urban ecology do not seem to be asking the same questions. In her essay in this volume, Barbara Finkelstein takes considerable pains to distinguish her approach from those of either the neo-Marxists or the Kaestle/Vinovskis school, using such terms as 'macro-structural' and 'material' to describe the interests of the latter and phrases such as 'the roles of the family and the church', 'small face-to-face social contexts and processes' and 'the consciousness of reformers' as evocative of her sense of what should be studied.[22] This is a call to study processes of educational development *within* the city, to move to the level of the neighbourhood, the parish, the ethnic enclave as a way of discovering the myriad patterns of adaptation and creative response to the pressures and opportunities of urban life. In simplest terms, it is a call to complement our grasp of the structural and material with equal attention to the psychological and cultural.

Yet, is this as different as it seems? Is not the generic question, 'what are the educational concomitants of urban growth?' with the concomitants now defined as psychological (as with Simmel and Wirth) or cultural (as with Gans and Fischer)? Finkelstein is keen to develop a research agenda that is rooted in the urban, suggesting, for example, that the city is 'a special kind of myth-inducing, myth-building environment'. A host of questions spring to mind. Were large cities more 'myth-inducing' than small ones (i.e., what is the importance of population size on this aspect of urban life?)? Was the impulse to school the young less intense in the countryside? Was the development of an array of educative institutions merely the result of population concentration (e.g., to have a Mechanics' Institute you need to have enough 'mechanics' in one place to start one)? Did the 'myth of the vulnerable child' arise in cities, or only in industrial cities, or only in immigrant industrial cities, or only in Eastern seaboard immigrant industrial cities? My point is that as interesting as are the questions posed by the attention to the psychological and cultural, without building in careful comparison, they will tell us little about *urban* educational history, including what it was about urban life that caused it to be such a myth-generating environment.

William Marsden's variant of ecological theory illustrates that Finkelstein's programme is not so far different from the 'macro-structuralists' as she suggests.[23] Marsden argues that his research illustrates 'the capacity of individual participants in schooling to adapt to changing social niches', and that 'the individual family retained considerable room for manoeuvre in making decisions about schooling', findings that are well within the range of concerns outlined by Finkelstein. Yet, these individual- and family-level responses are understood to be structurally patterned, forming 'an interactive trinity' of 'social stratification, territorial segregation, and educational gradation', patterns which might well have been discovered without considering individuals or families. To move beyond this point, the issue of whether one focuses on the 'domestic tensions' fuelled by the fact that 'clerkly and mechanical occupations were mingled in many families', or on the intense residential segregation characteristic of late nineteenth-century English cities is not as important as discovering, through comparison, what structural or cultural features of English society and law enabled the emergence of an elaborately graduated system of schooling as a way of expressing social stratification, for this, surely, was not the American way or the Canadian way or the Australian way.

It is only when we turn to the question of what is urban educational history for the neo-Marxists that we leave the generic question, 'what are the educational concomitants of urban growth?' For while they might study urban educational institutions and patterns, their search ultimately is for the urban forms of those educational processes generated by the concentration of capital and the class struggle, rather than for processes generated by urbanisation itself. Early on, neo-Marxists pursued a rather simple-minded view of how schooling could be understood as an adjunct of these more basic master processes of social change. Schooling was thought to be imposed on the poor by the rich as a way of creating a docile, clock-oriented, property-respecting working class. A number of pseudo- or crypto-Marxists continue to argue something like this, but more theoretically sensitive Marxists have developed new theory.

Whether because they were stung by the mounting array of contrary empirical evidence or because they realised the need for the continual revision of classical Marxism, they no longer see schools as the *outcome* of class struggle. As Samuel Bowles put it, 'this might have been good politics, but it is bad history'.[24] Schools are now seen as one of the many institutional arenas in which the class struggle occurs and in which myriad forms of capitalist social reproduction are played out. David Hogan is now stressing a distinction between classes as *categories* of people and class as a process of social formation.[25] The most important consequence of this for non-Marxists is that we can perhaps look for them to make a more useful contribution to our own interests in urban education than heretofore. The reason is that it is now in order to admit that the contribution of schooling to the furtherance of capitalist production might take many different forms, perhaps different forms in different countries, even different forms in different cities, or sizes of cities or types of cities, Marxists might develop a genuine curiosity about what actually happened in the past. If they do they will quickly see that comparison is as important for understanding the social reproduction of capitalism as a grand process taking many different forms in many different settings as it is for understanding the educational concomitants of urban growth.

Varieties of comparison

I am contending that with a little more attention to the nature of comparison by those who do history of urban education, the work can be more *cumulative*. Whether or not we can bridge the ideological gulfs that divide us or agree on a common research agenda, we can certainly expand the usefulness of our own research to others. The key to this is understanding and accommodating to the conditions under which comparison between studies is possible.

Not so long ago, 'textbook' discussions of 'the comparative method' tended to define comparison in narrow terms; the point seems to have been to outline a right way to do comparison so that certain approaches could be shown to be in error.[26] Lately, some scholars for whom comparison is essential have become quite reflective about the nature of comparison and quite expansive in recognising and defining a variety of legitimate approaches. I refer to those who do macro- or historical or comparative sociology. As cases in point, we will consider three recent attempts to develop a typology of comparison.

The simplest is by Victoria Bonnell. In a discussion of the key differences between the methodology of sociologists and historians, Bonnell focuses on the methods employed by historical sociologists such as Neil Smelser, Reinhardt Bendix, Charles Tilly, Immanuel Wallerstein and others. She argues that the use of comparison among such scholars takes two forms, 'analytical', in which 'the comparison involves an identification of independent variables that serve to explain common or contrasting patterns or occurrences ... between equivalent units', or 'illustrative', in which 'the main point of comparison is between equivalent units on the one hand and a theory or concept on the other'.[27] In this schema, the critical difference lies in whether the intention is to generate theory, or at least generalisation, or to illustrate the applicability of theory already developed. Even this simple typology begins to suggest that comparison is likely to serve different purposes for Marxist and non-Marxist scholars. It also suggests that, to the degree that Marxists are interested in 'illustrating theory' through historical writing, single city studies are inadequate to either establish or refute Marxist theory. For this reason, the debate over education in Chicago represented by the works of David Hogan, Julia Wrigley, Paul Peterson, Ira Katznelson and Margaret Weir, as closely joined as are the ideological issues, cannot really be thought to teach us much about generic social change processes.[28]

Theda Skocpol and Margaret Sommers argue for a three-category typology based on the purposes for which comparisons are made, their 'logics-in-use'. In their schema, Bonnell's illustrative comparison becomes 'the parallel demonstration of theory', the purpose of which is 'to persuade the reader that a given, explicitly delineated hypothesis or theory can repeatedly demonstrate its fruitfulness – its ability convincingly to order the evidence – when applied to a series of relevant historical trajectories'.[29] Bonnell's second category, analytical, is seen by Skocpol and Sommers to constitute two different 'logics-in-use', depending on whether the emphasis is on common or contrasting patterns. The latter is called the 'contrasts of contexts' in which the purpose of comparison is 'to bring out the unique features of each particular case ... and to show how these unique features affect the working out of putatively general social processes'.[30] While the parallel demonstration of theory places emphasis on explicit theorising, contrasts of context emphasise the historical integrity of each case.

The third type of comparison is called macro-causal analysis, the making of causal inferences about macro-level structures and processes. Here, 'the logic ... resembles that of statistical analysis, which manipulates groups of cases to control sources of variation in order to make causal inferences when quantitative data are available about a large number of cases'.[31] Within this type, there is a further distinction, with apologies to J. S. Mill, between the 'method of agreement' and the 'method of difference', though in most studies both methods are used.

Skocpol and Sommers go on to show that many of the best works in recent historical sociology combine these logics, but do so with a high degree of self-consciousness and care. For example, the Tillys' *The Rebellious Century* employs both parallel logic and macro-analytic logic. This works because the former is applied across nations while the latter is used to compare groups, regions and times. They suggest that segregating logics within separate levels of analysis helps make the combination less confusing.

This three-category typology allows us to make room under the comparative umbrella for those whose research impels them to argue that cities are not alike. Perhaps educational processes in cities do not vary concomitantly – perhaps each city is unique. But if this argument is made successfully, comparison is required. The approach will be 'contrasts of context'.

A more recent and still more elaborate typology appears in Charles Tilly's stimulating little book, *Big Structures, Large Processes, Huge Comparisons*.[32] Tilly categorises types of comparison by the 'sorts of statements they yield rather than with respect to the logic of comparison as such'.[33] He identifies four types: 'individualizing', 'universalizing', 'variation-finding', and 'encompassing'. Individualising comparison 'treats each case as unique, taking up one instance at a time, and minimising its common properties with other instances'. A universalising comparison, in contrast, 'identifies common properties among all instances of a phenomenon'.[34] A variation-finding comparison establishes 'a principle of variation in the character of intensity of a phenomenon having more than one form by examining systematic differences among instances'.[35] Finally, an encompassing comparison places different instances at various locations within the same system as 'a way of explaining their characteristics as a function of their varying relationships to the system as a whole'.[36]

The point is that all these various forms of comparison are useful depending on the 'intellectual task at hand'. All have their abuses as well: more on this later. It is no longer useful to argue that there is a right way and a host of wrong ways to do comparative history. What has become important is that we select our mode of comparison consciously, knowing its strengths, limitations and pitfalls, and keeping our intellectual objective clearly in mind and clearly stated.

Can these typologies be removed from the context of 'macro-social inquiry' which generated them and can they be made useful to urban educational historians? I believe they can. They provide a basis for seeing how comparison can be usefully employed at many different levels and for several different purposes. For those interested in the different educational experiences of different groups within cities, along the lines suggested by

Finkelstein, Marsden and Heward, comparisons that are individualising or universalising are likely to prove most apt. Those searching for similarities and differences between cities within a country or region will employ macro-causal analysis or the parallel demonstration of theory. Those bold enough to compare cities in different countries will likely find all of these, or combinations of these, useful.

Uses and abuses of comparison

The various types of comparison we have identified here have been used, and used to good advantage, in recent urban educational history. One of the commoner types is macro-causal analysis. Educational historians have examined a number of cities or communities of varying size to determine the patterns of variation associated either with size and density themselves or with other aspects of social life which provide a basis for categorising cities. A good example is the study by Kaestle and Vinovskis discussed earlier in which community size was found to vary concomitantly with age-specific school enrolment rates and with the length of the school year.[37] This sharpening of rural–urban differences is likely to contribute in a major way to the 'disaggregation' of a number of widely held generalisations about American schools.

Another is the recent collection of studies of educational development in Southern cities edited by Plank and Ginsberg.[38] This volume not only provides rich detail on a neglected area, Southern urban educational history, but in two essays, developments in the South are compared to those in Northern cities.[39] The work of John Rury also has explored regional variation by analysing data from large numbers of cities.[40] The focus on regional variation is particularly important in the American historiographic setting in which a strong tendency to generalise from Eastern cities to the country as a whole has been evident.

W. B. Stephens' comparison of literacy and school enrolment in England's provincial towns, 1640–1870, sets out to discover concomitant variation.[41] Instead, Stephens is impressed by the amount of variation he finds which resists categorisation. 'Once more we can find no "iron law", no easy categorization, but only a tendency against which to set the unique history of each particular town.'[42] While Stephens suggests that this result illustrates a limitation of the comparative approach, we can see that it is, in fact, a good example of a 'contrasts of context' approach in which the key finding is the frequency of deviation from a putatively general connection between industrialisation and literacy.

Nor is the Stephens study by any means the only example of comparison of this type. Marsden's essay in the same volume draws its explanatory power from a contrasting comparison of various sections of Greater London as that city's educational system developed against the background of rapid urban growth and residential segregation.[43] William Reese found substantial variation in the educational developments of three American cities in which socialists exercised considerable influence within the political arena.[44] David Ment's comparison of racial segregation in the schools of New York, New Rochelle and New Haven stressed the contrast of their experiences.[45]

Paul Peterson's comparison of the educational politics of Chicago, Atlanta and San Francisco has a somewhat curious status here.[46] On the face of it, Peterson seems intent to stress the 'complexity' of the political dynamics of these cities; but, while they were indeed complex, what Peterson really intends can best be understood as the 'parallel demonstration of theory', or, perhaps more accurately, the parallel refutation of theory. Peterson takes on the task of showing that Marxist and other revisionist accounts of urban educational reform in the 1880–1930 period do not adequately account for either the richness and unpredictability of political action or the shift he detects from the dominance of status politics in the nineteenth century to the dominance of class politics in the twentieth. While he comes close to generating a new theory of educational politics, this effort falls short, in part I think because of the intensity of his greater goal, the refutation of established theory.[47] Katznelson and Weir, interpreting the data from the same three cities in a rather different way, do indeed assert a new theory.[48]

A number of others have used this mode of comparison, some effectively, some not. Marvin Lazerson's *Origins of the Urban School* builds an integrated conceptualisation of the principles behind a wide range of nineteenth- and early twentieth-century developments on details drawn from ten Massachusetts cities.[49] The book has been criticised for 'taking a few towns in Massachusetts to be prototypical', but despite its somewhat expansive title, we are fairly warned that 'Massachusetts is not America in microcosm.'[50] Nancy Adelman's study of the influence of Columbia Teachers College on the school systems in its 'hinterland' showed important consistencies in the methods, values, intentions and results of the reform efforts of professors from Columbia despite major differences between the communities towards which reform efforts were directed.[51] Some of the major general works such as David Tyack's *The One Best System* and William Bullough's *Cities and Schools in the Gilded Age* suffer, I think, from a lack of attention to the conditions under which meaningful comparison can be made.[52] Appearing to be a general interpretation of trends and developments occurring in a large number of cities during the same period, presumably because there is something distinctively *urban* about what is going on, these works ought to be cast in the comparative mode of the 'parallel demonstration of theory'. Yet, there are important defects arising from, first, the failure to set out very clearly the 'theory' that is being demonstrated and, second, the failure to locate enough of a pattern of change in at least one city to show that it is indeed a pattern. In trying to be about all cities these books may be about no cities.

Certainly a share of this weakness stems from the fact that both of these works have a primary interest in the origins and consequences of educational *ideas*. This has always been a major concern in educational history, but in recent years there have been those who wished somehow to balance this concern with more attention to 'what really happened in schools', or, as they say in England, with 'developments on the ground'. Ideas do not have locations in the same sense that school systems or ethnic groups or production systems have locations. Thus, we have developed a tendency toward a bifurcated history in which those interested in 'what happened' look intensively at single cities, while those interested in ideas feel free to make sweeping statements about urban education without a reference to location at all.

This brings us to the point where we can suggest that abuses of comparison are more importantly understood as failures to employ comparison intelligently where and when it is actually required. The single most important fault in the work that has been done in the history of urban education is the widespread tendency to generalise well beyond the limits not only of the evidence we have gathered but the very scope of what we have examined. Probably no one does a better job than David Tyack of writing large-scale, sweeping works which synthesise large amounts of the research of 'toilers'. Yet, time after time, when the interpretive frameworks that Tyack develops are 'applied' to single cities, they simply do not work – they do not account for what is discovered at that level.[53]

Another form of this abuse is the assertion of general 'laws' or characteristics of urban historical change based on an intensive examination of a single city. Examples are legion, but the work of Michael Katz, because it is so influential, will suffice to make the point. Katz arrives on the educational history scene with a bold and sweeping reinterpretation of the 'origins of mass popular education' based on an analysis of a single momentary event in a single city.[54] True, once the basic evidentiary ground work is laid, he ranges beyond that city to muster bits and pieces of supporting evidence from other Massachusetts towns, but this casual lifting of evidence from a variety of places to shore up a theory derived from a single case is not good comparison by any definition. His failure to accomplish what he set out to accomplish was because he chose the wrong event at the wrong time in the wrong city.[55] The pattern continued with his studies of bureaucracy in Boston, and of class formation in Hamilton and Philadelphia.

By the same token, it is equally an abuse of comparison to imagine that a single city study can *refute* a theory, even one which is itself based on a single city.[56] The modal anti-revisionist work is the study of 'Americaville' that reveals a 'much richer complexity of events than is suggested by the revisionist model'. Much of this is 'straw-man' history in which the model which has been found to be too reductionist has in fact been reduced by its refuter rather than its originator.

This is not to say that single city studies are of no use or that they cannot be comparative in useful ways. We have already mentioned ways in which comparison between groups, times or areas within single cities can be enormously effective. But single studies can also be used to test theory, and out of such use can come suggestions for modifications in theory, for placing stricter limits around the scope of generalisations, for ways to categorise cities for further comparison, such as by region or developmental stage. I believe that this is done best when it is done self-consciously and when an effort is made to test more than one theory or interpretation at a time.[57]

Those who analyse data from large numbers of cities should not get off scot-free in this discussion of abuses. It is hard to think of a single useful generalisation that has emerged from a statistical analysis of a very large number of cities. Studies such as those by Rury and Stephens are at best preliminary 'sortings' of massive and complex data which need to be followed by more detailed analysis of a smaller number of cases to lead to important principle.

What should be done?

I began this essay with the hope that urban educational history might, in future, become more collective and more cumulative. There are certain prerequisites for this: that we all want to know what really happened and that this is possible, that our research agendas are not hidden agendas, that we will tell the truth about what we discover. It is *not* a prerequisite that we agree either in advance or along the way on a particular grand social theory or even on the ontological status of the concept 'urban'. Against these prerequisites, it may be vain to hope that we can go much beyond the ideological sparring, round by round, that seems to drive the field in circles.

Theory, as Kaestle argues, may be optional; comparison, in contrast, is essential. There are various, equally legitimate though perhaps not equally promising, ways to engage in comparison. There are also ways to abuse comparison by merely seeming to undertake it or undertaking it wrongly. What do I think needs to be done?

1 Those who insist on writing single city studies need either to structure their inquiry around the sorts of 'internal' comparisons described above

or to make possible the use of their work by others by being explicit about the interpretive models being explored and about those characteristics of the city which make it like or unlike others.

2 We need to remember that urbanisation, industrialisation and immigration are not inherently conjoined.

3 We need to avoid attributing any outcome to urbanisation in the absence of collected and presented data from appropriately selected non-urban social settings.[58]

4 We need to bring to consciousness and put to empirical test our deeply embedded sense that urbanisation is essentially disintegrative in its effects on groups, families and individuals. At the same time, we do not have to abandon the view that nineteenth-century urban residents *thought* that cities had these effects and behaved accordingly, though it is vital that we take care to discover who did and who did not believe this.[59]

5 Those who wish explicitly to compare cities need to be sharply aware of when they are crossing boundaries of habit, custom and law that materially effect the processes about which they wish to generalise. These boundaries may be state, provincial, regional or national, and the point is not that they should not be crossed but that the implications of this should be understood and acknowledged.[60]

6 Those interested in grand theory should suspend the *a priori* belief in a single, fundamental social process and be more open to history in the sense that specifically historical processes might be seen to determine what changes occur in specific groups in specific eras.

7 Those suspicious of theory should abandon the ridiculous requirement that, to be useful or true, a theory must account for every nuance, every rich detail of a given local situation.

This list neither inventorises our needs completely nor exhausts the value which may be derived from comparison. The intelligent, self-conscious use of a variety of different modes of comparison holds out the best hope for a re-invigorated urban educational history.

NOTES

1 Sol Cohen, 'The history of urban education in the United States: historians of education and their discontents', in David A. Reeder (ed.), *Urban Education in the Nineteenth Century* (London: Taylor and Francis, 1977), 119.

2 For a survey of the condition of the field see Derek Fraser and Anthony Sutcliffe (eds.), *The Pursuit of Urban History* (London: Edward Arnold, 1983), and a review, Terrence J. McDonald, 'The pursuit of urban history: to the rear march', *Historical Methods*, Vol. 18 (1985), 113–16.

3 References in the text are to Louis Wirth, 'Urbanism as a way of life', in Albert J. Reiss, Jr (ed.), *Louis Wirth on Cities and Social Life* (Chicago, IL: University of Chicago Press, 1964), 60–83.

4 *Ibid.*, 67.
5 *Ibid.*, 83.
6 Louis Wirth, 'Rural–urban differences', in Reiss (ed.), *Louis Wirth*, 221–5.
7 *Ibid.*, 223–4.
8 The two best-known revisions of Wirth's theory are Herbert Gans, 'Urbanism and suburbanism as ways of life: a re-evaluation of definitions', in A. M. Rose (ed.), *Human Behavior and Social Processes* (Boston, MA: Houghton Mifflin, 1962), 625–48, and Claude S. Fischer, 'toward a subcultural theory of urbanism', *American Journal of Sociology*, Vol . 80 (1975), 1319–41.
9 Ephraim H. Mizruchi, 'Romanticism, urbanism, and small towns in mass society: an exploratory analysis', in Paul Meadows and Ephraim H. Mizruchi (eds.), *Urbanism, Urbanization, and Change: Comparative Perspectives* (Reading, MA: Addison-Wesley, 1969), 243.
10 For a fuller discussion of the development of human ecology, see William E. Marsden, 'Ecology and nineteenth-century urban education', *History of Education Quarterly*, Vol. 23 (1983), 29–53.
11 Amos Hawley, *Human Ecology: A Theory of Community Structure* (New York: Ronald Press, 1950). The variant called 'social area analysis' traces from Hawley. See Eshref Shevky and Wendell Bell, *Social Area Analysis: Theory, Illustrative Application and Computational Procedures* (Stanford, CA: Stanford University Press, 1955).
12 Otis Dudley Duncan, 'Human ecology and population studies', in Philip M. Hauser and Otis D. Duncan (eds.), *The Study of Population* (Chicago, IL: University of Chicago Press, 1959), 678–716, and Otis Dudley Duncan and Leo F. Schnore, 'Cultural, behavioral, and ecological perspectives in the study of social organization', *American Journal of Sociology*, Vol. 65 (1959), 132–46.
13 Leo F. Schnore, 'The myth of human ecology', *Sociological Inquiry*, Vol. 31 (1961); Leo F. Schnore, *The Urban Scene: Human Ecology and Demography* (New York: Free Press, 1965); Philip M. Hauser and Leo F. Schnore, *The Study of Urbanization* (New York: John Wiley and Sons, 1965).
14 The variant of ecological theory most relevant to this last set of interests is called the socio-cultural approach, associated with Firey and Wilhelm. Walter Firey, *Land Use in Central Boston* (Cambridge, MA: Harvard University Press, 1947); Sidney M. Wilhelm, *Urban Zoning and Land Use Theory* (New York: Free Press of Glencoe, 1962).
15 For this brief description of Marxist theory I am most indebted to Enzo Mingione, *Social Conflict and the City* (Oxford: Basil Blackwell, 1981), 9–18.
16 M. Castells, *The Urban Question: A Marxist Approach* (London: Edward Arnold, 1977); see Ian Davey and Kerry Wimshurst in this volume, chs. 3 and 7, *passim*.
17 David Harvey, *Social Justice and the City* (London: Edward Arnold, 1973); Michael Dear and Allen J. Scott (eds.), *Urbanization and Urban Planning in Capitalist Society* (London: Methuen, 1981); Mingione, *Social Conflict*.
18 Henry Perkinson, 'the city and the schools', in *The Imperfect Panacea: American Education, 1865–1965* (2nd edn, New York: Random House, 1990) 67–102.
19 William A. Bullough, *Cities and Schools in the Gilded Age: The Evolution of an Urban Institution for Education* (Port Washington, NY: Kennikat Press, 1974).
20 For an example dealing with family structure, see Rudy Ray Seward, *The*

American Family: A Demographic History (Beverly Hills, CA: Sage Publications, 1978).
21 Carl F. Kaestle and Maris A. Vinovskis, *Education and Social Change in Nineteenth-Century Massachusetts* (Cambridge: Cambridge University Press, 1980).
22 See ch. 8, *passim*.
23 See ch. 5, *passim*.
24 Samuel Bowles, videotape of a conference, 'Schooling in corporate America', (Ann Arbor, Michigan, March 1974).
25 David Hogan, *Class and Reform: School and Society in Chicago, 1880-1930* (Philadelphia, PA: The University of Pennsylvania Press, 1985).
26 See, for example, Neil Smelser, *Comparative Methods in the Social Sciences* (Engelwood Cliffs, NJ: Prentice-Hall, 1976); R. L. Merritt and Stein Rokkan (eds.), *The Use of Quantitative Data in Cross-National Research* (New Haven, CT: Yale University Press, 1966).
27 Victoria E. Bonnell, 'The uses of theory, concepts and comparison in historical sociology', *Comparative Studies in Society and History*, Vol. 22 (1980), 156-73.
28 Hogan, *Class and Reform*; Julia Wrigley, *Class Politics and Public Schools: Chicago, 1900-1950* (New Brunswick, NJ: Rutgers University Press, 1982); Paul E. Peterson, *The Politics of School Reform, 1870-1940* (Chicago, IL: University of Chicago Press, 1985); Ira Katznelson and Margaret Weir, *Schooling for All: Class, Race, and the Decline of the Democratic Ideal* (New York: Basic Books, 1985).
29 Theda Skocpol and Margaret Sommers, 'The uses of comparison in macrosocial inquiry', *Comparative Studies in Society and History*, Vol. 22 (1980), 176.
30 *Ibid.*, 178.
31 *Ibid.*, 182.
32 Charles Tilly, *Big Structures, Large Processes, Huge Comparisons* (New York: Russell Sage Foundation, 1984).
33 *Ibid.*, 145.
34 *Ibid.*, 81.
35 *Ibid.*, 116.
36 *Ibid.*, 83.
37 Kaestle and Vinovskis, *Education and Social Change*.
38 David Plank and Rick Ginsberg (eds.), *Southern Cities, Southern Schools: Public Education in the Urban South* (New York: Greenwood Press, 1990).
39 David Angus, 'The origins of urban schools in comparative perspective', and Jeffrey E. Mirel, 'Progressive school reform in comparative perspective', in *ibid.*, 59-80, 151-76.
40 John Rury, 'Vocationalism for home and work: women's education in the United States, 1880-1930', *History of Education Quarterly*, Vol. 24 (1984), 21-44; John Rury, 'American school enrolment in the progressive era: an interpretive inquiry', *History of Education*, Vol. 14 (1985), 49-67; and John Rury, 'Urbanization and education: regional patterns of educational development in American cities, 1900-1910', *Michigan Academician*, Vol. 20 (1988), 261-80.
41 W. B. Stephens, 'Illiteracy and schooling in the provincial towns, 1640-1870: a comparative approach', in Reeder (ed.), *Urban Education in the Nineteenth Century*, 27-47.
42 *Ibid.*, 47.

43 William Marsden, 'Education and the social geography of nineteenth-century towns and cities', in Reeder, (ed.), *Urban Education in the Nineteenth Century*, 49–74.
44 William Reese, *Progressivism and the Grass Roots: Social Change and Urban Schooling, 1840–1920* (London: Routledge and Kegan Paul, 1985).
45 David Ment, 'Patterns of public school segregation, 1900–1940: a comparative study of New York City, New Rochelle, and New Haven', in Ronald K. Goodenow and Diane Ravitch (eds.), *Schools in Cities: Consensus and Conflict in American Educational Cities* (New York: Holmes and Meier, 1983), 67–110.
46 Peterson, *Politics of School Reform*.
47 *Ibid*. For a similar, but more modest, example, see David L. Angus, 'Conflict, class, and the nineteenth-century public high school in the cities of the Midwest, 1845–1900', *Curriculum Inquiry*, Vol. 18 (1988), 7–31.
48 Katznelson and Weir, *Schooling for All*.
49 Marvin Lazerson, *The Origins of the Urban School: Public Education in Massachusetts, 1870–1915* (Cambridge, MA: Harvard University Press, 1971).
50 *Ibid*., xvii.
51 Nancy E. Adelman, 'Sphere of influence: factors in the educational development of three New Jersey communities in the progressive era', in Goodenow and Ravitch (eds.), *Schools in Cities*, 111–62.
52 David B. Tyack, *The One Best System: A History of American Urban Education* (Cambridge, MA: Harvard University Press, 1974); Bullough, *Cities and Schools*.
53 See, for example, David Tyack, Robert Lowe and Elisabeth Hansot, *Public Schools in Hard Times: The Great Depression and Recent Years* (Cambridge, MA: Harvard University Press, 1984), and cf. Jeffrey E. Mirel, 'Politics and public education in the Great Depression: Detroit, 1929–1940', (PhD dissertation, University of Michigan, 1984).
54 Michael B. Katz, *The Irony of Early School Reform: Educational Innovation in Mid-Nineteenth Century Massachusetts* (Boston, MA: Beacon Press, 1968).
55 See Maris A. Vinovskis, *Re-Examining the Origins of Public High Schools: An Analysis of the Beverly High School Controversy in the Mid-Nineteenth Century* (Madison, WI: University of Wisconsin Press, 1986). See also the subsequent debate between these two historians in *History of Education Quarterly*, Vol. 27 (1987), 241–58, and an analysis of this debate, David L. Angus, 'What the Katz/Vinovskis debate tells us about the limits of quantitative history', *Journal of the Midwest History of Education Society*, Vol. 16 (1988), 1–9.
56 See the Hogan–Wrigley–Peterson battle mentioned earlier, and the Katz–Vinovskis comparison above. Marxism as a theory of history remains unscathed in all of this.
57 See, for example, David L. Angus, 'Common school politics in a frontier city: Detroit, 1836–1842', in Goodenow and Ravitch (eds.), *Schools in Cities*, 183–222.
58 Maris Vinovskis, 'Community studies in urban educational history: some methodological and conceptual observations', in Goodenow and Ravitch (eds.), *Schools in Cities*, 287–304.
59 Kaestle and Vinovskis, *Education and Social Change*; see also Tilly's discussion of the 'pernicious postulates' that twentieth-century social science has inherited from nineteenth-century social theory. Tilly, *Big Structures*.
60 An example is Ian Davey's suggestion that we abandon the rural–urban

distinction. If this is something other than an ideological ploy, then Davey should understand that rural–urban contrasts might well be different in a country in which educational policy is historically centralised from one in which local control prevails.

Index

Abbott, J., 98
Adelaide, 160-1, 168-9
Adelman, N., 235
administrative history, 17, 23
admission registers, 160, 168
adolescence, 31, 48
adult education, 5, 27, 29-30, 65, 143
Alberta, 90, 94
Alderson, C. H., 117
Allsobrook, D., 26
Althusser, L., 207, 210-11
American Federation of Teachers, 61
American Historical Association, 198
Angaston, South Australia, 161
Anglican schooling/influence, 30, 119, 121, 148-9
Angus, D. L., 2, 6-7, 222
ante-bellum period, 60, 65, 198
anthropological approaches, 198, 222
Anyon, J., 77
Apple, M., 77
Apter, D., 225
aristocracy, *see* social class perspectives
Arnold, M., 115, 118
Ashenden, D. J., *see under* Connell, R.W.
asylum concepts, 30, 48, 179
Atlanta, 235
attitudes towards the city, 31, 44, 66, 173, 178-9, 184-5

Badinter, E., 177-8
Bailyn, B., 5, 198, 221
Ballarat, Victoria, 79
Bamman, H., 93
Barman, J., 7-8, 95
Barnes, B., 29
Barossa Valley, South Australia, 160, 164, 166
Bate, W., *Lucky City: The First Generation at Ballarat, 1851-1901*, 79
Bender, T., 176
Bendix, R., 12
Bennett, P. W., 98

Bermondsey, London, 124
Berrol, S., 57, 177
Beverly, Massachusetts, 48
biographical approaches, 77, 79, 131, 178, 183, 198
Birmingham, England, 4, 21-2, 25, 27, 32, 129, 131, 134, 137, 146, 149-50, 153
Birmingham Centre for Contemporary Cultural Studies, 77
Birmingham Daily Mail, 150
Birmingham Education Society, 146-8
Birmingham Trades Council, 150
boarding schools, 25, 112-13, 119
board schools, 113, 120-4, 151
Bodnar, J., 57, 183
Bonnell, V., 232
Booth, C., 114, 121
Booth, W., 116
Bootle, England, 21
Boston, Massachusetts, 45, 49, 63, 236
bourgeoisie, *see* social class perspectives
Bowles, S., 197, 231
boys' work, 134-5, 137-9, 153-4, 165
Bradbury, B., 96
Bradford, England, 22, 218
Brenzel, B. M., 174, 177
Brereton, J., 112
Bristol, England, 27, 29, 33
British Columbia, 90, 94-5, 97-8
'British' schools, 117-18
Brown, R. D., 197
Brown v. Board of Education, 62-3
Bryant, M., 25
Bullen, J., 96
Bullough, W., *Cities and Schools in the Gilded Age*, 228, 235
bureaucracy, 4, 49, 53, 55, 59-60, 75-6, 93, 175, 236
Burgess, E. W., 208, 223, 225
busing, 63

Cairo, 213
Calgary, 91

243

244 Index

Calhoun, J., 174, 176, 184–5
Canadian Historical Review, 92
Canadian Social History Project, 94
capitalism, 13–14, 16, 18, 27, 30, 46, 48, 50–1, 57, 59, 62, 77–8, 80, 82, 95, 169, 181, 201–2, 209–10, 226–7, 231
Careless, J. M. S., 90
Carpenter, M., 116
Castells, M., 15, 158, 207, 209–11, 217
catchment areas, 21–2
Catholics and education, 50–2, 56, 64, 91, 94, 97, 113, 118, 121, 149, 177, 229
Cavallo, D., 178
census/census enumeration schedules, 21, 74, 89, 131, 136–7, 153, 160
centralisation, 4, 60, 65, 75–6, 180
Chalmers, J. W., 90
Chamberlain, J., 148–9, 151
charity schools, 45, 47, 115, 202
Chartists, 32
Cheshire, 117
Chicago, 52, 54–5, 57–8, 61, 63–4, 232, 235
Chicago School, 6, 158, 208, 225
Chicago Teachers Union, 60–1
childhood history, studies of, 17, 30–1, 78, 81, 89, 96–7
child labour, 88–9, 96–7, 130, 141–5, 159–60, 164–6, 168
child minding/help, 135, 145, 167
Children's Employment Commission, 132–3, 137–9
Chuen yan Lai, D., 98
Church of England *see* Anglican schooling/influence
Cincinnati, 50
cities as myth-generating, 3, 5, 176–9, 182, 233
citizenship, 3, 26
civic colleges, 28
civil rights movement, 60, 62–3, 73
Civil War, American, 5, 49–51, 133, 142
Cleveland, 52, 57, 63
Clifford, G., 60
Cockerton judgement, 122
coeducation, 47
Cohen, M., 58
Cohen, R. D., 3–4, 54, 174, 176; *Children of the Mill*, 64-5
Cohen, S., 221
colonial colleges, 45
colonial education, 45, 75, 96
Columbia Teachers' College, 235
common schools, 47, 50, 55, 115
comparative approaches, 1, 6–8, 196, 201–2, 208, 211–14, 218, 221, 230–8, 276
comprehensive schools in Britain, 17, 23

compulsory schooling, 33, 76, 117, 121, 129–30, 134, 140, 142, 144, 148–9, 151–2, 154, 158–61, 168–9
Conant, J. B., *Slums and Suburbs*, 64
Congregational Training College, 119
Connell, R. W., Ashenden, D. J., Kessler, S., and Dowsett, G. W., *Making the Difference*, 83
Cook, P., 77
Copp, T., 96
Couett, P., 97
Coulby, D., 2–3, 7
Coulter, R., 97
Cremin, L., 5, 13, 177, 221; *American Education: The Colonial Experience*, 45; *American Education: The National Experience*, 47; *The Transformation of the School*, 52
Cross Commission, 123–4
Cuban, L., 64
curriculum history, 18
Curtis, B., 95

dame schools, 113, 131
Danylewycz, M., 93
Davey, I., 8, 77–8, 81, 93, 96, 159, 174, 177, 185, 222
Davis, W. J., 142, 151
Davison, G., *The Rise and Fall of Marvellous Melbourne*, 79
Dehli, K., 97
delinquency, 30–1, 48, 97–8, 224
DeMause, L., 178
demographic influences, 5–6, 19, 22, 29, 95, 200, 208, 212–14, 218, 228
Demos, J., 198
denominational education, 20, 118, 162, 182
Denton, F., 93
dependency: childhood, 135, 158; social, 7–8, 213–14, 218
determinism, 23
Detroit, 61, 206
Dewey, J., 55
division of labour, 134
Dixon, G., 148–9
Dobbs, A. E., 32
domestic budgets, *see* family economy/strategies
domestic workshops, 88, 133–5, 139, 141, 167
Donzelot, J., 177–8
Doucet, M., 174
Dowsett, G. W., *see under* Connell, R. W.
Dublin, T., 5
Dumont, M., 94
Dumont-Johnson, M., 96

Index

Duncan, O., 225–6
Durkheim, E., 198, 223
Dyos, H. J., 14, 79

ecological approaches, 6, 13, 15, 19, 21–3, 28, 32, 34, 111, 114, 158, 173, 208–9, 222, 225–6, 228, 230
economic history, 14, 117
Edinburgh, 24, 29
Edinburgh Review, 117
Edmonton, 97
Education Act 1870, 120, 122, 130, 134, 148
Education Act 1876, 130
Education Census 1851, 120
Education Department, 124
Education (Revised) Code 1862, 119
Education Reporter, 116
educational/social policy, 2, 4–5, 7–8, 15–16, 18, 22, 30, 73, 96, 206, 208–9, 212–13
elementary schooling hierarchy, 22, 50, 113–14, 116, 120–3, 125, 146
Endowed Schools Commission, 22, 25
ethnicity/race influences, 4–5, 44, 49–52, 54, 56–9, 62–5, 73, 83, 93, 97–8, 125, 179–80, 182, 185, 200, 202, 206–7, 213, 216–18, 223–4, 228–9, 236
ethno-historical approaches, 33

Fahmy-Eid, N., 94
family economy/strategies, 5, 18–21, 32–4, 47–8, 51, 54, 57, 65, 78, 80–3, 88–9, 93, 95–6, 99, 111–12, 129, 131, 133–7, 139–43, 145–7, 150, 153–4, 159, 166–8, 173, 182–3, 222, 228–30
Fearon, D., 119
feminist perspectives, 18, 47, 76–7, 82–3, 158, 184, 222
Fingard, J., 96
Finkelstein, B., 3–4, 178, 183–4, 222, 229–30, 234
Fischer, C. S., 229
Fleming, T., 94
Foster, J., 197
Foucault, M., 30, 78, 95
Fox-Genovese, E., 197
Frankfurt School, 226
Franklin, V. P., 58, 174, 177
Fraser, J., 115
free education, 46, 76, 134, 149, 151, 158
French Canada, 96
functionalist approaches, 197, 202

Gaffield, C., 94
Gans, H. J., 229
Gardner, P., 32
Garner, A. D., 29

Gary, 62–5, 176
Gaskell, J. S., 95
Geertz, C., 173, 182, 196–7, 199
gender perspectives, 17, 47, 51, 54, 57–8, 61, 73, 77–80, 82–3, 88, 94–6, 98, 131, 135, 142, 158, 166, 169, 184–5, 206
Genovese, E., 197
geographical approaches, 5–6, 15, 21, 28, 75, 198
George, P., 93
Gidney, I., 94
Gilmore, W. J., 45
Gintis, H., 197
girls' education, 17, 24, 31, 47, 58, 61, 78, 94
girls' work, 134, 137–9, 153, 162, 165, 167
Goodman, C., *Choosing Sides*, 56
Grace, G., 16, 207–8, 215–16
Graff, H. J., 20, 93
grammar schools, 25, 45
Gramsci, A., 199
Greenwich, 121
Grubb, W. N., 178
Guelph, 91

Habermas, J., 212, 226
Halifax, Nova Scotia, 93, 96–7
Hall, P. D., 177
Hall, S., 169
Hamel, T., 97
Hamilton, Ontario, 93, 96, 160, 236
handicap *see* special needs
Handlin, O., 79
Hansot, E., 177; *see also under* Tyack, D.
Hareven, T., 200
Harrigan, P., 94
Harvey, D., 15
Hauser, P., 225–6
Hawes, J., 177
Hawley, A., 225–6
Hays, S. P., 44, 52
hegemony, 30, 32, 73, 95
Heward, C., 4, 32–3, 132, 136, 141, 145, 152, 234
Higham, J., 176, 182
higher elementary/higher grade schools, 27, 113–14, 122
Hindmarsh, South Australia, 160–3, 165–7
historicism, 212
historiography, 1, 3–4, 8, 13, 16–17, 54, 73, 76, 125, 158, 172–3, 205
History of Education Society of Great Britain, 16–17
Hogan, D., 53–4, 174, 222, 231–2
Holley, J. C., 133
Holmes, B., 208, 211–13
Homerton College, 119

Index

Hoselitz, B., 225
Houston, S. E., 92–4, 178
Hurl, L. F., 96
Hurt, J., 18, 111

ideological issues, 3, 7, 17, 30–1, 34, 73, 76–7, 80, 97, 124, 172, 180–2, 200, 209–11, 221, 231
illness, 147, 150, 162, 164–7
immigration, *see* migration
Indiana, 62
Indianapolis, 62
industrialisation, 3–4, 13, 18–19, 24–5, 53, 81–2, 89, 95, 130, 137, 178, 181, 195, 197, 214, 229, 234, 238
industrial revolution, 19–20, 112, 124
industrial schools, 30, 113, 115, 179
inequality, 21, 44, 49–51, 55, 59–60, 62, 64, 76–7, 93–4, 125, 202, 205, 216–17
infancy, 177
infant departments/schools, 24, 79, 162
Inkster, I., 29
inner city schooling, 2, 14, 16, 63, 65–6
Inner London Education Authority, 206
Innis, H., 89–90
integration, 49, 58, 62–3
interdisciplinary approaches, 14, 22, 73, 80, 222
Irish and education, 34, 50, 80
irreguarl attendance, 158–62, 164–6, 168; *see also* truancy
Isaac, R., 197

Jackson, N. S., 95
Jakarta, 213
Jefferson, T., 44, 66
Jenkins, E. W., 29
Jewellery Quarter, Birmingham, 21, 129–35, 139, 141, 143, 146, 151, 153–4
Jews and education, 34, 52, 56–8, 98
Johnson, D., 91
Johnson, F. H., 90
Johnson, P., 198
Johnson, R., 29
Johnston, A. J. B., 94
Jones, A., 92
Journal of American History, 5
junior high schools, 55
juvenile employment, 129–30, 135, 137, 142

Kaestle, C. F., 1, 6, 45, 76, 222, 227–9, 234, 237; *Pillars of the Republic*, 49–50
Kaestle, C. F., and Vinovskis, M. A., *Education and Social Change in Nineteenth-Century Massachusetts*, 228
Karier, C. J., 77, 81

Katz, M. B., 8, 51, 76, 82, 92–3, 95, 177, 222, 236; *The Irony of Early School Reform*, 48–9
Katznelson, I., 6, 14, 232, 235
Kelly, M., 79
Kelso, J. J., 97
Kessler, S., *see under* Connell, R. W.
Kett, J. F., 177
kindergartens, 27, 56
King, M., 88–9
Kingston, Ontario, 92
Kirp, D., *Just Schools*, 63
Klassen, H., 97
Krug, E., *The Shaping of the American High School*, 54
Katznelson, I., and Weir, M., *Schooling for All*, 54

labour history, 125
Lagerman, E. C., 184
Lake, M., *The Limits of Hope*, 80–1
Lambeth, 123
Lancashire, 159, 197
Lancasterian schools, 45–6, 87
Lasch, C., 177
Lawr, D., 94
Lawrence, Massachusetts, 48
Lazerson, M., 55, 76, 177–8; *Origins of the Urban School*, 235
Leeds, 21, 25, 29
Lerner, D., 225
Levine, R. A., 179–80
Levy, M., 225
Lewis, N., 97
Life Adjustment Movement, 61
Lim, S., 88
Lingen, R., 118
linguistic analysis, 184
literacy, 17, 19–20, 32, 45–6, 94, 130, 143, 153, 173, 180, 184, 201, 234
Liverpool, England, 119
local/case study approaches, 18, 20, 29, 32–3, 35, 62, 73, 91
local history, 14, 33
London, 7, 21–2, 24–6, 30–1, 33–4, 90, 113, 115, 120–4, 206, 213, 216, 235
Lowe, Robert, *see under* Tyack, B.
Lowe, Robert (Viscount Sherbrooke), 111
Lowe, Roy, 22
Lukas, J. A., 63

Maciejko, B., 95
McKenzie, R. D., 225
McLennan, G., *Marxism and the Methodology of History*, 199
MacLeod, D., 97

Index

MacNaughton, K. C. N., 90
Manchester, England, 24–5, 28–9, 119, 123
Mann, A., 198
Mann, H., 46, 55, 120
Mannheim, K., 199
Manpower Services Commission, 215
Marcus, S., 9
Marlyn, J., 98
marriage registers, 19
Marsden, W. E., 4–6, 21–2, 32, 34, 230, 234
Marxist/neo-Marxist approaches, 1, 15–16, 18, 27, 30, 76–7, 82, 95, 158, 196–7, 209, 211–12, 222–3, 226–8, 230–2, 235
Massachusetts, 46, 48, 56, 81, 199, 235–6
mass schooling, 2–3, 18, 46, 49, 51, 75, 82, 120, 129, 135, 169, 180, 185
Mechanics' Institutes, 29, 177, 230
Medick, H., 137
Melbourne, 79–80
Mennell, R., 177
Ment, D., 235
meritocracy, 26, 124–5
Merseyside, 21
Mexico City, 213
Miami, 218
middle class, *see* social class perspectives
migration, 3, 5–6, 22, 32–4, 47, 50–2, 56–8, 80, 93, 177–9, 183, 202, 213, 228–30, 238
Mill, J. S., 232
Millar, W. P. J., 94
Miller, P., *Long Division: State Schooling in South Australian Society*, 77–8
Milwaukee, 56
Mohl, R., 54, 174, 176
Mohraz, J. J., 177
Montague, C. J., 116
Montferrand, J., 87
Montreal, 88, 90, 93–4, 96–8
Moogk, P., 96
Moor, W., 225
Morell, J. D., 118–19, 121
Morrell, J., 29
Morrison, T., 96, 98
Mulcahy, M., 97
Mulligan, J. S., 177
Mutual Improvement Societies, 32

Nash, G., 44–5
National Education League, 148
National Society, 148
Nelson, J., 114
neo-Marxist, *see* Marxist/neo-Marxist approaches
New Brunswick, 94
Newcastle, England, 123
Newcastle Commission, 111, 115–19

New England, 45, 201
New Haven, 235
New Orleans, 52
New Rochelle, 235
New York City, 7, 45–9, 52, 56–8, 61, 63, 90, 213, 235
New York Free School Society, 46
Nicolson, M., 98
nonconformist schools, 118, 120–1
Notting Dale, 124
Notting Hill, 124
Norris, J. P., 117

Oakeley, H. E., 123
O'Gallagher, M., 97
Oneida County, New York State, 46
Ontario, 90, 92–8, 159, 161
Ontario Institute for Studies in Education, 92, 222
oral history approaches, 33–4, 129, 132–3, 138–9, 142–3, 150, 168
O'Rooke, P. T., 97
Ottawa, 91
Owen, R., 32
Oxford Review of Education, 16

Pahl, R., 217
Palmer, B., 95
parental attitudes/choice, 4, 32, 118–20, 122, 125, 159, 164–6, 179
Paris, 208
Park, R. E., 125, 172, 208, 223, 225
parochial schools, 50, 64
Parsons, T., 196
Past and Present, 17
patriarchy, 78, 80, 82
patriotism, 57, 59
Pennsylvania, 56
Perkinson, H., *The Imperfect Panacea: American Education, 1865–1965*, 227–9
Perrault, J.-F., 87
Peterson, P., 232, 235; *The Politics of School Reform*, 53–4
Petroff, L., 98
Philadelphia, 45, 49–50, 55, 58, 62, 236
Phillips, C. E., 90
Pittsburgh, 56
Plamenatz, J. P., 199
Plank, D., 234
pluralism, 4, 7, 54, 63, 211, 218
political history, 23
Polyzoi, E., 98
Popper, K., 212, 222
population, 5, 51, 89, 91–2, 116, 125, 153, 167, 201, 223–5, 227–8

poverty, 30, 59, 122, 130, 133, 146–7, 150–1, 154, 159, 164, 166, 212, 217–8
Powell, T. E., 123
Prentice, A., 92–5, 178; *The School Promoters*, 92
Preston, 21
private schools, 22, 25–6, 32, 45–6, 49–50, 64, 112–13, 117, 119, 162, 167
progressive influences, 3, 31, 52–4, 56–8, 60–2, 65, 75, 173, 184
proprietary schools, 22, 25–6, 113–14, 119
Protestant influences/schools, 46, 50, 57, 64, 176, 181, 200–2
psycho-social/psychological approaches, 6, 174–6, 179–81, 184, 198, 222–3, 229–30
Punch, 154–5

Quaker schools, 143
Quebec City, 87, 94, 97
Quebec State, 93–4

race/racism, *see* ethnicity/race influences
ragged schools, 113, 116, 120, 146
rates, 120
Ravitch, D., *The Troubled Crusade*, 62
Redfield, R., 175, 225
reductionism, 1, 237
Reeder, D., 2, 6–7, 174, 178, 222, 227; *Urban Education in the Nineteenth Century*, 6, 16, 73
Reese, W. J., 3–4, 235; *Power and the Promise of School Reform*, 54
reformatory schools, 113
reformers, 1–2, 23–4, 31–2, 45–8, 52–4, 56, 76–7, 81, 90–1, 93, 95–6, 116, 158, 169, 173, 176–9, 184–5, 200, 202
reform schools, 48
regional variation, 19–20, 234
Reiger, K., *The Disenchantment of Home*, 80–1
respectability, 25, 32, 88, 112, 114, 117, 121, 125, 146
revisionists, 4, 18, 51–2, 54, 62, 76, 92–3, 98, 111, 215–16, 235
Richardson, M., 97
Richler, M., 98
Rochester, USA, 198
Roe, J., 79
Rooke, P., 97, 177
Rothman, D., 177
Rowe, F. W., 90
Royal Commission on Education (Australia) 1913, 168
rural–urban dichotomy, 50, 59, 78, 80–3, 90, 94, 124, 158–61, 228
Rury, J., 59, 234, 237

Rutman, L., 97
Ryan, M., *Cradle of the Middle Class*, 46–7
Ryerson, E., 90, 95

Saint John, New Brunswick, 94
Saint John's, Newfoundland, 97
Salisbury, England, 115
Salverson, L. G., 98
Samuel, R., 33
Sanders, J. W., 50, 57, 174
San Francisco, 7, 52, 90, 235
Sault Ste. Marie, 98
Saunders, P., 217
Schlereth, T. J., *Material Culture in America*, 183
Schlesinger, B., 79
Schlossman, S., 177
Schnell, R. L., 97, 177
Schnore, L., 225–6
school attendance, 20–1, 33, 52, 93, 112, 129–30, 143, 145–6, 151–4, 158–69, 179
School Board Chronicle, 117, 120
school boards (England and Wales), 23, 33, 120–3, 130, 148–51, 153–5
school–community links, 6, 34
school enrolment, 19–21, 52, 54, 59, 61, 94, 153, 201, 234
school fees, 22, 33, 112, 118–24, 129, 145–6, 149–51
school gradation, 21, 50, 112, 114, 116, 119–20, 125, 230
School Guardian, 120–1
school strikes, 34
Schrag, F., 197
Schultz, S. K., 49
science associations/institutes, 24, 28–9
Scott, J., 119
Scriptural Education Union, 150
secondary schools, 25, 27, 87, 113–14, 122–3, 169
segregation, residential/social, 21, 44, 58, 62–3, 97, 114, 116, 124–5, 223, 230, 235
Seliger, M., 199
Selleck, R., and Sullivan, M., *No So Eminent Victorians*, 77
Seller, M., 177
Sennett, R., 176, 182
Service Bureau for Intercultural Education, 63
Shapin, S., 29
Sharpe, T. W., 126
Sheffield, 24, 27, 122, 206
Silver, H., 17, 34
Sharpe, T. W., 120
Shropshire, 117
Simmel, G., 175, 184–5, 223, 229

Index

Simon, B., 27
Skeats, H. S., 119–20
Skocpol, T., 232–3
slavery, 51, 202
slums, 32, 79, 132
Smelser, N., 197, 232
Smith, D., 27
social class consciousness, 114, 124, 184
social class perspectives, 4, 16–17, 20–2, 24–6, 28, 31–4, 44–9, 53–8, 62–3, 73, 77–9, 82–3, 88, 93, 95–8, 111–22, 132, 135–7, 139, 143–6, 150, 152–3, 158–9, 165–9, 173, 177, 185, 196, 202, 206, 210, 213, 216, 223–4, 226, 228–31, 235–6
social control, 4, 17, 29–31, 53, 56, 58–9, 73–9, 92, 111–12, 175, 201, 207, 215, 228
social history, 2, 7–8, 14–15, 17, 30, 47, 65, 73–5, 78, 81, 92, 125, 158, 173
socialisation, 4, 45, 51, 99, 111
socialism, 54, 222, 235
social mobility, 5–6, 22, 47, 57
social orders, 114–15, 124
social science/theory, 3–4, 7, 15, 32, 195–202, 205–11, 216–18, 222, 225, 235–8
social status, 22, 112, 116, 124–5, 131
social stratification, 21, 111, 125, 215
social structures/systems, 7, 15, 20, 22, 75, 81, 92, 117, 195, 199, 209
socio-cultural approaches, 173–6, 180
socio-economic groups/influences, 15, 21, 24, 93, 95, 125, 134, 200
sociological approaches, 2, 16–17, 27, 64, 76, 78, 83, 92, 158, 172, 197–9, 211, 224–6, 231
Sommers, M., 232–3
South Australia, 77, 160–1, 166
South Australian Education Act 1875, 160
South Australian Education Act 1915, 169
Southport, England, 21
Southwark, London, 123
spatial factors, 19, 21, 184, 209, 224, 226
special needs, 60, 206–7
Spring, J. H., 76; *Education and the Rise of the Corporate State*, 53
Staffordshire, 117
Stamp, R., 90, 94
Stanley, T. J., 98
Stephens, W. B., 19–20, 234, 237
Stone, L., 178, 200
Strickland, C., 177
Strong-Boag, V., 94
structuralilsm/post-structuralism, 6, 13–15, 18, 24, 27–9, 32, 78, 158, 174, 197, 221, 229–30

Studies in Urban and Social History, 79
suburbanisation, 22, 59, 62–5, 79, 81, 131, 160–2, 165–8, 207
Sullivan, M., *see under* Selleck, R.
Sunday schools, 27, 30, 115, 122, 143
Sutherland, N., 7–8, 90–1, 94, 96–7, 174, 178
Swann v. Charlotte Mecklenburg, 63
Sydney, 79
Sydney Labour History Group, *What Rough Beast?*, 80
Synge, J., 96

teacher strike, 64
teacher unions, 60–1, 207
technical education, 27, 88
tertiary revolution, 112, 124
Thackray, A., 28
Thebarton, South Australia, 168
Theobald, M., 78
Thompson, E. P., 198
Tilly, C., 232; *Big Structures, Large Processes, Huge Companies*, 233
Tilly, C., *et al.*, *The Rebellious Century*, 233
Timmins, S., 134
Tonnies, F., 223
Toronto, 88, 89–93, 97–8
trade unions, 54–6, 60, 112, 142, 151, 210
Training Agency, England and Wales, 215–16
transfer, international/educational, 1, 3, 6, 8, 185, 208, 213–14, 217–18
Trimmer, S., 115–16
truancy/truant schools, 113, 161–2, 166
Tyack, D., 177, 197–8; *The One Best System*, 49, 73, 235–6
Tyack, D., and Hansot, E., *Managers of Virtue*, 53, 198
Tyack, D., Lowe, R., and Hansot, E., *Public Schools in Hard Times*, 61

Unitarians, 24
United States Supreme Court, 63
universal schooling, *see* mass schooling
University of Cambridge, 26–7
University of Harvard, 92
University of Oxford, 26–7
Unwin, W., 119
upper class, *see* social class perspectives
urban biographies, 79, 81, 91
urban consciousness/urbanism, 173–4, 223
urban educational history, 1–2, 6, 8, 13–43, 73–5, 78–9, 172–5, 180, 215, 221–2, 230, 236, 238

urban education/studies, 14, 73, 205–18, 227
urban experience of education, 18, 20, 22, 31, 173–4, 233
urban growth, 5, 51, 55, 59, 176, 179, 229, 235
urbanisation, 3–4, 8, 13–15, 18, 29, 34, 78, 81–2, 89–93, 98, 130, 201, 211, 213–14, 225, 227–8, 238
urban settlement movement, 30
Utica, 47
utilitarianism, 24, 26

Vancouver, 88, 91, 95, 97
Verrette, M., 94
Vick, M., 77
Victoria, Australia, 80
Victoria, British Columbia, 98
Vinovskis, M., 50, 81, 199, 222, 234; *see also under* Kaestle, C. F.
Virginia, 197
vocational education, 27, 53, 55, 79, 89, 169, 211
voluntary schools, 22, 113, 120–4, 149

Wallerstein, I., 232
Walters, R., 199
Warren, D. R., 174
Washington, DC, 63
Watson, W., 116
Weber, M., 197, 211, 223
Weir, M., 9, 232, 235; *see also under* Katznelson, I.
Weiss, J., 55
Weiss, N. B., 177
welfare, child, 54, 65, 79, 91, 96
welfare state, 14
Wesleyan schools, 117–18, 123
Wesleyan Training Institue, 118–19
Whig interpretations, 76, 173
White, J. E., 132
White, M. I., 179–80
Wiebe, R., 176
Wilson, J. D., 94, 96
Wimshurst, K., 8, 160–1, 222
Windsor, Ontario, 98
Winnipeg, 90, 95
Wirt, W. A., 65
Wirth, L., 29, 175, 223–5, 227–9
women's education, *see* gender perspectives
Woodward, C. V., 198
Worcester, Massachusetts, 56
Working Men's Auxiliary, 148
Workshops Act 1867, 142
World War I influences, 58, 60, 65
World War II influences, 61–2
Wrigley, J., 54, 232

Zelizer, V., 129
Zuckerman, M., 177

Printed in the United States
25296LVS00005B/301-303